Bridging Divides

Bridging Divides

The Channel Tunnel and
English Legal Identity
in the New Europe

EVE DARIAN-SMITH

University of California Press

BERKELEY   LOS ANGELES   LONDON

University of California Press
Berkeley and Los Angeles, California

University of California Press, Ltd.
London, England

© 1999 by the Regents of the University of California

Library of Congress Cataloging-in-Publication Data

Darian-Smith, Eve, 1963–
  Bridging divides : the Channel Tunnel and English legal identity in
the new Europe / Eve Darian-Smith.
      p.   cm.
  Includes bibliographical references and index.
  ISBN 0-520-21610-5 (alk. paper).—ISBN 0-520-21611-3
(pbk.: alk. paper)
    1. Law—Great Britain.   2. Law and anthropology.
3. Nationalism—Great Britain.   4. International and municipal
law—Great Britain.   5. Channel Tunnel (England and France).
6. European Union—Great Britain.   I. Title.
KD640.D37   1999
340'.115—dc21   98-46627
                                                                      CIP

Manufactured in the United States of America

9 8 7 6 5 4 3 2 1

The paper used in this publication meets the minimum requirements
of ANSI/NISO Z39.48-1992 (R 1997) (*Permanence of Paper*).

An earlier version of chapter 2 was previously published in Eve
Darian-Smith, "Legal Imagery in the 'Garden of England,' " *Indiana
Journal of Global Legal Studies* 2, no. 2 (1995): 395–411. An earlier
version of chapter 5 appeared in Eve Darian-Smith and Peter
Fitzpatrick, eds., *Laws of the Postcolonial* (Ann Arbor: University of
Michigan Press, forthcoming), by permission of The University of
Michigan Press. Chapter 6 is based on Eve Darian-Smith, "Rabies
Rides the Fast Train," which appeared in *Law and Critique* 6 (1): 75–
94, and is republished here, in revised form, with the permission of
Deborah Charles Publications.

For Peter and Shelby

Contents

Illustrations

MAPS

GRAPH

Preface

Having studied the Channel Tunnel and why it has taken on a particular symbolism in the English imagination over the past twenty years, I was excited about finally taking the Tunnel train, or Eurostar (earlier "Le Shuttle"), as it is officially known, that was scheduled to transport me from London to Paris in just over three hours. Passengers on Eurostar depart from a terminal more like an airport than a traditional train station. There are boarding passes, luggage trolleys, loudspeaker announcements of departure times in English and French, fast-food smells, and anxious rummaging in luggage. Unfortunately, no duty-free sales are allowed. I was greeted by electronic security and staff wearing fancy blue-and-gold uniforms, looking very similar to the attendants on airlines. I was impressed by the computerized turnstiles, through which you are meant to feed your ticket, and the general efficiency of proceedings. However, in the general confusion, I just walked around the surveillance system, and my luggage was not checked at any stage of the journey. Apparently, too, my experience was not unique, judging from numerous complaints about the level of security on the trains and an escalation of popular fears about terrorist activities.

The trip under the Channel was a bit of an anticlimax. We descended into blackness for half an hour and could see nothing. I had hoped for something to happen, but my ears did not even pop. Still, I wasn't about to complain, because on 12 April 1995, a week before I traveled, hundreds of people coming from France were stranded on the tracks for seven hours after power lines came down in Kent. With no air-conditioning, food, or information, tempers flared before passengers were finally put on a bus to continue their journey to London. "Delayed passengers were offered distraction by the 35-strong choir of New College, Oxford, on its return from a 10 day tour of France," according to reports. "The group said, with pride, that it had sung 'various songs' to cheer people up, although one French conductor had tried to stop them" (*Independent*, 13 April 1995, p. 3).

Once the train ascended into daylight on the French side, the train's speed picked up. A group of four Englishwomen, all dressed up, who had been talking in loud, excited tones about their plans for a slap-up birthday lunch at an expensive French restaurant, cracked a bottle of champagne and drank from plastic glasses. The other passengers, in true English form, averted their eyes and pretended not to notice. The rush through the French countryside at 180 mph was certainly exhilarating. Upon arriving at the Gare du Nord, people quickly grabbed their belongings and headed out past a group of French gendarmes, all standing in a very relaxed manner on the platform. I had the sense the police were there more for show than anything else. I did not have to present my passport at any point.

But upon our return to London, things were very different. When we disembarked at Waterloo and headed toward customs, citizens of the European Union were marshaled into three lines, while those classified as "Other," including Australians like me, had to line up in one. Considering that many of the passengers were North Americans or Japanese, and that most of these tourists had a great deal more luggage than the English and French business crowd, getting cleared through passport control and the checking of bags was a very tedious process. Conforming to national stereotypes, one irate American, upon being told he had to return to the back of the line, yelled out above the heads of the quietly standing Japanese families and their metallic suitcases that he would sue Eurotunnel. All in all, it was a complete shambles, reflecting on the part of the English a general lack of foresight, planning, and care of what others might think.

Most impressive about the whole travel experience between London and Paris is Waterloo International Station, a lovely steel and glass structure that evokes memories of the Crystal Palace and echoes nineteenth-century railway terminals such as St. Pancras. Despite some initial French objections to arriving at a station called Waterloo, its charms are openly acknowledged. Late in 1994, the architect, Nicholas Grimshaw, was awarded the prestigious Royal Institute of British Architects award. One of its fans has described the old-style romance of the terminal thus:

> Look at those big analogue clocks counting down the minutes to departure; no digital nonsense here. Look at the bright yellow, Meccano-like cog-wheels that raise and lower the lifts from concourse to security gates. And—look—how, inside or outside, you can see the elongated trains purring in and out of the terminal. . . . Waterloo

International is an inspired building, an adventure in steel and glass, a
place that promises, like the wardrobe in *The Lion, the Witch and the
Wardrobe,* to spirit us away to a more glamorous life, one in which
the champagne flows and foie gras abounds, and evenings resound
with Edith Piaf.

(*Independent*, 26 April 1995, p. 22)

An English author and French singer are evoked here to encapsulate
the romance and spirit of the Channel Tunnel project, but neither epitomizes it very well. For the Tunnel is, in a profound sense, neither English
nor French, and so is incapable of being represented by either country's
respective cultural icons. Other contradictions and ambiguities mark the
Tunnel, which is at once a triumph of science and modernity and yet at
the same time an embodiment of the tensions and confusion that continue
to plague the shaping of the unfolding postmodern European Community.
Inasmuch as the Tunnel is grounded in English and French national, regional, and local contexts, it is also a significant feature in the emerging
pan-European political, economic, and cultural spheres.

This book highlights the competing and overlapping views of the Tunnel's significance that make studying it so fascinating. In the context of
the New Europe, the Tunnel operates in a very tangible way as a catalyst
for renewing and rearticulating similarities and differences between peoples and across towns, regions, nations, states, and global divides. As a
symbol of the breaking down of European state borders, the Tunnel pre-
cariously affirms the ideal of a united Europe. At the same time, however,
the increasing threat portrayed in the British popular media of postcolonial
peoples from places such as Africa and India boarding the train in Paris
and illegally entering London highlights a continuing need to demarcate
differences between "east" and "west," first and third worlds, colonizers
and colonized, and, in a rather circular move, again between the English
and French legal systems and national and regional social values. In a world
of increasing talk about unity and transnationalism, what the Tunnel helps
articulate is that there are also simultaneously emerging expressions of
neonationalism and parochial exclusivity.

I want to make clear from the outset that the purpose of this book is
not to treat the Channel Tunnel simply as a concrete entity and so to
analyze how people living in England are responding to it, positively or
negatively. I do not take the Tunnel as a given thing with an attached set
of fixed meanings. Rather my purpose is to ask why it is that the Tunnel
has come to have the object status that it has, and what the conceptual,
discursive, and practical effects of power are that have helped crystallize

this supposedly technical apparatus of "connection" into an icon of political, moral, and ideological focus.

In treating the Tunnel as a dynamic "field" of analysis that overlaps, bridges, undermines, divides, disconnects, and reconnects with other symbolic domains and imagined visions of nature, nation, sovereignty, landscape, and legal practice, this project directly engages with a growing body of literature in anthropology that seeks to deconstruct and critically reflect upon the nature of the field in "fieldwork" (see Gupta and Ferguson 1997). Inasmuch as ethnographers are now acutely aware, at least since the mid 1980s, of their role in the mediation of knowledge and the production of texts, the "reflexive turn" in anthropology is taking a further twist toward interrogating what we mean by fieldwork and the geographical "where" that spatially contextualizes what are considered appropriate objects of study (Gupta and Ferguson 1997; Comaroff and Comaroff 1992; Greenhouse n.d.; Marcus 1995; Appadurai 1991; Fardon 1990; Marcus and Fischer 1986; Clifford and Marcus 1986).

I take seriously the viability, and indeed the necessity, of doing ethnographies of transnational processes and globalization. Given my critical reflection on what constitutes a field of analysis, this book presents a rather unconventional ethnography in both its subject matter and methodology. My subject is the articulation of law as social practice and how this both "bridges" and "divides" neighbors, enemies, immigrants, and citizens in the new transnational contexts the Tunnel iconically represents. Since social practice does not operate in a vacuum, it is also an ethnography about the significance of law and its relationship to the mapping of particular epistemological, political and cultural geographies that inform a (post)modern global production of locality (Appadurai 1996a: ch. 9). In the process of exploring these interrelations, both what we consider as law and what we accept as somehow natural geopolitical boundaries are brought into question and challenged.

Methodologically, attempting an ethnography of globalization raises numerous problems for anthropologists who continue to define themselves intellectually on the basis of their "face-to-face" communications with the other. However, it is critical that such methodological limitations be overcome if anthropology's fieldwork tradition is to endure. As Akil Gupta and James Ferguson argue, there is a need for "attentiveness to different forms of knowledge available from different social and political locations" (Gupta and Ferguson 1997: 39). Drawing upon my intellectual background in law, art theory, history, and anthropology, as well as my work experience as a lawyer, waitress, art gallery administrator, and teacher, I collected a wide range of materials and evidence in support of my analysis. The more obvious of these are local voices, press reports, political cartoons, interviews with foreign visitors, television and radio programs, conversations with Eurotunnel representatives, official government statements, tourist postcards, law archives, newspaper advertisements, representations of national icons, maps of transportation networks, minutes of environmental and community project meetings attended, and discussions with judges and local politicians. These materials are interwoven with theoretical discussions from a range of perspectives and bodies of scholarly literature, including but not limited to works classified as anthropology, cultural geography, socio-legal studies, sociology, history, literature, cultural studies, and jurisprudence. All of these pieces go toward building the multifaceted dimensions and "layers" of my argument. Of course, there may be many pieces that I have overlooked and that could be included. As with most narratives, stories about the Channel Tunnel require constant retelling.

The Tunnel's crystallizing of similarities and differences between peoples and places is an ongoing and dynamic process. Categories of identity and cultural affiliation and their linking to institutions of law and economic power are never static, even when they outwardly appear so. This insight has been reinforced through my own experiences as an Australian citizen. Having practiced in Melbourne as a lawyer and been obliged to pay symbolic homage to Queen Elizabeth II, and then trained in the United States as an anthropologist supported by U.S. funding, my personal biography created a microcosm of postcolonial and global ironies that I felt befitted a researcher studying the significance of the Channel Tunnel in England.

In 1993–94, I lived in the picturesque southern English town of Canterbury, Kent, in a very small apartment above a health-food shop and a "fish-and-chippy." My evenings were broken by the constant squeak of the fish-and-chip shop door as students from King's School, the oldest school in England, on which I voyeuristically looked down from my kitchen window, bought their late night munchies. I was fascinated by these kids in black suits and white wing-tipped collars gulping down greasy chips and sausages in batter as they clutched their books, pens, and calculators. Here, it seemed, was a slice of living history. The students seemed to epitomize the incongruities between the trappings of tradition, clung to so dearly in Canterbury, whose real and quasi medievalism make it one of the most touristed places in England, and the presence of an encroaching modern world. Incongruities of past and present pervaded my everyday world as I sat at my desk, looking out toward the towers of Canterbury Cathedral over the rooftops, tapping out my notes on the Channel Tunnel at a laptop computer in a wheezing old building supposedly owned in the 1370s by Geoffrey Chaucer.

I am in no doubt that my being an Australian placed me in a favorable position with Canterbury and Kent residents, although at times I found it hard to explain that I was funded by U.S. institutions. Some English anthropologists from the University of Kent showed explicit signs of discomfit in being the "objects" of fieldwork when I talked to them about my research, but ordinary people were pleased to be "investigated." Most took it as appropriate and fitting that an Australian should return, as it were, to Mother England. I had a sense that people could relax with an Australian in ways they might not be able to do with a "European" or American. At times, I still found myself face to face with what Paul Theroux has called the quintessential England: "not just coastal, seaside holiday, retirement England, but secretive, rose-growing, dog-loving, window-washing, church-going, law-abiding, grumpy, library-using, tea-drinking, fussy and inflexible England" (Theroux 1983: 42). But the very imperial chauvinisms fostered by such personal inflexibility, which gave those I talked to a certain understanding of an Australian's curiosity about the English, actually offered me insights and experiences and tales that I might not otherwise have been privy to. This may help explain why a journalist from the magazine *L'Express*, whose mother is English and father French, sought me out to comment upon the impact of the Tunnel in Kent for his article on the Channel Tunnel's inauguration in 1994. I had value as a foreigner, but one considered by my English hosts as not too far "outside" or "beyond the pale."

There are many people to thank, the most important being the many, mostly anonymous people whom I observed, casually talked to, and interviewed in the process of research, and who gave their time and energy so generously. In terms of friendship, support, advice, and careful reading of numerous drafts, I thank Peter Fitzpatrick, without whom this book would not have been written. I also especially thank John Comaroff, Sally Falk Moore, and Marshall Sahlins. People who have been extremely generous in commenting on drafts are (in alphabetical order) Arjun Appadurai, Mathieu Deflem, William Felstiner, Elvin Hatch, Bernard Hibbitts, Andrew Kirby, Mark Leichty, Richard Mohr, Ann Plane, and Terrence Turner. I am also indebted to those who read individual chapters, some of which were presented as conference papers, and thank Fred Aman, Daphne Berdahl, Roger Cardinal, Jane Collier, David Engel, James Fernandez, Carol Greenhouse, Chris Hann, Gary Marx, Alexander Murphy, Colin Perrin, Nigel Rapport, Paul Silverstein, Leo Stable, Chris Stanley, Susan Sterett, and John Torpey. Thanks also to Lesley Grayson, associated with the Science Reference and Information Service of the British Library, for her encouragement and help with bibliographic details. I sincerely acknowledge Donna Merwick and Greg Dening, my history professors at the University of Melbourne, who have always provided inspiration and supported my academic career. Finally, I thank my parents, my twin sister Corinna, and my partner, Philip McCarty, for helping me put the writing of this book into proper perspective.

I am very grateful to the National Science Foundation, the Wenner-Gren Foundation for Anthropological Research, and the Australian Federation of University Women for providing doctoral dissertation grants that funded the research on which this project is based. I am also indebted to copy editors of the Dartmouth Publishing Company, the *Indiana Journal of Global Legal Studies, Political and Legal Anthropology Review, Law and Critique,* and the University of Michigan Press for comments and advice that have in part been incorporated into the book. I'm further indebted to James Clark, director of the University of California Press; Peter Dreyer, who copyedited the manuscript; and Katherine Bell and Rachel Berchten, who both helped to bring this project to completion. Lastly, I want to thank Professor Vincenzo Ferrari and the Selection Committee at the University of Milan for awarding this project the Renato Treves International Sociology of Law Prize in 1997.

Santa Barbara, California
November 1998

Introduction

In 1994, after eight years of construction, the Channel Tunnel between the county of Kent in England and Nord–Pas de Calais in France was completed (map 1). More than just another rail connection, the linking of Kent to Calais by way of the Channel Tunnel represents the first physical, geopolitical joining of Britain to the European mainland. The Tunnel links historical pasts to unfolding futures, and serves as a unique site on which turn important issues surrounding national, regional, and local identities, as well as new challenges to traditional territorial, economic, cultural, and legal boundaries. As the following quotations indicate, the significance of this historic bridging is often simultaneously understood from diverse and even opposing perspectives:

> Something unique is afoot in Europe, in what is still called Europe even if we no longer know very well *what* or *who* goes by this name. Indeed, to what concept, to what real individual, to what singular entity should this name be assigned today? Who will draw up its borders?
>
> (French philosopher and social theorist Jacques Derrida, *The Other Heading* [1992][1])

> While the British were angrily debating their relationship with Europe 1in 1992, a weird landscape was being bull-dozed behind the Kent coast in the south-east; a futuristic network of roads, bridges and railway lines which narrowed into two holes likes nostrils in the ground. The raw excavations and straight lines have a quite different geometry from the surrounding Victorian towns and winding lanes; and the expected rush of traffic from the Channel Tunnel will eventually bypass

1. Derrida 1992: 5.

the local economies, as passengers from the fast special trains race on to London and the north. But the psychological shock goes far deeper.

(British historian Anthony Sampson,
The Essential Anatomy of Britain: Democracy in Crisis [1992][2])

[T]he Channel Tunnel . . . is nothing less than a revolution in habits and practices . . . the whole of Community Europe will have one nervous system and no one country will be able indefinitely to run its economy, its society, its infrastructural development independently from the others.

(French President François Mitterrand[3])

The Channel Tunnel combines French and English ingenuity—the dining car has horrible food served by obnoxious waiters.

(American comedian Conan O'Brien on NBC's
"Late Night with Conan O'Brien Show," 7 May 1994)

Who has paid for all the bally-hoo?

(Lord Ferrier, House of Lords,
second reading of the Channel Tunnel Bill, 16 February 1986)

From one standpoint, the Channel Tunnel can be seen as an enormous national icon of unqualified technical and engineering success that deserves pride of place alongside other modern marvels like the Eiffel Tower and the Empire State Building. Yet the inherently transnational aspects of the Tunnel and its development make it possible to interpret the continuing controversies surrounding it in ways that bring to light ambiguities and contradictions more characteristic of postmodern approaches to complex social issues. When understood as a step in the unification of the New Europe, the Channel Tunnel is often interpreted by English observers less as a modernist triumph and more as an intrusive continental penetration of sovereign island soil. I am careful in my use of "English" rather than "British," since people in Wales, Scotland, and Northern Ireland appear to think about the Tunnel rather differently (see Appendix 2). Thus for many English people, the Channel Tunnel marks the beginning of a new postnational era identified with the ever-increasing power of the European Union (EU)[4] and a continuation of the territorial losses associated with the end of the British empire.

2. Sampson 1992: 108–9.
3. Mitterrand quoted in Holliday, Marcou, and Vickerman 1991: 190.
4. When the European Union was first established in 1957 under the Treaty of Rome, it was called the European Economic Community, or EEC, reflecting its origin as an economically based free-trade zone and customs union between the

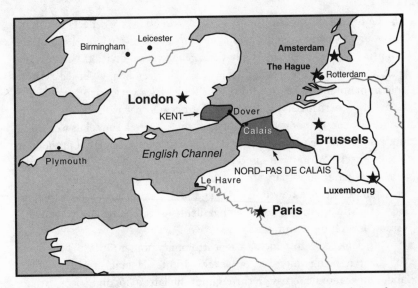

Map 1. The Channel Tunnel in geographical context. Courtesy of Dirk Brandts.

I interpret the Channel Tunnel as both a tangible technology of "connection" and a symbolic metaphor, which together form a dynamic "field" that represents shifting attitudes in England at national, regional, and local levels, to the experience of an ever-encroaching EU. By implication, this interpretation turns upon how the English define themselves vis-à-vis their conception of mainland Europe. As English attitudes about being part of a united Europe continue to vacillate, both new connections and new divides will continue to form between England and the EU. As the social theorist Georg Simmel noted, bridges not only connect a former separation, but can also mark new divisions. According to Simmel, "In the immediate as well as the symbolic sense, in the physical as well as the intellectual sense, we are at any moment those who separate the connected, or connect the separate" (Simmel 1994: 5).

original six member-states, Belgium, France, the Federal Republic of Germany, Italy, Luxembourg, and the Netherlands. In response to the Single European Act (1986) and an emerging recognition that it involved much more than only economic concerns, the EEC came to be called more simply the European Community, or EC. Now, under the Treaty on European Union, or Maastricht Treaty (1992), the name has evolved into European Union. Technically, EC is used to refer to matters within the scope of the Treaty of Rome, such as trade, while EU is used to refer to matters that involve the Maastricht Treaty, such as foreign policy and security issues.

The title of this book, *Bridging Divides*, deliberately reflects the ambiguity of the point Simmel was trying to demonstrate. In the past the English Channel operated as a natural geographical division between England, France, and the rest of Europe. As such, the Channel served a critical role in maintaining what many English felt was a very important distinction between themselves and other Europeans, particularly the French. Hence the contemporary significance of the Channel Tunnel as a connecting bridge between historically quite distinct identities. Yet, I argue, that it is precisely owing to unprecedented levels of social, political, and economic integration, in part attributable to the Tunnel, that there are now emerging in Europe new hostilities and practices through which the illusion of distinct national and regional identities can be reasserted and necessary differences maintained.

This book seeks to punctuate a postcolonial moment in which a former colonizer is being colonized on several fronts. Having gravely suffered under an economic recession throughout the late 1980s and 1990s, Britain is no longer a great imperial power but now one of the poorest countries in northwestern Europe in per capita terms (see graph). Increasingly, England finds itself taking on the role of the colonized, subject to the politico-economic power of the EU and its laws. This external challenge to English authority plays out in numerous ways, creating an internal fragmentation of the state itself as Wales, Scotland, and Northern Ireland demand increasing autonomy, spurred on by their expanding ties to and financial assistance from the EU (Lovering 1991). This is a move that resists and in a way goes toward reversing an earlier phase of internal colonization, most notably described by Michael Hechter, when England subjugated Wales and Scotland under the Act of Union in 1707 to form the modern nation-state of Great Britain (Hechter 1975).

Another feature of postcolonialism related to the EU's breaking down of barriers between and within member-states is its facilitating of movement to England by immigrants from Britain's former colonies. Among other things, the Channel Tunnel is seen by many English as a conduit by which foreigners can enter the country illegally. France, it should be noted, has more illegal immigrants in its territory than any other European country. The presence in the EU of illegal immigrants in search of labor markets and better living conditions directly ties movements of people to the forces behind the global political economy. So any discussion of the Channel Tunnel and how it relates to issues of nationalism, sovereignty, or citizenship in the English imagination necessarily links the postcolonial

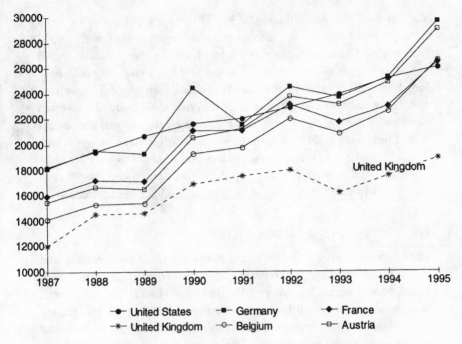

Gross Domestic Product, per capita 1987–95, for the United Kingdom and other nations. Source: *Statistical Yearbook* (New York: United Nations, 1997).

condition with globalization, transnationalism, and modernity (Darian-Smith 1996). And all these elements simultaneously relate to the unfolding cultural, legal, political, and economic tensions between England and the EU.

Today, as much as in the past, the Tunnel embodies a culmination of values associated with the Enlightenment, such as progress and the harnessing of nature by scientific rationality. Like the first railways, invented by the English in the 1820s, the Tunnel and the trains that speed through it are particularly powerful icons of modernity, publicly declaring its builders to be masters of great skill and daring. The Tunnel, in short, "is the ultimate nineteenth-century project completed just before we enter the twenty-first century" (Barnes 1995: 327). There is no denying that the Tunnel is a great engineering feat, but it should be noted that the necessary technology, construction plans, and political proposals to complete such a tunnel have been repeatedly put forward since the mid 1800s. In fact, with the invention of Colonel Edward Beaumont's rotary boring machine in

1875, and the sinking of tunnel shafts at Shakespeare Cliff near Dover and Sangatte near Calais in 1881, construction had begun in 1882, and a tunnel of nearly a mile long was completed before fears of a French invasion again halted tunnel works. An insistent question is if the engineering skills have long been available to build the Channel Tunnel, then why did it take until 1994, over one hundred years, to build it? What is highlighted is an often overlooked dimension in analysis of scientific progress and the much-touted increasing globalization of the world, which is that all projects such as the Tunnel are as much moral and political products as they are technological. And as a "technical" apparatus of "connection," the Tunnel embodies particular ethics, values, politics, and subjective experiences.

THE BUILDING OF THE CHANNEL TUNNEL

The Channel Tunnel bores under the Kentish coast in southern England beneath a point called Shakespeare Cliff—an irony that has often been noted. Shakespeare Cliff, where Edgar leads his blind father, Gloucester, in *King Lear*, is a chalk cliff rising some 300 feet above the sea, epitomizing the chalk downs that line the Dover coast. As the last image of the island on the horizon when crossing the Channel on the way to Europe, Shakespeare and the Dover Cliffs are emblematic of England and have been written about profusely in poems, songs, and fiction.[5]

The Tunnel itself is composed of three parallel tunnels fifty kilometers (thirty-one miles) long, which come to the surface some distance inland in England and France at the Folkestone and Coquelles terminals respectively (fig. 1). The two outer tunnels each contain a single, one-way railroad track. These are joined at intervals by a smaller central tunnel, which provides ventilation and access for support and emergency services. All three tunnels are about forty meters (forty-four yards) below the seabed, and run for thirty-eight kilometers under the Channel, making it the longest undersea railway. Japan's Seikan tunnel, linking the islands of Hokkaido and Honshu, is nearly four kilometers longer in total length, but its underwater section is a few kilometers shorter.

5. In the late nineteenth century, a colliery was established at Shakespeare Cliff's base when coal was discovered during an attempt to dig a Channel Tunnel in the 1880s. Today, in the course of constructing the present Tunnel, this base platform has been extended 250 meters into the sea as a result of 4.75 million cubic meters of excavated tunnel spoil being deposited in artificial lagoons along a 1.5 kilometer stretch at the base of the cliff. Eurotunnel is landscaping this platform to provide public access to a recreation area and environmentally designed foreshore there.

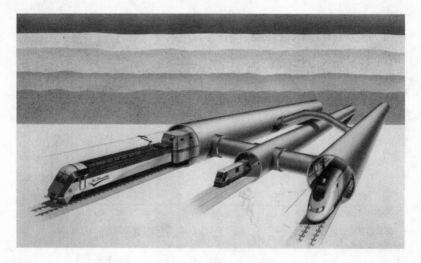

Figure 1. Schematic drawing of the Channel Tunnel. By kind permission of Eurotunnel.

The digging of the Channel Tunnel began on 1 December 1987 on the English side. Huge tunnel-boring machines weighing over 1,000 tonnes were used. Crews worked around the clock at times, in eight-hour shifts, and reached a record 428 meters of construction in a single week. The breakthrough finally came on 1 December 1990, when Graham Fagg and Philippe Cozette bored through the remaining last few layers of chalk to exchange a historical handshake in the service tunnel. The official word was that the meeting of the tunnels in mid channel was out of alignment by about three centimeters. "When we opened up the gap, there was a massive airflow between the two sides," said Fagg, recalling the historical moment. "Once we were on the French side, we got absolutely frozen" (*Kent Messenger*, 5 May 1994). But despite the chill, and some embarrassment that Fagg could not speak a word of French, festive celebrations marked the long-awaited handshake under the sea. After two hundred years of waxing and waning enthusiasm for the project on both sides of the Channel, the Tunnel finally existed.

However, the building of the Tunnel, and its physical linking of states, people, commodities, and communications along new transnational transport networks, represents only part of the still-unfolding narratives about its significance for the people of Kent and its representation in the English and British imagination (Anderson 1991; and see Appendix 2). There is no doubt that the Tunnel has had enormous effects, both positive and negative, on Kent and its quintessential English landscape. Among other things, it has destroyed old farms and orchards, threatened endangered animals, reinvigorated the ferry industry, boosted property prices, heightened tourism, and prompted many English schoolchildren to learn French. The other part of the tale is the significance of the Tunnel as a sign of transitional change. As Anthony Sampson has noted, "the psychological shock goes much deeper" (1992: 109). In its metaphorical and literal undermining of Shakespeare Cliff, Dover, and the wider region of Kent, the Tunnel embodies a piercing of historical narratives and accepted commonalties about what it means to be "Kentish," "English," and "British," and so distinct from mainland Europeans.

Recurring themes of exclusion and inclusion, injustice and state irresponsibility, fear of invasion, and despoliation of Kent's "garden" landscape mark, in different ways, public debates about the building of the Channel Tunnel, both within Kent and at the national level. This book explores these themes over the course of the Tunnel's construction between Kent and Calais in the ten-year period approximately from 1984 to 1994. Uniting my discussion of English responses to the Tunnel is a concern with how they explicitly and implicitly raise issues of law, identity, and territory. This convergence of interests is most marked in a country that has one of the oldest and most stable western systems of democracy, isolated and contained within its island borders. For that very reason, the Tunnel's perceived puncturing of the country's "natural" island borders provides a focus for examining more pervasive public anxiety about the nature of England and its people's future place as citizens of the New Europe.

THE SOCIO-LEGAL AND CULTURAL IMPLICATIONS OF LINKING ENGLAND TO MAINLAND EUROPE

Primarily owing to the Single European Act (1986) and the Treaty on European Union, or Maastricht Treaty, as it is commonly known (1992), the cultural-spatial implications of EU policy have acquired legal and political prominence (Barry 1993; Williams 1993). In part this is due to the fact that in economic terms, the EU seems to be progressing toward its goals, as stated in Article 8a of the 1986 Act, to break down internal state borders, introduce a common currency, and promote the free movement of goods, services, people, and capital. I find it interesting that these goals can in many ways be interpreted as a continuation of the historical development of uninhibited "free trade" characteristic of modern capitalism that dates back over the centuries (Wallerstein 1983; McMichael 1995). Just how the current relaxing of economic borders will affect various legal identities, as well as national, subnational, and transnational cultures, is difficult to predict, precisely because this is a complex and dynamic process.

In modernist terms, law is conventionally defined as a body or system of rules authorized by general consensus and applied and enforced through a central government. As an Enlightenment discourse, modern European law is based on assumptions of sovereignty at multiple levels, and the autonomy of the individual is guaranteed through a person's legal rights as a member of an autonomous, self-governing nation-state (Derrida 1990; Fitzpatrick 1990; Collier et al. 1995). Assumed within this modernist mode is the view that persons, governments, economies, and cultures are units that can stand alone, or have meaning outside of the social context in which they are relationally defined. Following this logic, from the early eighteenth century on, the state became spatially redefined as the bounded geopolitical entity called the nation-state. Used in this way, the hyphen in nation-state designates a conflation of bounded, sovereign territory with the idea of one homogeneous ethnic nationalism.

Today, new subnational and transnational legal interactions are currently challenging these conventional understandings of modern liberal law, and particularly its unquestioned attachment to the bounded modern nation-state (O'Neil 1994). A monopoly over the means of control no longer defines the state; nor does a capacity to be enforced any longer define what is regarded as legitimate law (Weber 1946: 77–83). For example, the EU relies upon members to enforce EU regulations, but the nation-state's authority to produce law and control the terms of coercion have dramatically altered. In Europe, the direct relationship between a system of law and the territorial integrity of the nation-state is gone. More significant, the autonomy of nation-state-based structures of territorial democracy is gone too (Connolly 1991: 199–222). Or, to put it another way, since legal meaning may be perceived on one level as a narrative, the particular (state-bound) discursive spaces in which the narrative of law has existed are in the process of being reshaped (see Dumm 1990; Foucault 1977).

The EU's undermining of the illusion of an autonomous legal state calls into question the mythology surrounding the island nation of Britain. This mythology of Britain being an island entity has in the past given English law a centrally structured form and internal consistency. Today, however, the EU intrudes to question the hyphenated relation between nation and state, bound together through law. The EU imposes policies that expressly seek to dismantle national borders, intentionally loosening the ties between Britain's dominant national culture and the perception of a bounded territorial state. By becoming subject to EU law, Britain in part gives up the material and symbolic capacity to determine whom it will and will not allow to qualify as being a citizen. Changing, then, I argue, are the legal conditions that in the past sustained the cultural ideologies through which Britain's island status embodied Englishness and English nationalism. This raises a central question that is asked in various ways and from various perspectives throughout the book: What is the significance of the European Union's legal blurring of the material and symbolic borders around what people imagine as England and the British nation-state?

From this description of change in Europe, it becomes easy to postulate that the EU constitutes a new legal and political entity that, in transcending member states' powers, goes beyond modern forms of nationalism (Hobsbawm 1990: 163–92; Smith 1997; McGrew 1992). The EU, according to this rationale, is a postnational entity and thus reconfigures the idea of citizenship (see Habermas 1992). This is the rhetoric of Brussels bureaucrats and politicians and many who support them (Shore and Black 1994a; Shore 1995). But whether this rhetoric accords with reality any more than accompanying claims about the nation-state's demise is not altogether evident. Some critics of Brussels argue that the EU's almost total lack of accountability, and of popular support and perceived legitimacy, are in fact creating a new super-state that seeks to promote Anglo/European dominance and so echoes the west's strategies of colonization and racism in the nineteenth century (Bunyan 1991, 1993: 32–33; Webber 1991; Wieviorka 1993). In other words, the EU does not so much represent a breaking down of nation-states as the reproduction of the nation-state's structure in a more expansive and powerful form (Bergeron 1998).

This book takes into account a range of possible interpretations of the relationship of England to the New Europe. I do not contend that the EU is either good or bad, but only that it exemplifies change in legal, political, economic, and cultural cohabitations and (dis)integrations within its ever-expanding territory. To what degree such cohabitations and (dis)integrations ultimately alter existing state structures and state nationalisms remains a critical open question, about which this research can only make preliminary suggestions. The territorially or spatially oriented ethnography that I present here may provide new insights for understanding legal processes and cultural identities not necessarily bounded by a territorially defined state.

In attempting to contextualize the experience of local people and events through the wider contexts of transnational legal, political, and economic shifts, this study links up with new theoretical and methodological approaches emerging within anthropological studies of Europe (Goddard et al. 1994; Macdonald 1993a; Abèles 1991; Herzfeld 1987, 1992; Wilson and Smith 1993; Nadel-Klein 1991; Nelson and Viet 1992). Scholars are now taking seriously the critiques in the 1970s of a European anthropology predominantly focused on village studies and small rural communities (Macdonald 1993b: 5, 11; Grillo 1980: 3–9). In contrast to this earlier scholarship, there is now much interest in the impact of large-scale legal, political, and economic change, and the people in positions of power affecting such change, on cultural formations (Shore and Black 1994b; Wilson 1993). The more interesting of these studies, from which I take my cue, seek to understand how cultural diversity in the context of the idea of a united European citizenry forces a merging and colliding of arenas of power, in turn disrupting the linear symmetry presupposed in a local/global ordering of society.

Current research focusing on the concepts of borders and frontiers also points to the cultural complexities of identity politics, particularly evident in moves toward the breaking down of national boundaries in the European Union (e.g., Donnan and Wilson 1994; Wilson and Donnan 1998). While "boundaries" have for a long time been a theme in anthropology (Evans-Pritchard 1940; Barth 1969; Leach 1954; Cohen 1987; Prescott 1987), what these new studies introduce is an approach derivative of new directions in cultural geography (Rumley and Minghi 1991: 1–14). Highlighted are the more subtle and less well articulated frontiers of cultural conflict operating through and between people and places inside (and outside) geopolitical lines (Beynon and Hudson 1993). These studies represent a move away from the presumption of a state-centered discussion in an attempt to examine how what is happening between nations at international borders has as much to do with demarcating the others beyond state lines as the others within (see Berdahl 1999; Buchanan 1995; Bhabha 1994; Gupta and Ferguson 1992; Borneman 1992). In contrast to earlier anthropological explorations, what these recent studies suggest, rather than treating boundaries as primarily marking community and state divisions, are the multiplicity and simultaneity of cultural identities generated through border redefinition.

THE INTERSECTIONS OF LAW, IDENTITY, TERRITORY, AND LANDSCAPE

In treating Kent as a border region *and* as a site of power differentiation through which competing legal regimes operate and interrelate, it becomes clear that analyzing shifts in legal identity and consciousness cannot be contained by reference to localities within the framing totality of the state. The tensions between English and EU law illustrate that areas of English legal competence are not static, and that there is not a simple hierarchy of power between local and state governments. This is not to suggest that English law or the British state will matter less in the future (Milward 1992; Kahler 1987; Wallace 1997; Brenner 1997; Wallace 1997; Ross 1990). What I argue throughout the book, however, is that the landscape, the nature, the ground on which England's "iconic unity of law" is based can no longer be assumed to be solid or fixed (Goodrich and Hachamovitch 1991: 167; Goodrich 1992: 15; Fitzpatrick 1998). Land or, more specifically, the island state, as a point of reference through which English law is invested with cultural meaning is being held up as vulnerable and open to re-representation. Hence one important dimension of an increasing cross-border blurring of the taken-for-granted relations between territory and national identity is its highlighting of the nonorganic relationship between law, geography, and state.[6]

6. Notwithstanding that spatial metaphors have a long history (e.g., William Blackstone's "general map of the law" of 1765, discussed in chapter 1), there is a marked absence of research into the relationships between law and political-geographical space, or the implications of space as a concept in legal discourse (see Ford 1994: 1857; Pue 1990: 566; Economides et al. 1986: 162; Blomley 1989a). There have been a few studies that highlight the geographical viability of national laws by focusing on different enforcement agencies and techniques (Blomley 1989b; Kirby 1990), describe the uneven distribution of legal resources (Blacksell et al. 1988), or point to racial boundaries and segregation in the spatial differentiation of particular areas within cities (Ford 1994). But space as a concept has been generally ignored in legal analysis. This is despite theories of place, space, and territoriality, and their relationship to nationalism, postcolonialism, and identity, increasingly attracting attention in the social sciences (Carter and Squires 1993; Keith and Pile 1993; Bird et al. 1994; Friedland and Boden 1994; Godlewska and Smith 1994).

I suggest three interrelated reasons why law and its relationship to spatial differentiation are overlooked. First, the dominant formalist conceptions of law are anti-contextual. Since they are supposedly abstract, universal rules, there is no necessity to ground law in specific context; rules have no history and no geography. Wesley Pue argues that, bleak as it might sound, all contexts, be they of gender, race, class, history, or space, are the enemies of law. "Law is the antithesis of region, locality, place, community" (Pue 1990: 566, 577). The credibility of law

Michel Foucault's theory of governmentality, and its basis in strategic power relations that extend beyond any one state, plays a central role in my analysis (Foucault 1991; Rose and Miller 1992). Building on Foucault's arguments, which I discuss in chapter 1, I suggest that territory or landscape plays a critical role as a mechanism of governmentality in its conflating of juridical and disciplinary forms of power. Landscape, in other words, embodies particular logics of order and authority that represent the places and spaces in which people live, but that are not necessarily state-bound. Treating landscape as a form of governmentality opens up our thinking about what constitutes the realms of law. It suggests a need to move beyond explicit legal change, accounted for in the more obvious arenas of courtrooms, parlia-

---

depends upon its capacity to be universally applicable across social and geographical divisions. A belief in this universalism was, of course, critical in the colonial expansion of the eighteenth and nineteenth centuries, when imperialist nations presumed a capacity to transport their own legal systems and impose them in entirely different geographical locations. The basic legal premise was that the wilderness of Africa was equivalent to metropolitan London or Paris. This points to a second reason why law ignores space, which is that law is abstract. Law generalizes, and in so doing, it displaces any geographical context. Generalized rules diminish the specific details of any one case. Rules depersonalize, freeze time, and displace actual events and circumstances. In this way, legal rules gain kudos as scientific truths. Able to be objectified and abstracted, rules apply because of their very rationality, generality, and naturalized logic. Rules embody a principle. Thus a law cannot be valid in one part of the country and invalid in another. Such a localized contextualization is characteristic of custom, which as explored further in chapter 7 with respect to the revival of the custom beating the bounds, is the conceptual opposite of modern formal law. Third, law needs to serve the ideals of universalism and equality that underpin modern western law. For law to be legitimate, it must be presented as accessible to all and accountable to each. It has to persuade, in ways similar to belief in a god, that it is the highest authority. Space is rarely discussed in the context of law, because it disrupts its overarching mythical logic and undermines its explanatory power. According to Pue, if it were accepted that legal knowledge is context-specific:

> all the hallmarks of professional training in common-law countries would be swept away . . . : gone would be the case method, Socratic teaching, obsession with judge-made law, the myopic focus on courts, contempt for the workaday world of law, the public-private distinction, the over emphasis on commercial law subjects, . . . the denial of history and place, . . . and all the spoken and unspoken cues in "training for hierarchy." (Pue 1990: 578)

Against intrinsic opposition from within the law, some legal geographers and legal scholars have been opening up the field of law's spatial implications over the past ten years (see Blomley 1994; Blomley and Clark 1990; Clark 1989; Johnston 1990; Stanley 1995). There is an emerging acknowledgment that law is, in the words of David Engel, "self-consciously spatial in orientation, and its first concern is to define the boundaries within which it operates" (1993: 130). The overriding concern in this call for a legal-spatial reorientation is to stress the site-specificity or place of legal analysis (e.g., Costonis 1989; Karp 1990).

ment, legislation, and the legal profession, and focus on an aesthetics of law. By this I mean the ways in which law is intimately connected to visual, sensual, and textural phenomena, and hence the need to explore how an aesthetic redefinition of people's view of their material, symbolic, and metaphoric landscapes influence how they experience the powers that order specific territories and shape related forms of morality. In the 1950s, Edmund Leach argued that "[l]ogically, aesthetics and ethics are identical. If we are to understand the ethical rules of a society, it is aesthetics that we must study" (1954: 12). More recently, Peter Goodrich has explicitly connected aesthetics with legal practice, noting: "A reading of the legal text which ignores the power of its imagery or the aesthetic of its reception is a reading which is in many senses beside the point in that it ignores precisely that dimension of the text and its context which performs the labour of signification and so gives the text its effect" (1991: 236–38).

Legal aesthetics highlights persisting indeterminacies between statehood, territory, and subjective identity and focuses attention on how we may understand law in practice (Coombe 1989). It adds one more dimension to an exciting body of literature in anthropological approaches to law that deals with both subnational and transnational constructions of difference (Merry 1992; Maurer 1997; Coutine n.d.; Gupta 1992; Collier et al. 1995; Santos 1995). Up until recently, much of the work by socio-legal scholars has tended to take as given a structural state context against which individual agency and resistance can be posited (e.g., Merry 1990; Lazarus-Black and Hirsch 1994: 13; McCann and March 1994: 19; Greenhouse et al. 1994). However, if we accept that the state is not a given entity and must be constantly interrogated as a subject of investigation (Abrams 1988; Taussig 1996), new questions emerge that ask in what ways other than through state structures we understand the operation and power of law itself. In the context of the Channel Tunnel, I ask: *How is legal intervention by the European Union reorganizing Kent's local politics and opening up to local government through alternative decision-making processes new possibilities, participations, and purposes that transcend national borders? In what ways does the EU's supervision and endorsement of the transnational Euroregion of which Kent is a part challenge the nature of England's control of law and politics? And is the overlapping of English and EU legal systems contesting the authoritative basis of law and so determining new forms of legal understanding, subjectivity, and consciousness? In sum, can it be argued that the presence of a European legal order is undermining (or reinforcing) the conditions sustaining nationalism through which state law is accepted and acceptable?*

It is, I suggest, issues such as transnationalism, globalization, and post-colonialism that a legal anthropology will have to increasingly identify and negotiate in integrating shifts in legal systems with new configurations of cultural identity not necessarily defined through and against the state (Certeau 1998; Darian-Smith and Fitzpatrick 1998a). In anthropology, it has been an important step to move away from a perceived need to compare, differentiate, and implicitly rank customary law and colonial law as though they were distinct and separate entities (Geertz 1983; Comaroff and Roberts 1981; Gadacz 1982), and more explicitly focus on issues of power (Moore 1973, 1976, 1986; Cohn and Dirks 1988; Starr and Collier 1989; Just 1992; Fuller 1994). The result is the now familiar interpretation of legal systems as indicators of and strategies for asserting nationalist sentiments, be these conceived of as inherently racist, gendered, or otherwise (Fitzpatrick 1995b; Pateman 1988; Rhodes 1989; Smart 1989). However, if it is accepted that legal and cultural orders are mutually defining, and that "'nationhood' mandates a congruence between cultural and legal entities" (Starr and Collier 1989: 12), it is important to then ask how new legal alignments below and beyond the state fit into this formula and what kinds of nationalism they generate. In other words, if the unity of a nation is equivalent to its national law, as Goodrich maintains (1992: 10), and it is thus the case that "to create a legal order is to write into law a sense of national unity and purpose" (Starr and Collier 1989: 11), how can this be understood in the context of the EU, which embodies a new form of transnational legal order, and, following this logic, substantiates a new form of overarching nationalism?

In the following chapters, I examine such things as a local land ritual, the historical role of railroads, transnational policing of terrorism, fear of the plague, and the garden landscape as pivots on which turn the larger theme of the shifting relationships between law, identity, and territory. My aim is to criticize the use of these categories as static or independent units. By focusing on the impact of the Channel Tunnel upon the relationships between people living in Kent, England, Britain, France, and the emerging New Europe, this book explores some of the ways in which the EU blurs the linear association between law, geography, and culture. This exploration highlights how these various and overlapping regional identities, and their associated legal and cultural structures, are continually redefined both in relation to, and as resistance against, the EU and its separate member-states.

1 Landscape and Law in the English Imagination

One of the most powerful symbols of the English constitution and its connection to land is the oak tree, which explicitly links law and order with earth and water and the ancient roots of history.[1] In England, the most symbolic of all trees is the oak. The value of the oak as a source of fuel and, perhaps more critically, as the most suitable shipbuilding material, and so vital to the maintaining of the English navy, ensured its prominence throughout the sixteenth, seventeenth, and eighteenth centuries (Schama 1995: 153–83). The oak tree was emblematic of native freedom and a marker of patriotism. Particularly during the Napoleonic wars, when wood became scarce, among those lords with political aspirations, it became almost obligatory to plant oak plantations as a signal of one's loyalty and commitment to the nation, as well as a symbolic affirmation of national power (Schama 1995: 168; Daniels 1988: 47–48; Williamson 1995: 124–30).

The English oak, native to the island, represented a particular relationship, evoked through the national imaginary about its people and the land. It historically symbolized—as does the Latin derivation of the word "forest," in which the oak stands—the exclusive property of the king or state "outside" the reach of the ordinary person (Schama 1995: 144). At times

---

1. "Now of all European trees none has such claims as the oak to be considered as pre-eminently the sacred tree of the Aryans," writes Sir James Frazer. ". . . We have seen that it was not only the sacred tree, but the principal object of worship of both Celts and Slavs" (1981 [1890–1915], 2: 291; see also Fernandez 1991: 11–12). English history is inextricably linked with oak trees. For instance, the future King Charles II hid in the branches of an oak tree after the battle of Worcester in 1651 and following the Restoration planted oaks as a symbol of authority and national power.

this exclusionary symbolism was contested by poor peasants, as expressed in local outbursts of resistance against the propertied elite, who felled many trees in the clearance of enclosed land. But more readily the oak was appropriated by the wider English population as a symbolic barrier to outside intervention and foreign attack. William Hogarth summed up this sentiment in a cartoon called *The Invasion* published in 1756 on the outbreak of the Seven Years' War with France. In it, British soldiers and a sailor amuse themselves outside an inn, while another soldier draws a caricature of the French king on the wall. The inscriptions include extracts from James Thomson's song "Rule Britannia," and end with the verse:

Britons to arms! and let em come . . .
No Power can stand the deadly Stroke
That's given from Hands & Hearts of Oak
With Liberty to back em.

Simon Schama in a chapter in *Landscape and Memory* entitled "Hearts of Oak and Bulwarks of Liberty?" expands upon the symbolic imagery of English woodlands as infused with a sensibility of freedom and justice (Schama 1995: 153–74). Schama argues that stories and mythologies about woods and trees and their linking to laws and outlaws—such as the tale of Robin Hood of Sherwood Forest, who robbed the rich to give to the poor—filter through the national sensibility (ibid.: 142). Curiously, oak trees symbolized both a landed conservatism, in their protection and cultivation by the gentry, and the radicalism epitomized by Tom Paine's appropriation of the oak tree as symbolic of North America's independence (Daniels 1988: 43–57).

Today, the oak is still associated with freedom from external influence and its symbolism is used as a strategy for conservation and defining of the "proper" rural landscape. In Kent, there exists a group called "Men of Trees." Established in 1923 by a former South African colonist, it currently attracts about 300 people from the county, mostly over 40 years of age, and, it can be safely presumed, mostly from middle- and upper-class Conservative backgrounds. According to the group's chairperson, Peggy Stevens, Men of Trees sponsors tree plantings and competitions in villages but not towns. When I asked her what criteria were used to make this distinction, she replied, "I have been born and bred in Kent and I know my villages from my towns!" (interview, 30 Nov. 1993). She proudly announced that at the queen's sixtieth birthday celebration, the group had planted an avenue of oak trees at Lyton Park, and then proceeded to tell me a long list of other sponsored oak plantings in Kent.

What appeared most important for Peggy Stevens was that the trees sustained her insider's knowledge as a native of Kent as to what constituted a village. Moreover, in being able to recognize an "authentic" village, the group could take satisfaction in protecting and perpetuating a village-based community that spoke of traditional values and a nostalgia for a golden past. Hence only those villages that meet the criteria established by Men of Trees are deemed worthy of improvement and so eligible for free oak trees, grown locally at Ashford. No doubt its members would agree with Uvedale Price, in his 1794 essay on the picturesque, that trees "alone form a canopy over us, and a varied frame to all other objects which they admit, exclude, and group with, almost at the will of the improver" (quoted in Daniels 1988: 57–59). Today, these trees symbolize a sense of freedom in their being used to acknowledge, commemorate, and help sustain small communities that have resisted the outside intervention and modernization that taint larger Kentish towns.

This linking symbolism of the oak tree with the ownership and ordering of the land and the reproduction of a timeless English justice helps explain the transfer of Biggins Wood, an ancient oak woodland that was situated in the middle of the Channel Tunnel terminal site at Cheriton, Folkestone.[2] This transfer of a forest was the largest conservation project of its kind in Britain and attracted a great deal of local and national attention. Because the mature oak trees were too big to shift, thousands of acorns were collected and 2,000 saplings grown and then planted on the edge of the terminal. This was accompanied by the redistribution of two and a half acres of topsoil from the old to the newly constructed woodland. The project's importance, at least to those volunteers to whom I talked from local environmental groups and students from Wye College who had taken part in its operation, went beyond the immediate satisfaction of replanting a woodland. Transferring the new trees reflected stoicism in the line of defense, a determination not to be beaten, and resistance to historical change.

In the 1989 BBC Keith lecture, Jacques Darras comments:

2. In Kent, numerous tales and legends about trees and woodlands exist. The Headcorn Oak, in Headcorn, is the only remaining tree of a group of oaks claimed to be more than 1,000 years old and part of the original ancient forests of the Kentish Weald. The last tree is very gnarled and crooked, but still managing to produce foliage every year. Legend goes that John Hessel was wrongly accused of stealing sheep and was imprisoned in a room overlooking the tree. He escaped by climbing along its branches, and so lived to prove his innocence (Bignell 1983: 58). Again justice is linked here to the symbolism of a magisterial old oak tree.

To this day, British—especially English—nationalism is an organic nationalism of dissent, where each individual interiorises personally a social and political contract all presume to have the force of Nature. On the Continent, certainly in France, systems of law and politics are made by people and changeable by people. In English common law each case is considered an offshoot of what preceded it, a new scion of an old legal bough, unlike the bureaucratic new laws that keep turning up tied in European red tape and postmarked Brussels. Indeed our respective nationalisms seem to me to carry the mark of a deeper, almost theological cleft.

(Darras 1990: 91–92)

In this chapter, I examine some of the relevant connections between legal aesthetics and its symbolic connection with land, property, and nationalist ideals. This discussion is not irrelevant to understanding current legal transformations unfolding in the New Europe. In the context of the EU as an overarching legal entity, state laws, now more than ever before, operate as markers of national identity and local distinctiveness. The extent to which law marks difference—the significance of a legal identity—should not be overlooked. Important to current politics is how legal distinctiveness is being drawn, argued, and justified through interpreted histories of modern western nation-building and mythologized genealogies of certain peoples living in specific terrains.

I begin an analysis of legal aesthetics and legal identity by first highlighting my theoretical frames as they relate to the relationship between landscape and nationalism. This leads into a historical exploration of the links between law and landscape in the establishment of an English legal identity, which, I argue, was critical to the forging of a nationalist sentiment and British processes of state-building. I analyze how English common law developed in the seventeenth and eighteenth centuries in direct contrast to that envisioned as occurring across the Channel in France. English common law, and the related principles of parliamentary sovereignty, was what the French codified law introduced by Napoleon could never be. The mythology surrounding English law was that it was deeply embedded over time immemorial in an idealized image of the (is)land, its stoic peoples, and a particular landscape of property ownership and aesthetics that marked borders and a rational ordering of the land. Finally, I link this discussion of the past to contemporary responses to the Channel Tunnel and argue that historical attitudes toward law and legal identity in England are now resurfacing in connection to the Tunnel's despoiling of an old, cherished, nationally symbolic Kentish landscape.

LANDSCAPES AND NATIONALISMS

The imperative to account for constructions of space as a particularized territory—be this a state territory or otherwise—is crystallized in any discussion of landscape. The meaning of "landscape," like the "places" that occupy it, is complicated and involves a long intellectual genealogy that parallels the rise of modern nation-states and capitalist economy (Johnston 1990). Of course, a landscape represents different things for different people at different times, seen through different perspectives. In his essay "The Beholding Eye," Donald Meinig illustrates this with ten different versions of the same scene, saying, "Thus we confront the central problem: any landscape is composed not of what lies before our eyes but what lies within our heads" (Meinig 1979: 34). Moreover, a landscape is capable of defining a collective imagination. Any landscape does not just exist, but is to be thought of as a form of "cultural practice," a particular way of observing, a strategy of encoding. I thus adopt W. J. T. Mitchell's aim to "think of landscape, not as an object to be seen or a text to be read, but as a process by which social and subjective identities are formed" (Mitchell 1994a: 1; see also Inglis 1990; Zukin 1991: 16–20). This approach questions the proposition suggested by Barbara Bender that landscapes can be divided into horizontal and vertical planes, and that in contemporary western societies, the landscape involves only the surface or topography of the land (Bender 1993: 1). Against this, I argue that in western as much as in nonwestern contexts, landscapes reflect cosmologies and epistemologies that transcend the lie of the land. The "taken for-granted landscapes of our daily lives" (Cosgrove 1989: 131) are thus part of our "unwitting biography, reflecting our values, our aspirations and even our fears in tangible, visible form" (Lewis 1979: 12; and see also Daniels and Cosgrove 1988, 1993). Landscapes influence people's thinking and social relations in important ways, helping to make tangible categories of thought and spatially articulate social relations.

As a constructed social space, landscape is an expression of ideology, and as such it is political, contested, and dynamic. And as manifestations of social value and mythologized collective vision, landscapes in Europe "remain compelling icons of *national* identity" (Lowenthal 1994: 30), calling to mind Claude Lévi-Strauss's discussion of "mythical geography" in the construction of tribal identities (Lévi-Strauss 1966: 166). Scholars are increasingly recognizing the significance of the English landscape in the foundation and maintenance of the modern island-state (Cosgrove 1993; Wright 1985; Daniels 1988; Helsinger 1994; Bermingham 1994). Alongside today's roaring heritage industry, there is a growing market for coffee-table magazines full of glossy imagery of a parochial "south country" recognized as quintessentially "English." Magazines such as *This England*, *The Field*, and *Great Britain: The Conservation of Our Heritage* merge ecological and heritage issues in the assertion of a nostalgic rural idyll (Walsh 1992: 126). Clearly, this mythical landscape has a "semiotic structure rather like that of money, functioning as a special sort of commodity that plays a unique symbolic role in the system of exchange value" (Mitchell 1994b: 14).

While it is certainly problematic to speak of England as representative of the rest of Britain, the protection and commodification of the localized English countryside through governmental (and, increasingly, nongovernmental) bodies should be historically considered first and foremost a nationalist project (Claval 1992: 348). The reification of the countryside was and is a strategy for gathering in the national territory and for reasserting the autonomous sovereignty of a bounded and cohesive state. This process is succinctly illustrated by a 1994 issue of postage stamps depicting Prince Charles's watercolor paintings. Landscape views of Scotland, Wales, and England draw together the separate regions of Britain and position the viewer "inside" looking out onto a delimited island horizon. These views are devoid of actual people, and questions of race, poverty, unemployment, and regional differences are thus masked in a glorious, golden hue of naturalized empty ruralism. This is an explicit—although not necessarily conscious—instance of a particular construction of territoriality being used as a strategy and cultural practice in the imposing of order and reinforcing of a central state authority.

Moreover, infused as it is with legal meaning and legalities, landscape provides one way of breaching the distinction between what Foucault calls juridical and disciplinary notions of power. Judiciary power refers to a centralized state system of rules and norms, authorized through a theory of sovereignty. In contrast, disciplinary power is fragmented, diffuse, normalizing, and "more pervasive than a set of state laws or state apparatus," resulting in it having no fixed center (Foucault 1980: 158; see also Gordon 1987; Burchell et al. 1986). According to the legal theorist Boaventura de Sousa Santos, this distinction is defective for two reasons. First, although Foucault rightly posits power relations that transcend state entities,

> he goes too far in stressing their dispersion and fragmentation. He is left with no theory of hierarchy of power forms and consequently no theory of social transformation. He obscures the central role of the

power forms of the citizenplace and the workplace in our societies, domination and exploitation, respectively.

On the other hand, it must be noted that, in other respects, Foucault does not go far enough. He takes the conventional critical wisdom about the state for granted, in that he conceives state power and law as a monolithic entity and reduces it to the exercise of coercion. This leads him to overstate the mutual incompatibility of juridical power and disciplinary power and to overlook the subtle interpenetrations between them.

(Santos 1985: 325)

With respect to the first critique, according to Santos, Foucault's stressing of the intricate workings of power taken for granted in cultural practices does not adequately take into account how power is promulgated through state institutions. This relates to Santos's second critique, that while Foucault consciously avoids privileging the state and state law, he in fact reiterates conventional assumptions about the state as a totalizing entity.[3]

3. This helps explain Foucault's ignoring of territory as a strategy of governmentality precisely because he considered it an adjunct to the state. Territory, according to Foucault, is a secondary matter to governmental rationality, his central concern, and in effect equates to the state. By governmental rationality, Foucault refers to the tactics and technologies employed by the modern state for the purposes of social control, such as statistics, surveillance, police, hospitals, prisons, and records (Foucault 1991: 99). By contrast, governmentality is concerned with the ordering and management of whole populations, referring to issues of social control and security and also to the managing of the singular person, the subjectivity of the individual, through what Foucault calls the technologies of the self (Foucault 1988). Central, then, to the concept of governmentality is the idea that power and control are not only the work of state institutions. But, says Foucault, "I don't want to say that the state isn't important; what I want to say is that relations of power, and hence the analysis that must be made of them, necessarily extend beyond the limits of the state" (Foucault 1980: 122; see also pp. 72–73). Because governmentality extends beyond the state, law, as a result of its connection to the state, plays a secondary role in the context of power. In Foucault's words: "One impoverishes the question of power if one poses it solely in terms of legislation and constitution, in terms solely of the state and the state apparatus. Power is quite different from and more complicated, dense and pervasive than a set of laws or a state apparatus" (Foucault 1980: 158). According to Foucault, the disciplinary mechanisms of power are not the application of a central law but an apparatus of punishment (Foucault 1984: 337–38). Therefore power should not be confused with law. "What we need today. . . . is a political philosophy that is not erected around the problem of sovereignty, nor therefore around the problems of law and prohibition. We need to cut off the King's head" because "power is always already there" (Foucault 1980: 121, 141). Yet Foucault does not deny the importance of legal phenomena. While discipline is not an extension of the juridico-

Against this position, I suggest that relations among law, identity, and territory should not be so neatly conflated with the institutional structure of the state. Landscape, as the cultural reproduction of territory and an icon of national identity, may transcend state boundaries. For this reason, landscape should, I argue, be approached as a strategy of governmentality. In being infused with legal meanings and multiple forms of legality, landscape highlights the necessary compatibility of the juridical and disciplinary forms of power that together inform Foucault's concept of governmentality. Landscape is subject to legal norms that in part determine its use, value, and appearance, and, at the same time, is a normalizing social space implicated in the networks of power relations among the individuals who inhabit it. Foucault's discussion of cemeteries and gardens as particular spaces highlights the significance of these localized landscaped projections in the construction of modern cities, which banished the cemetery to the suburbs and reified the zoological garden "as a sort of happy, universalizing heterotopia" (Foucault 1986: 25–26). Expanding these insights to encompass the context of governmentality indicates that the concept of landscape as a cultural practice is one way of approaching the apparent divide between judiciary and disciplinary power and focusing on their intrinsic interpenetrations.

With the above theoretical issues in mind, I now turn to the history of English law as it developed up to and beyond the French Revolution. My argument is that English legal identity today cannot be disassociated from its long historical relationship to a very specific construction of land and local landscape. In the current historical moment, this relationship is widely perceived by many English people to be under attack by the European mainland, an assault dramatically experienced through and symbolized by the building of the Channel Tunnel.

PROTESTANT ISLE OF LIBERTY

Up until the French Revolution of 1789, it was a widely held presumption amongst European philosophers and politicians that England possessed the most liberal democratic system in Europe. To bolster this claim, they cited

---

political structures of society, it is not independent of them. The techniques of surveillance represented by Jeremy Bentham's panopticon, for instance, generalize the power to punish, but do not represent a universal consciousness of law. So in a way law follows discipline. Law is secondary in that it sustains and legitimates what the technologies of power have already established as norms (Foucault 1980: 95; see also Hunt 1992; Silbey 1992; Simon 1992; Hunt and Wickham 1994).

England's unique system of common law based on customary legal practice, as evidenced in the doctrine of precedent (Pocock 1987: 31). In the seventeenth century, English customary law was contrasted to other European systems, which incorporated various versions of Roman law and, as written texts, had been imposed upon the people by a dominant sovereign (Helgerson 1992: 63–104). By contrast, as Sir John Davies, attorney-general for Ireland, wrote in 1612, English common law is

> nothing else but the *Common Custome* of the Realm: and a custom which hath obtained the force of a Law is always said to be *Jus non scriptum*: for it cannot be made or created either by Charter, or by Parliament, which are acts reduced to writing, and are alwaies matter of record: but being onely matter of fact, and consisting in use and practice, it can be recorded and register no-where but in the memory of the people.
>
> (Davies quoted in Pocock 1987: 32–33)

Davies expressly pointed to a "natural" conflation between law and state, claiming that English customary law is:

> so framed and fitted to the nature and disposition of this people, as we may properly say it is connatural to the Nation, so it cannot possibly be ruled by any other law. This Law therefore doth demonstrate the strength of wit and reason and self-sufficiency which hath been always in the People of this Land, which have made their own Laws out of their wisedome and experience, (like a silk-worm that formeth all her web out of her self onely), not begging or borrowing a form of a Commonweal, either from *Rome* or from *Greece*, as all other Nations of *Europe* have done. . . .
>
> (Davies quoted in Pocock 1987: 33–34)

This emphasis on the immemoriality of law was endorsed by Sir Edward Coke in the preface to his *Fourth Reports* (ca. 1610) where he supported the idea of judge-made law on the basis of its refining customary law and not creating new regulations (Pocock 1987: 35–55; see also Helgerson 1992: 70–93). The common law's immemoriality justified its fixity, surety, and central place in the defining of English people's mythologized loyalty to an ancient constitution that had developed in a pre-sovereign historical age. The merging of myth, law, and land is powerfully visualized in the title page from Thomas Hobbes's *Leviathan* of 1651 (Hobbes 1985), where the Leviathan is depicted as a great giant presiding over a tidy landscape composed of a walled town with a large cathedral (Canterbury?) in the foreground and smaller towns in the distance. Leviathan literally embodies the body politic, composed of thousands of individuals, all facing inwards to a central core. Above Leviathan, the Latin inscription reads, "There is no power over earth than compares to him."

According to the legal theorist Sir William Blackstone, in his famous *Commentaries on the Laws of England* (1765), the unique qualities of English law articulated a cartography or a "general map of the law, marking out the shape of the country, its connexions and boundaries, its greater divisions and principal cities" (Blackstone 1765: 34). This spatial dimension had helped England weather "the rude shock of the Norman conquest" (ibid.: 11).[4] Moreover, "in our law the goodness of a custom depends upon its having been used time out of mind. . . . This is what gives it its weight and authority: and of this nature are the maxims and customs which compose the common law, or *lex non scripta*, of this kingdom" (ibid.: 67). The Irish-born poet, playwright, and novelist Oliver Goldsmith (1728–74) supported the superiority of custom over written law, arguing nostalgically that the former "partakes of the nature of parental injunction; it is kept by the people themselves, and observed with a willing obedience. The observance of it must, therefore, be a mark of freedom" (Goldsmith 1759: 208).

Montesquieu in 1729 and Tocqueville a century later were both enchanted by England's legal system. "This nation is passionately fond of liberty," Montesquieu wrote, speculating that "the inhabitants of islands have a higher relish for liberty than those of the continent." A sense of liberty was also believed better suited to Protestantism than Catholicism, and Tocqueville saw in English law the reason for Britain's prosperous trade and precocious modernization (cited in Macfarlane 1978: 165–69).

Considering the country's extensive naval power and trading networks, this image was comparatively easy to maintain. William Hogarth's satirical cartoon *The Gates of Calais. O the Roast Beef of Old England* (fig. 2) contrasts England with a starved France oppressed by its Catholic faith and monarchy. In the foreground, Hogarth portrays those objects of English scorn, the Highland Scottish refugee and the degraded Irish mercenary, both employed in the French military service. The main focus of the cartoon is a rotund French friar greedily watching a skinny French cook staggering under the weight of a huge sirloin of beef just arrived by boat from

4. However, it has been convincingly argued that English law is, paradoxically, essentially French, in having been introduced by the Normans in the eleventh century (see Caenegem 1973: 85–110).

England and being carried to a hostelry for English travelers.[5] Hogarth, who can be seen drawing the scene in the left-hand corner, had the misfortune to be arrested as a spy while sketching the fortifications of Calais (note the hand of the arresting soldier on his back). Wrote Hogarth:

> The first time anyone goes from hence to France by way of Calais he cannot avoid being struck with the extreme different face things appear with at so little a distance from Dover, a farcical pomp of war, a parade of religion and bustle with very little business, in short poverty, slavery, an insolence with an affection of politeness. . . . I mean to display to my own countrymen the striking difference between the food, priests, soldiers, etc. of the two nations.
>
> (British Museum 1992: 1; see also George 1959: 114)

Comparing the French, North American, and English legal systems in the 1830s, Tocqueville concluded that Britain's island isolation from continental Europe had protected it from the "new phenomenon of the Revolution," which he considered a "virus of a new and unknown kind" (quoted in Drescher 1964: 195). As a consequence, there was no other country in Europe, according to Tocqueville, in "which, even in Blackstone's time, the great ends of justice were more fully attained than in England; not one where every man, of whatever rank, and whether his suit was against private individual or sovereign, was more certain of being heard, and more assured of finding his fortune, his liberty, and his life" (quoted in ibid.: 205).

Tocqueville's insights spoke to what he believed were medieval traces

5. The symbolic linking of beef with English identity has taken a nasty turn with the panic over bovine spongiform encephalitis (BSE), or "mad cow disease." This fatal affliction, a degenerative condition of the brain resulting from eating contaminated meat, came to public attention in the mid 1990s amid great controversy. It became apparent that the Tory government had deliberately held back information and put the British population and others at considerable health risk. The EU immediately imposed bans on the export of beef and beef products to the Continent, which has in effect crippled English beef production. Countless cattle have been slaughtered in an attempt to eradicate the problem.

Quite apart from the economic ramifications of BSE, the attack on the beef industry has taken a heavy psychic toll on England. "In the ebullient infancy of the British empire, beef was not just the dinner . . . of choice; it was an entire gastronomic constitution, the marrow of political freedom," Simon Schama observes (1996: 61). Today, beef—or rather its likely absence from the table owing to BSE—evokes images, not of the wealth and power of the empire, but of its demise and internal decay. "The monarchy may have become soap opera, and the national cricket team a bad joke, but the extinction of the Sunday lunch of Roast Beef and Yorkshire Pudding has tabloid soothsayers prophesying the death knell of British culture," according to Schama (ibid.: 62).

Figure 2. *The Gates of Calais*, by William Hogarth (1749). By kind permission of the Founder's Library, University of Wales, Lampeter.

of communal vitality in the English parish system of local government, which formed the "foundation of the English constitution and English habits" (ibid.: 204). The French parish, by contrast, had been swamped by a dictatorial and centralizing government that in dispelling the power of the French nobility had also dissolved a sense of participation and mutual responsibility among French people. Under the *ancien régime*, according to Tocqueville, the withering away of political life had resulted in a disproportionate growth of bureaucratic power and strategies of secrecy, irresponsibility, and resignation, which became the dominant traits of French public life (ibid.: 201).

Tocqueville's focus on what his great intellectual confident and collaborator Gustave de Beaumont called the "democratic-Saxon parish" taps into a central theme of locality underpinning how the English viewed their own legal and political system. The parish system exemplified the power of Protestantism, and thus above all the freedom of the English in the face of a Catholic France and Ireland. For it was precisely this sensibility of independence that was shaped by and shaped the particular form of English liberalism that was the envy of foreigners like Tocqueville. "Specific free-doms—free subjects, free speech, free ideas, free religion, free contracts, free enterprise, free markets, free trade—were the *historic* liberal induce-ments of an *ideal* Englishness" (Colls 1986: 31).

THE DECLINE OF LEGAL CUSTOM IN ENGLAND

The myth of England's customary law existing from time immemorial was strengthened, not weakened, by the codification of modern British law in the seventeenth and eighteenth centuries that exemplified the emergence of Britain as a modern nation-state (Shapiro 1974). This process of legal centralization was both cause and consequence of a range of social and political changes that accompanied the decline of church and aristocratic powers, the rise of capitalist ideology, and an emerging industrial economy in which wages slowly replaced former tenant-farmer arrangements. Of course, these historical changes happened slowly over time—it has been argued, for example, that ecclesiastical authority began declining in the Middle Ages (Holmes 1962). Moreover, change often met with resistance.[6] Yet despite local pockets of opposition to change in Kent and elsewhere, by the mid nineteenth century, village life was dramatically different from what it had been in 1800 (Jessup 1974: 134–42). Industrial regions in the west and north were superseding the agriculturally based southeastern counties as the primary focus of politics.[7]

Law played a central role in these social, political, and economic trans-formations. Industrialization, although it did not have such an overt impact in Kent as in other areas, nonetheless drastically altered the infrastructure of its parish/county community relations. This was primarily owing to the grounding of capitalism in a laissez-faire ideology of contractual liability

6. For instance, the economic depression that followed the Napoleonic wars harshly affected rural Kent, giving impetus to popular movements such as the Swing Riots of 1830–31 and the Courtney Rising of 1838, when the poor demanded higher wages and lower food prices (Mingay 1989a; Mingay 1990: 154–64). Across the nation, events such as the Peterloo Massacre of 1819 and the Chartist cam-paigns in 1839, 1842, and again in 1848, helped raise popular consciousness of the poor and electorally underrepresented.

7. There is an interesting correlation between the first official census taken in England in 1801, and the rise of the regional scale of differentiation (and fall of public concern in smaller localities below the region) at roughly the same time. As been noted, this was partly because many government-administered data col-lections and surveys, such as the *General Household Survey* and *New Earnings Survey*, adopted the regional scale and so officially enshrined its spatial value (Sav-age 1989: 247; on the relationship between state-building and the use of statistics, see Cohn 1987: 231; Appadurai 1996a: 114–38).

dependent upon a uniform, predictable, and enforceable legal system (see MacDonagh 1980). Peculiarities of Kent law such as the intestate rule of *gavelkind* could no longer be tolerated under the rubric of English common law (Elton 1867; Sandys 1851). Such local legal inconsistencies were eliminated through the enclosure acts and streamlining of property devolution, leading in some cases to the criminalization of customary legal practices (King 1989). These legal changes made landlord-tenant relations a matter of "free contract" by abrogating customary responsibilities and village obligations.[8] Thus through enclosure and the breaking up and fencing of land, what were tangibly represented were the possessory rights of individuals over rights held by the collective community. Land privatization effectively annulled landlords' traditional responsibilities to the poor, and thus undermined "an alternative notion of possession" located in the "petty and particular rights and usages which were transmitted in custom as the *properties* of the poor" (Thompson 1993: 184; Williams 1973: 137).[9] This shift of power to landlords also affected the existence of older public rights-of-way and bridlepaths that formed complex walking and horse-transport networks crucial to a localized agricultural community (Shoard 1987: 321–70). E. P. Thompson has written powerfully about the dismantling of local land customs surrounding the village common. According to Thompson, "Common right, which was in lax terms conterminous with settlement, was *local* right, and hence also a power to exclude strangers. Enclosure, in taking the commons away from the poor, made them strangers in their own land" (Thompson 1993: 184).

Industrial growth, then, was necessarily accompanied by a reassessment

8. The history of English property law leading up to the general enclosure acts of 1836, 1840, and 1845 is very complicated (see Turner 1984; Burt and Archer 1994; for analysis of the second half of the nineteenth and twentieth centuries, see Douglas 1976; Cox 1984). Parliamentary enclosure involved the reorganization of over 21% of English land, but did not affect some places as dramatically as it did others (Turner 1984: 133).What is important for this discussion are the ideological assumptions enclosure embodied and promulgated.

9. Furthermore, it brought about much hardship by denying small farmers their rights to pastoral commons (sometimes called "wastes") and eliminating a valuable safeguard against economic hardship. "I learnt to hate a system that could lead English gentlemen to disregard matters like these! That could induce them to tear up 'wastes' . . . 'Wastes' indeed!" William Cobbett exlaimed in his *Political Register* (1821: 520–21). "I am convinced that Paper-money, Large farms, Fine houses, Pauperism, Hangings, Transportings, Leprosy, Scrofula and Insanity, have all gone on increasing regularly together" (ibid.: 508). This list reflects the degeneration of public health resulting from the decline in village life, where formerly the poor and mentally ill would have been accommodated and supported.

of the function of law with respect to land rights and state control that made local people "strangers" and altered the reproduction of community identity within the rural landscape. The diminishment of local rights-of-way points to an intended, but often unremarked upon, consequence of legal centralization. This was the puncturing of any remaining social and cultural ties local villages had with their long-standing lords. For a codified law better served an emerging culture of entrepreneurs, many of whom lived in London, and diminished the need to recognize the legal and social particularities of a locality.[10] Railways embodied the new spirit of the age, bursting through the spatial particularities of villages and the significance of local practices. And as a result, local moral codes that had sustained premodern rural customs based on a reciprocity of needs and acknowledged rights between the have and have-nots were, by the mid nineteenth century, severely shattered.[11] Normative legality, existing in informal and unidentified local communities without legal standing, and so outside the logic of British state governance and a philosophy of corporate individualism, was denigrated and eventually abandoned. Explicit in this dismantling of the village parish system was the declining significance of legal customs and norms in the reproduction of locality. Thus the very qualities of community and independence in English law that Tocqueville so greatly admired were refashioned by nineteenth-century legal reforms, not according to the concerns of community welfare, but according to the demands of rampant capitalism.

THE CONCEPT OF PARLIAMENTARY SOVEREIGNTY
AND THE IMPACT OF THE FRENCH REVOLUTION

One of the key concepts sustaining England's ideology of freedom and its linkage to the state territory was the doctrine of parliamentary sovereignty. Having no codified legal system, English common law derived its legitimacy from having existed since time immemorial, thus predating sovereign authority. This immemoriality was promulgated through the

10. After the 1834 introduction of the poor laws, the parish was not held morally responsible for rural poverty. Nor was defense and protection against crime any longer within the parish domain. Moreover, the remapping of new county court districts in 1846 limited the powers of local justices of the peace—the traditional enforcers of village law and order (MacDonagh 1980: 118).

11. It would take the franchise-widening Reform Bills of 1867 and 1884, the first driven by the enthusiasm of the Conservative leader Benjamin "Dizzy" Disraeli and the second put through under the Liberal William Gladstone, to lay the basis for the emergence of the British welfare state.

unique principle of parliamentary sovereignty, which declared a limited monarchy and the population's supposedly voluntary acquiescence in a representative system of governance (Harden and Lewis 1986: 22–36; Waldron 1990: 56–87). The Glorious Revolution's culmination in a "constitutional monarchy" in 1688–89 was viewed as the highest expression of English freedom. According to T. B. Macaulay in his celebrated *History of England* (1848), "Our liberty is neither Greek or Roman, but essentially English. It has a character of its own" (quoted in Colls 1986: 33).[12] Parliament, and more specifically the doctrine of parliamentary sovereignty as the "recognized pillar of constitutional law," granted English law autonomous distinction and a unique particularity (Carty 1991: 198). "In France, sovereignty means the sovereignty of the nation, never mind whether it is Napoleon or Louis Philippe, de Gaulle or Mendès-France who speaks for it," Ralph Dahrendorf observes. "In Britain, sovereignty means the sovereignty of Parliament which is of course the parliament of the unitary state of Britain. Thus, democracy comes before the nation, or rather, the nation is defined by its democratically elected Parliament" (Dahrendorf 1982: 129).

Despite England's widespread reputation as a land of freedom, the cries of liberty, equality, and fraternity sounded throughout the late eighteenth century by the French revolutionaries fundamentally destabilized English law, based as it was on a mixture of monarchy, aristocracy, and democracy (Blackstone 1765: 50; Black 1986: 185–203). The ensuing inversion of national oppositions was picked up by the eighteenth-century English cartoonist James Gillray whose *French Liberty—English Slavery* (1792) contrasts a hearty Englishman deploring English taxes for "starving us to death" as he makes his way through a huge side of beef, while a scrawny Frenchman glories in his freedom as he gnaws on a garlic weed. A statuette of Britannia looks down on the Englishman with a sack of "sterling" in place of her standard shield. By playing on national stereotypes, Gillray's cartoon lampoons essentializing imagery. But it also bespeaks a deep-seated disquiet among the English about the impact of the French Revo-

12. For connections between the myth surrounding the English nation's Saxon descent and its implications of racial purity, liberal law, and democratic institutions that accompanied a growing English nationalism in the mid seventeenth century, see Francis Whyte's *For the Sacred Law of the Land* (1652) and Richard Hawkins's *A Discourse of the National Excellencies of England* (1658), both discussed in MacDoughall 1982: 62–70. With respect to Sir Edmund Coke and the connection between common law and Anglo-Saxonism, see Pocock 1987: 56–57. On Anglo-Saxonism as an exported myth and its relationship to nineteenth-century racial discrimination in North America, see Cosgrove 1987: 59–94.

lution and can be interpreted as an attempt to deflect the French questioning of traditional English ideals of monarchy and state. Jacques-Louis David's 1793 painting of the French revolutionary Marat stabbed to death in his therapeutic bath at the hands of Charlotte Corday epitomized the extent to which the old world had been turned upside down to make way for a new era "when the state breaks with Christian faith and Christian temporality" (Bryson 1988a: 91).

The French Revolution took the English by surprise (Black 1986: 198). William Pitt the Younger, the prime minister, initially welcomed it as a valuable distraction from internal political tensions. But in the ensuing years, and particularly with the ascendancy of Napoleon Bonaparte in 1799, England became more and more alarmed by the growing power of France. Napoleon issued a new law for France, the Constitution of the Year VIII, and under the authority of the Consulate, he instigated widespread administrative, educational, and judicial reforms. He consolidated the legal transformations that had been taking place since 1789 and, in 1804, announced the Code Napoléon as France's first integrated national legal system. While this new legal code reflected the French dictator's authoritarian aims and conservative character, it was nonetheless sufficiently liberal to have widespread appeal among those who considered themselves more enlightened and socially progressive.

English leaders looked on in horror at what was happening in Europe. Austrian forces were soundly defeated by Napoleon in his victory at Marengo in June 1800. In February 1801, the Austro-French Treaty of Lunéville left Italy and much of German territory open to Napoleon's control. But despite Austria's domination, war between France and England continued, broken only by the short peace that followed the agreement at Amiens on 27 March 1802. Among other things, this treaty required that Britain renounce the claims of the British sovereign to the throne of France and restore captured French territories, including the port of Calais. Unfortunately, the peace settlement did not last long, and the two nations were soon at war again. William Wordsworth fled France in 1802 and wrote the following words of relief upon his arrival in Dover, on the coast of England:

> Here, on our native soil, we breathe once more.
> The cock that crows, the smoke that curls, the sound
> Of bells—those boys who in yon meadow-ground
> In white-sleeved shirts are playing; and the roar
> Of the waves breaking on the chalky shore—
> All, all are English. Oft have I looked round

With joy in Kent's green vales; but never found
Myself so satisfied in heart before.
Europe is yet in bonds; but let that pass,
Thought for another moment. Thou are free,
My Country! and 'tis joy enough and pride
For one hour's perfect bliss, to tread the grass
Of England once again . . .

The poem exemplifies recurring themes of battle and invasion, on the one hand, contrasted with the peace and liberty of the island nation distant from the chaos of Europe, on the other. The dramatically intense writing of Thomas Carlyle's *The French Revolution* (1837) also evokes the disorder, confusion, and turmoil of French bids for liberty (see, e.g., Carlyle 1891: vol. 2, bk. 5, pt. 2). In this context, the Channel assumed heightened meaning in its sustaining of Britain's island mythology as a means of distancing the nation from continental Europe. In England, it was widely believed, order and tranquillity and freedom from tyranny uniquely coexisted, sustained and naturalized through a superior legal order that—in contrast to the fabricated Code Napoléon—was as old as the Romans and drew its strength from the idealized woods, streams, commons, farmlands, and village communities of the English landscape. This led Edmund Burke to contrast the soft, shadowy, wooded landscapes of England with the harshness of "experimental landscapes" like the "geometrical constitution" of revolutionary France. For Burke, the revolution changed everything: "All the pleasing illusions which made power gentle, and obedience liberal, which harmonized the different shades of life, and which by a bland assimilation, incorporated into politics the sentiments which beautify and soften private society, are to be dissolved by this new conquering empire of light and reason" (quoted in Daniels 1988: 46; see also Lock 1985).

LAW AND LANDSCAPE

As discussed above, English law, unlike French law, is interpreted by many as having existed from time immemorial. The distinctiveness of English law, which Anthony Carty notes was and remains the principal form through which English people express their identity, drew its particular quality from the insularity that consolidated the idea of nation-state within a specific juridico-political territory (Carty 1991: 183). By the end of the eighteenth century, the conflation of English law with English identity, island territory, and British institutions of government was virtually complete. It was impossible to segregate perceptions of English law from the idealized English landscape and culture through which authority, power, and class relations were inscribed and spatialized across the whole of Britain, as well as being visually and aesthetically affirmed through gardens, public parks, and town planning.

Simon Schama has argued that the importance of landscape, a word imported into England at the end of the sixteenth century from the Dutch, derived its signification as "a unit of human occupation, indeed a jurisdiction, as much as anything that might be a pleasing object of depiction" (Schama 1995: 10). In England, the common law is the land, and the imagery evoked "is of old England, an England that is eternal: it is our ground and our circumstances, our landscape, our nature, both mystical and thoughtless" (Goodrich and Hachamovitch 1991: 167). Moreover, a reliance on legal precedent complements a belief in "this naturalness of a law inscribed in nature itself, in the heart, that guarantees that it will return, again and again, as the 'same' law" (ibid.: 163; on precedent, see Cross 1977: 4).

However, A. V. Dicey, in his *Introduction to the Study of the Law of the Constitution* (1915), cautions against equating law with nature, attesting, in his rejection of the idea, to its common use. According to Dicey, it is "the current but misguiding statement that the 'constitution has not been made but has grown.' This dictum, if taken literally, is absurd. . . . Men did not wake up on a summer morning and find them [political institutions] sprung up. Neither do they resemble trees, which, once planted, are 'aye growing' while men 'are sleeping'" (Dicey 1915: 191). Nonetheless, Dicey has to concede that:

> the dogma that the form of a government is a sort of spontaneous
> growth so closely bound up with the life of a people that we can
> hardly treat it as a product of human will and energy, does, though in
> a loose and inaccurate fashion, bring into view the fact that some politics, and among them the English constitution, have not been created
> at one stroke, and, far from being the result of legislation, in the ordinary sense of that term, are the fruit of contests carried on in the
> Courts on behalf of the rights of individuals. . . . Here flow noteworthy distinctions between the constitution of England and the constitutions of most foreign countries.
>
> (Dicey 1915: 192)

Dicey's formulation of law and government "as a sort of 'spontaneous growth'" resonates with wider cultural ideas of the naturalness of law and order and a sense of justice. It echoes Edmund Burke's late-eighteenth-century critique of the French Revolution as introducing harsh light and geometric legal form, in contrast to England's harmonized and softly shadowed legal and social landscape. According to Burke: "The French builders, clearing away as mere rubbish whatever they found and, like their ornamental gardeners, forming everything into an exact level, propose to rest the whole local and general legislature on three bases of three different kinds: one geometrical, one arithmetical, and the third financial" (Burke 1955: 203).

Of course, Burke's claim to a picturesque legal aesthetic was challenged by the coming of the Industrial Revolution, which celebrated geometrical form as an indicator of progress and rational thought. In London around 1800, the first residential squares were landscaped with houses surrounding a garden common, replicating the format of English cathedral towns and setting up "exclaves of the country in the town" (Pevsner 1956: 179). The vegetation in these squares, according to John Loudon, the Scottish landscape gardener, in his plans for metropolitan improvements in 1803, should be natural and soft. Plantings should be of masses of trees, shrubs, and plants that united and blended as in a natural wood. In Loudon's view, "edgy" lines of turf and deep ruts for drainage were unnecessary (Simo 1988: 211).

This concern for the blending of nature with rationalized form was slowly eroded throughout the nineteenth century. For instance, John Nash's original plans for the residential terraces of Regent's Park, published in 1812, include some fifty villas dotted among woody groves, with a serpentine lake, a great double circus, and a central church. However, because of the Treasury's financial cutbacks, these picturesque elements were not executed, leaving today a grand sweep of formalized, dramatic, but rather regimented terraces (Summerson 1945: 181–82). Financial priorities exerted more and more pressure on urban architectural form, resulting in the bland and grandiose High Victorian terraces of South Kensington and a proliferation of workingman's cottages in inner city areas divided up into long, narrow street strips, all in regular size and format. This standardizing of land titles into basic square plots affected all property holdings in the late eighteenth and nineteenth centuries. But as has been convincingly argued by the art historian Sir Nikolaus Pevsner, property standardization was peculiarly bound up with a sense of justice and liberty:

> The planning of Bath with circus and crescents and the planning of Bloomsbury with its squares is liberty in the sense of an informal composition taking into consideration sites, conditions of property, balance of building to open spaces and so on. South Kensington and the poorer suburbs are liberty in the sense of *laissez faire*, that is of

letting the philistine, or the Francophile, or indeed the callous specula-
tor have his way and his money's worth.

(Pevsner 1956: 184–85)

While the spatial frames through which law, land, and property con-
verged were predominantly geometrical in form, what was treasured inside
the square plot was the idealized cottage garden as a particular symbol of
individual liberty (Rotenberg 1995: 66–87). Thus in the English reaction
against rapid industrial growth and the profusion of regimented, deper-
sonalized homes that began in the 1870s, the picturesque was again turned
to as a guiding principle, resulting in plans for the garden suburb and
garden city. These garden ideals "succeeded in the blending of small-size
housing with nature and the application of the principle of variety to the
layout of streets, the provision of footpaths and so on" (Pevsner 1956:
185). And, as discussed further in chapter 2, it is the peculiar quality of
the cottage garden—in essence a controlled and intimate "wilderness"—
that sustained a romantic claim on law as the protector of individual life,
home, and liberty, and perception of it as the embodiment of naturalized
justice.

Today, these concerns with a particular legal aesthetics again resurface
in discussions about the Channel Tunnel. Katherine Kershaw, Eurotunnel's environmental manager, noted that in contrast to the French side of
the Tunnel, where motorists are greeted with formal lines of planted trees
and flowers, "the whole area this side of the tunnel follows the English
landscape tradition. A total of 220,000 trees and shrubs have been planted
around the tunnel entrance, the railheads and slip roads, from 18 inch
saplings to 15-year-old oaks and maples. The planting around the edges is
intended to merge with the surrounding countryside, and the shrubs are
designed to be calming and easy on the eye" (*Observer*, 8 May 1994, p.
10).

The disparity between English and French landscapes around their respective Tunnel terminals on the two sides of the Channel points to a
critical element in the grounding of law in the mythologized rural English
landscape. At the same time as ensuring confidence in the doctrine of legal
precedent, an image of an "olde England" allows people to distance themselves from more explicitly fabricated—and presumably superficial—legal
systems and cultures such as that of the French. The English merge the
new Tunnel buildings and tracks with the preexisting woodlands and try
to pretend the Tunnel does not exist. In telling language, "the former
construction site is introduced to country life," and areas have been de-

signed around the terminal "where nature can take over" (*Kent Today*, 30 March 1994, p. 17). The French, in comparison, are quick to respond by planting an exuberant and ostentatious "formal scene, with miles of pink roses and other flowering shrubs on the central reservations of the motorways," openly celebrating the Tunnel as a symbol of progress and dramatic change (*Observer*, 8 May 1994, p. 10).

In a revealing interview with a leading member of the Kent Conservation Society, a retired lawyer who worked in London and now lives in Barham, Kent, these two themes of law and environment constantly overlapped and merged throughout our two-hour discussion, only interrupted (much to my joy and amazement!) by the production of a tray of cucumber sandwiches. Incomprehensible to my informant was the "strange" lack of concern by the French for nature and the preservation of ancient wildlife and woodlands—an attitude it seemed that could not be disentangled from their "barbaric" system of law. According to the retired lawyer:

> The French, you see, have much more control over people there. They haven't got democracy there in the same way as you have here. Here you've always meetings and discussions. People have time to think and opportunities to defend what is important to them like nature and wildlife. There it goes right back to Napoleon—the French, if they want something done, it's done you know. . . . It's a law dictatorship the French system of government, funnily enough, despite the French Revolution.
>
> (interview, 25 Feb. 1994)

CONCLUDING COMMENTS

In the unfolding of the New Europe, legal identity and the cultural practices and territorial strategies through which such an identity is marked visually on the landscape continue to be of great significance. As stated at the beginning of this chapter, under the overarching legal entity of the EU, state laws, now more than ever before, operate as markers of national identity and local distinctiveness. Perceptions of the Channel Tunnel marring an idealized Kentish, and English, landscape, raise a critical question: How is legal distinctiveness being drawn, argued, and justified through interpreted histories of modern Western nation-building and mythologized genealogies of certain peoples living in specific terrains?

This question turns on the rise of modern nation-states and their enduring stability in the New Europe. Neil Smith, a well-known cultural geographer, notes that while states are defined most obviously by their legal jurisdictions and formalized boundaries, the state:

> can justify and define its authority over society only through such abstract principles of social intercourse as democracy, liberty, moral right etc. Such principles are themselves products of particular class societies. Thus while particular states may have a distinct and limited territorial basis, the social principles underlying such states are readily mobile. A given state, and the society that belongs to it, therefore find themselves more spatially rooted than ever before and simultaneously more mobile. . . . The first intimations of a spaceless conception of society, and abstract spaceless second nature (social space), becomes [*sic*] possible with the explicit spatial definition of the state.
>
> (N. Smith 1984: 80)

This loosening of territory from relations of power may explain Foucault's classification of territory as a secondary matter, a variable, in modern governmental forms of management (Foucault 1991: 93–94).[13] Yet as Smith notes, at the same time that territory is rendered less important because its borders are defined on the basis of ideological principles that help consolidate a given population, such principles heighten the imperative for government to be spatially grounded in its claim over a specific territory. And this need to claim is only intensified when the mythic principles sustaining the state are themselves challenged. Santos calls this a process of deterritorializing and reterritorializing deriving from a dialectical relation between globalization and localization (Santos 1995). While I, and others, hesitate to accept this neat polarization of scales between the global and local that characterizes much theory on globalization, what this process indicates is that territoriality, and its manifest reproduction through landscape, remains of critical and enduring importance.[14]

In the context of the New Europe and the challenge to democratic ideals that the central legal administration of the EU in Brussels poses, claims to territory have in fact escalated, as evidenced by the rising tide of spatially expressed nationalist xenophobia. In England, the conflation of landscape and law in popular imagination has taken on new dimensions and symbolic imperatives. Building upon long-standing historical narratives of a mythological freedom embodied in a natural island independence, now, perhaps

13. See n. 3 above.
14. For more critical interpretations of the local/global rhetoric, see Amin and Thrift 1994; Brenner 1997; Cvetkovich and Kellner 1997; Darian-Smith 1998b.

more than ever before, law constitutes a platform and defense upon which a particular aesthetics, lifestyle, ideology, and interpretation of self rest. In the current push toward transnational legal processes and what Santos calls "a plurality of legal orders" (Santos 1995: 114), the question that is being made explicit is: Whose definition of law prevails in any given context—that of the town of Canterbury, of the county of Kent, of the national region of England, of the state of Britain, or of the Union of Europe?

2 Kent

Garden of England and
Gateway to Europe

Down in the valley it's all green and brown and patchy, woods
marked off with neat edges and corners, hedges like stitching.
There's a splodge of red brick in the middle with a spire sticking
up. It looks like England, that's what it looks like.

Graham Swift, *Last Orders* (1996)

THE KENTISH GARDEN IN THE ENGLISH IMAGINATION

"[T]he mythical English landscape is drawn from a highly localized region," the geographer Denis Cosgrove has written (1993: 299; and see also
Pugh 1990: 239; Howkins 1986: 54). Kent, the so-called Garden of England,
embodies the highly symbolic landscape of London's "home counties"
(originally Kent, Surrey, Essex, and Middlesex, with the more recent inclusion of Buckinghamshire, Berkshire, Hertfordshire, and Sussex) that
has come, through a roaring heritage industry, to represent the "authentic" England both to its residents and foreigners. Thus, for instance, a 1995
United Airlines advertisement explicitly conflated garden, England, and
Britain with a picture of an idealized rambling old house and cottage flower
garden captioned: "You can dream about a place this beautiful or you can
visit England. United Airlines can make Britain a reality for you. . . ."

As the capital's backyard, Kent has long enjoyed a special place in English history. With its rolling downs, hop fields, oast houses, and church
spires, Kent is popularly conceived of as both a mysterious secret garden
and an accessible scene of pastoral tranquillity. Through aggressive tourism and marketing, the county is evoked as the scene of a past golden age
of local community spirit and rural idealism (fig. 3). Key to this representation is Kent's spatial confinement between London and the sea, which in
its very boundedness frames the landscaped imagery with a naturalized
order and calculability.

Kent, of course, is not all green rolling hills, just as its approximately
1.52 million residents are not uniformly conservative in their politics and
neither all live in manor houses nor all go foxhunting and bird shooting.

41

Figure 3. Contemporary postcard depicting Kent as the "Garden of England." By kind permission of J. Salmon Ltd.

Such caricatures mask how the majority of people live in Kent and the seedier, less attractive aspects of the county. At one extreme, there still exist wealthy estates and large old homes, many of which are protected by the National Trust.[1] Indeed, the Trust has more properties in its care in Kent than in any other region in England. At certain times of the year, it remains possible to see foxhunting. And from what I have been told, the season of balls and coming-out parties is still taken very seriously amongst the "old families." But the other extreme is that there are pockets of grave poverty in the rural areas and along the coast away from the major Channel ports, such as in the Isle of Sheppey, Herne Bay, and the Isle of Thanet, incorporating Margate, Ramsgate, and Broadstairs. In these peripheral out-

1. The National Trust was established in 1895, and by 1907 it had been given the legal authority to protect sites and "preserve them for the nation." However, it was not until the period after World War II that it emerged as a powerful institution. Other conservation groups created in the second half of the nineteenth century included the Commons, Footpaths and Open Spaces Preservation Society (1865) and the Society for the Protection of Ancient Buildings (1877). These societies were concerned with preserving a particular image of "tradition" and heritage that focused predominantly on what was deemed "English." For instance, Irish monuments were originally excluded from the Ancient Monuments Protection Act of 1882 (Walsh 1992: 70–71).

skirts of Kent exist some of the most deprived council housing projects in England, marked by extremely high unemployment rates (Buck et al. 1989: 166).[2] Beach pollution, power stations, industrial development, and most conspicuously the Channel Tunnel do not fit the idealized Kentish countryside either. Kent's garden landscape as it exists in the Kentish and English popular imaginations and the realities that imagery elides clearly do not correspond.

Yet what these contradictions do allow for are multiple interpretations both of what the garden is and of what it means. What is interesting is the extent to which the garden mythology still resonates with a vast number of people in Kent who are only too well aware of its illusory qualities. Garden imagery appears to speak to a wide cross-section of the community and to unite those who in many other ways are mutually opposed. What struck me in my conversations with people was that the evocation of a garden landscape appealed alike to people of conservative and more progressive political persuasions, various generations, the unemployed, farmers, green activists, and London commuters fleeing the city. All of these various individuals seemed at times to be coming together as a relatively united front. Many of them, for different reasons and motivations, have vested interests in defending the remnants, or, if not the remnants, then the return, of a naturalized garden landscape.

The defense of a rural idyll was brought home to me very strongly at a photography exhibition by Patrick Sutherland called "The Garden of England," staged at the Kent Institute of Art and Design in February 1994. Commissioned by the Cross Channel Photographic Mission, the photographs resulted from a year Sutherland had spent in and around Ashford, Kent, now the site of the new International Rail Passenger terminal for the Channel Tunnel. Sutherland directly confronted local objections to the terminal on the basis that it would spoil the countryside. His photographs, which show the seedier side of village life such as car boot (trunk) sales, mobile homes, a bed-and-breakfast interior, and so on, graphically expose the superficiality of the beautiful Kent countryside mythology. As I walked

2. East Kent has been isolated from the rest of the county and has limited transport, health, educational, and general welfare services. The scale of unemployment has, for example, given Thanet Assisted Area status, which qualifies it for EU funding and government aid. Dover and Shepway are classified as Intermediate Areas, meaning that they, too, receive limited regional and national aid on the basis of projected high unemployment figures, especially in the ferry industry (Kent County Council 1991; Church and Reid 1994: 204).

around the exhibition, the receptionist at the front desk asked me whether I liked the photos. I responded enthusiastically, whereupon she got up and came across the hall, leaving her phone and duties, to tell me that she thought the display was disgusting. "You know that Kent is the garden of England," she told me emphatically, "and these pictures put us all in such a bad light" (conversation, 4 Feb. 1994).

The metaphor of the Tunnel penetrating Britain's island boundaries, and its further desecration of the orderly and contained symbolic garden landscape of Kent, provides a point of departure from which to slice across one instance of emerging relations crisscrossing state borders in the New Europe. In this new context, how are English people, and more generally British people, distinguishing themselves from European and postcolonial others? As discussed in the Introduction, these ongoing concerns surround the Tunnel itself, and its evocation of other pertinent local and national emblems associated with the Kentish landscape, garden imagery, law, and property, as well as with the state and its enduring maintenance of cultural homogeneity. Of course, someone else might read the Tunnel, Kent, gardens, law, and state in very different ways and contexts. I am not presenting the only meanings embodied in these terms of reference. But I am pursuing an interrelated set of interpretations to show why the Tunnel, and especially its influence on a relatively small area of southern England, carries greater significance in local, regional, and national identities than its particular geographical impact would initially suggest.

In the first section below, I briefly discuss Kent's mythologized history and how this cannot be divorced from the region's concurrent inland relations with London or its transnational relations with Nord–Pas de Calais on the opposite side of the Channel. I want to stress that understanding any given community in any national context requires looking at it within the wider domestic setting of the state, as well as the state's external relations to its neighboring countries.

In the next section, I turn to Kent and its historical embodiment as the Garden of England. I show how this essentialized representation of Kent resonates with the historical and contemporary development of an English national imagination that in its current manifestation embodies certain features of an idealized English heritage. Rolling green hills in an idyllic pastoral landscape embody profound and fiercely defended icons of a timeless, Anglo-Saxon imperial power brimming with class hierarchy and feudal patronage. Kent—at least the characterization of Kent as projected most obviously through tourism and the heritage industry—manifests old world charm and embedded traditional values.

This leads me into the second half of the chapter with a discussion of the garden metaphor and its linking up with historical reconstructions of Britain's past imperial age. The English garden cannot be seen as innocent of historical accretions of power and privilege. It was (and still is) a symbol of control and civilization. In its transplantation across the country, the English domestic garden played a role in consolidating the multinational British nation through the cultivation of a visual aesthetics associated with southern England and London. As early as the seventeenth century, settled agrarian pursuits were seen as a remedy for the "wild Irish," whose hostility and savagery were believed to be related to their semi-nomadic lifestyle (Comaroff and Comaroff 1992: 246). Cultivation became an important ontological frame, and, through its linkage to the English garden landscape, translated into a visual aesthetics of power. The imposing of the English garden across the whole of Britain is a dramatic visual and experiential demonstration of how England was conflated with, and came to represent, the greater British nation. What is important for my purposes here is that analogous to Kent embodying certain English ideals, it is critical to remember that after the Act of Union of 1707, which joined Scotland to England and Wales, England in turn historically embodied and stood for "one united kingdom by the name of Great Britain," with one legislature, one government, and one policy of free trade (Colley 1992: 11).

At the same time as the English garden helped to unite Britain, it also consolidated British power abroad in its transplantation throughout the colonial periphery. In its first manifestation as the mission garden,[3] and then later as the scientific botanic garden,[4] public gardens helped to create and spatially map new public spheres of control. Alongside courthouses, jails, statehouses, and other administrative buildings in peripheral outposts around the world, almost all centers of colonial authority had (and many still do) an officially run public botanic garden, as well as large private

3. Mission gardens, used to illustrate the value of labor and the division of male and female work, and the local political battles waged over their irrigation created much tension and threatened the ontological basis on which chiefs ruled the Tswana in southern Africa (Comaroff and Comaroff 1992: 240–50).

4. A remarkable illustration of the conjunctures between imperialism, science, and geography occurred in the mid nineteenth century in the Calcutta Botanic Gardens, to which Robert Fortune, a Scottish plant hunter who stole seeds and cuttings from China, sent numerous boxes of tea plants for cultivation. Nearly 20,000 plants were grown, and toward the end of the nineteenth century, tea was one of north India's main exports to Britain, which effectively supplanted the dominance of the Chinese tea industry. Such appropriation of plant species, which L. H. Brockway calls "botanical imperialism," occurred throughout the colonial periphery (Brockway 1979; Hoyles 1991: 96–110).

estates, complete with English garden landscapes. Although the style and function of the English garden changed over time between the late seventeenth and the early twentieth centuries, it remained a particularly important symbol in the interconnected internal and external maintenance of the British empire (Ranger 1975: 166–67). What I argue is that with today's great political and cultural instabilities, the ideals of garden orderliness, containment, and control are, perhaps more than ever, powerful and appropriate symbols, not only for the people of Kent, but for England and its representation of the whole British nation.

KENT AS PLACE AND SYMBOL

Long-standing historical claims present Kent as once joined to Calais, "by an Isthum which reached from Kent to about Calais in France" (Harris 1719: 3–5). Whether this is true is not known. In any event, it is generally accepted by archaeologists that Kent was the first area of England to be occupied by humans, as evidenced by Neolithic burial chambers such as Kit's Coty House which has stood for 4,000 years overlooking the Medway Gap. Over time, these people built up small communities and villages. According to the nineteenth-century historian Christopher Greenwood, the name "Kent" is of Gallic origin and suggests a corner, alluding to Kent as the corner of the island continent (Greenwood 1838: v; see, for an earlier account, Harris 1719: 2). The *Oxford English Dictionary* derives "Kentish" from the Old Celtic *kanto-* meaning either (i) rim, border, or (ii) white.

Kent was invaded in 55 B.C. by Julius Caesar, who honored its people by declaring them the most civilized in England, placing Kent on par with occupied Gaul. After the Roman legions abandoned England and returned to the defense of Rome, Kent reached its full potential as an autonomous and separate Jutish kingdom by the end of the fifth century. In fact, King Ethelbert (560–616) governed so well in making Kent one of the most advanced of all English kingdoms that its prestige caught the attention of Pope Gregory I, who sent a monk named Augustine (later canonized as St. Augustine, or Austin, of Canterbury) and forty missionaries to preach Christianity to the Anglo-Saxon "heathens." On their way to London, Augustine and his religious messengers stopped and settled in Canterbury and later in Rochester, building at each site grand cathedrals. As a result of Augustine's fondness for Canterbury, the pope established the position of archbishop of Canterbury and declared the town the ecclesiastical see of England—the source and cradle of religious authority. Although Catholicism was expunged when Henry VIII declared himself the head of the new Church of England in 1530, Canterbury Cathedral maintained its historical import as the center of state religion. The significance of Canterbury Cathedral in contemporary negotiations of national politics involving the Channel Tunnel will become apparent in chapter 4.

After the Norman Conquest in 1066, Kent's ports, dockyards, trading fleets, church administration, and unique legal system further developed, and throughout the Middle Ages and into the sixteenth century, the county remained an independent region with its own character and qualities. It is of interest that Kent was seen as both complementary and in opposition to the growing London metropolis, supposedly full of sin and social alienation, as well as to its nearest neighbor on the European mainland, the flat and rather dreary Nord–Pas de Calais.

Divided by a deceptively narrow strip of often dangerous sea, Kent and Nord–Pas de Calais are the English and French regions surrounding the tunnel terminals on either side of the Channel. Today, relations between Kent and Nord–Pas de Calais can be considered as a smaller but not equivalent instance of more general communication between England and France. And similarly to the national realm, one cannot be understood without the other. Kent and Nord–Pas de Calais, England and France, Kent and England, Nord–Pas de Calais and France (not to mention Kent and France!)—each of these sets of political relations and their related cultural and social communications reflects and impinges upon the others. And within each set of relations the reified polarities are defined in negation— and thus as a complement—to what the other is not (see Gibson 1995; Black 1986). In short, the county of Kent requires the region of Nord–Pas de Calais to define itself to itself and the rest of England and greater Britain, as much as the people of Kent seek to distance themselves from the "French peasants" (interview with local resident of Kent, 14 Mar. 1994).

KENT AS THE GARDEN OF ENGLAND

Contrary to popular narratives, which always stress the differences between them, Kent and Calais share a long and complex history of overlapping genealogies, kinship, kings, queens, foods, tastes, desires, trades, markets, and languages. Generally being the first port of call on the way to and from England and the European mainland, Kent has always experienced much through traffic and so enjoyed the transfer and exchange of ideas, goods, and peoples that a clientele of travelers and migrants carries.

That being said, many of the numerous historical accounts of Kent treat the county as rather enclosed and independent (Everitt 1986; Wright 1975;

Jessup 1974; Brandon and Short 1990; Lincoln 1966; Hasted 1788; Harris 1719; Greenwood 1838). One of the earliest and certainly most famous of these histories was written by Edward Hasted in 1788 on the brink of the French Revolution and entitled *The History and Topographical Survey of the County of Kent*. In it, in mind-boggling detail, are presented extensive descriptions of the land and customs of Kent, suggesting the level of interest and local knowledge among the community for whom the book was written.

Kent was also well known within England. Famous interpretations of the county of Kent exist such as those found in Celia Fiennes's *Illustrated Journeys* (1682–1712), Daniel Defoe's *A Tour of the Whole Island of Great Britain* (1724–76), William Cobbett's *Rural Rides* (1830), and more recently, but in the same traveling-around-the-countryside genre, Paul Theroux's *The Kingdom by the Sea* (1983). In all of these accounts, there is an undercurrent of intrigue with the region and its curious paradoxes. For at the same time that Kent was considered the most cosmopolitan region (outside London) in terms of the presence of European influences, the county retained its essentially rural domestic character throughout the Industrial Revolution and the rapid transformations wrought by railways, tourism, and increasing cross-Channel traffic. Thus Fiennes could write as early as 1682 that in Canterbury "there is a great number of French people in this town which are employ'd in the weaving and silk winding," and at the same time remark upon Kent's agricultural landscape and particular cottage customs (Fiennes 1982: 120).[5]

Hence alongside its image in England as the most "European" of the country's regions, Kent was also known in southern England for representing more than anywhere else the most desired charms and mythologized features of an idealized English countryside. By the late sixteenth century, Kent was widely known at home and abroad as the Garden of England. In the words of Greenwood, "from Blackheath to Gravesend, it is literally one scarcely interrupted garden. The whole county indeed is entitled, by its general fertility, to the appellation of the garden of England" (Greenwood 1838: v). This reference to Kent as the garden of England has a long and complex genealogy. According to Schama, by "the time of the Domesday Book in 1086, areas whose very names signified

---

5. An estimated 80,000 Huguenot refugees fled France to England between 1670 and 1690. Many French refugees settled in Kent and made a significant impact on the local communities. In Canterbury Cathedral, a special chapel (with separate entrance) dedicated solely for the use of the French Huguenots is still signposted as a reminder of this history.

woodland, like the Kentish Weald, had been converted into pasture, orchard and arable" (Schama 1995: 142). This agricultural domesticity helped define the recognizable landscape of Kent. Hasted in his famous survey of Kent in 1788 wrote:

> The *general face* of this country is very beautiful, not only from the wealth and abundance with which it is constantly covered, but from the great variety and inequality of the ground, the former of which is so great, that it may almost be called from thence an epitome of the whole kingdom. Indeed, it has most advantages that the rest of the kingdom enjoys, and many that are not to be found elsewhere.
>
> (Hasted 1778: 266)

Travelers through Kent such as Defoe, Cobbett, and Fiennes—each with his or her particular economic, social, and agricultural interests—all mention the glories and bountifulness of the rolling countryside. Kent is described as having "Very neate market towns," "fine hopp-yards," and "Kentish Cherrys" from Flanders, and was certainly some of "the most pleasant beautiful country" in England, with "the wholesome rich soil, the well wooded, and well watered plain on the banks of the Medway" and "every where spangled with populous villages, and delicious seats of the nobility and gentry" (Fiennes 1982: 124; Defoe 1971: 147, 132). Of course, the "deep foggy marshes" and foul airs of the poor, chalky downs were also remarked upon, as were the pockets of poverty, poor roads, and the debauchery of the larger towns, but the predominant image is one of "prosperity" and "purity," lending itself naturally to a local community of "figure and quality" (Defoe 1971: 131–32). This image was enhanced by the fact that the best wages for agricultural laborers and hop pickers in the eighteenth century could be found in Kent—4 to 5 shillings an acre in harvest time and a food allowance (Defoe 1971: 12 n. 14). Of course, it is wrong to assume that because the landowners were wealthier than in other areas, the laborers were correspondingly better off (Winstanley 1981: 627). But the image of bountifulness was sustained by Kent's supplying London and parts of the Continent with fruit and linen.

With the rising interest in holidays and leisure trips from London and northern cities to the country and seaside throughout the late eighteenth and nineteenth centuries, the people of Kent were keen to maintain its reputation as a prosperous region of rural and coastal delights (Urry 1990: 16–39; Pimlott 1947). This image has been sustained throughout the twentieth century, as evidenced by postcards issued early this century detailing the glamorous train travel from London railway stations where one could make a southbound connection. But as has been asked by Alan Everitt, a well-known historian of Kent, to what extent did the distinctive features of Kentish settlement actually set it apart from other counties? How untypical was Kent?

> Taken together there can be no doubt that these features gave rise to the unusual society and went far to shape the unique Law and Custom of Kent as it came to be codified after the Conquest. When examined individually, however, it becomes plain that none of them was peculiar to the county; it was rather their *conjunction* that was unusual. The absence of common fields, the dispersal of settlement, the prevalence of woodland, the sudden contrasts between one type of country and another, the predominance of pasture, the development of transhumance, and the peculiarities of Kentish custom were all echoed more or less distinctly elsewhere, though there was no other county where they all seem to have characterized the community as a whole.
>
> (Everitt 1986: 333)

It is this sense of a homogeneous landscape and a united community—despite the variations of the topography and the different local customs, religions, class divisions, and political and manorial loyalties across the entire county—that helped forge a Kentish identity. A consciousness of regional identity has waxed and waned in intensity over the centuries and decades. It seemed particularly strong before vast numbers of people started to cross the country by train in the early half of the nineteenth century. Throughout the 1900s, Kent served increasingly as a rural ideal in contrast to the evils of inner-city London and working horrors of the industrial north, and local writings confirm a general sense of the Kentish people's unblemished values and agriculturally based sensibilities.

In the past decade, a Kentish identity has now again been enthusiastically reconfirmed by many locals (see chapter 7). Admittedly, many residents have a vested interest in representing themselves in this light, given the economic benefits of buoyant heritage tourism in Canterbury, Dover, and other Kentish towns. However, along with many others, I suggest that a reclamation of local roots, however they may be constructed and remembered, is not unique to Kent and is in fact now occurring across English counties, Wales, Scotland, Ireland, and in fact many parts of the world.[6]

6. Since the 1997 general elections in Britain and the voting in of Tony Blair and his Labour party, devolution of state power has occurred at a remarkably rapid rate. In referendums held in Scotland and Wales, moves toward regional independence and separate parliaments based on local historical claims have gained popular

This retreat to localized collectivities runs alongside a growing distrust in the British state to manage and represent local interests in an increasingly globalized New Europe. It is also being aided by the European Union's modification of the sovereign powers of its member countries. In Kent, it is possible to see these dual processes of distrust of the national government and retreat to localism more clearly articulated and sharpened in the context of events surrounding the building of the Channel Tunnel. The Tunnel, in other words, has brought clearly to the fore what was already emerging in Kent and refocuses attention on garden imagery as a metaphor for both change and the continuities of tradition.

GARDEN BORDERS AND WALLS

The garden is a complex, contradictory concept that constantly changes meaning (Ross 1998; Foucault 1986: 25; Moore et al. 1989). As Edward Casey has argued, even the most formal gardens "remain *liminal* phenomena" (Casey 1993: 155). Gardens have historically been used to evoke pastoralism, romanticism, naturalism, and anti-barbarism, among other ideologies and philosophies (see Leo Marx 1964). As its referential applications shift over time, the garden as a stable figural representation defies specificity, highlighting its constructed quality and unnatural origins. That said, gardens, as statements of fashion and embodiments of ideology and symbolism, do represent a certain coherence of design and format at particular historical moments. In the eighteenth century, the garden's recurring themes and motifs complemented the emergence of Britain as a modern nation-state and imperial power—what Zygmunt Bauman calls the emergence of the "garden culture of modernity" (Bauman 1987: 50–67). The garden was a symbol of cultivation, and by association its protectors were deemed cultivated.[7] Spatially representing a new way of seeing that transcended class and political hierarchies in England, the garden was used as a metaphor for civilization, as expressed in Voltaire's *Candide* of 1759.

---

support. While Scotland, led by the Scottish Nationalist Party, is much more strident than Wales in its calls for separation, these moves do indicate that the so-called "unbundling of Britain" could occur sooner than anyone had predicted (*Guardian*, 8 May 1998, p. 23). For interesting historical analyses of the turbulent legal relationship between Scotland and England and how this has been modified by the European Union, see Campbell 1993; McCrone 1993.

7. "On every side, as far as the eye can reach, you behold the finest country in the universe, the most populous, the most animated, the most cultivated, the most varied in all kinds of products," the duke of Nivernais said of southeast England in the mid eighteenth century (quoted in Brandon 1979: 167).

Concurrently, the garden image underscored a collective difference and distance with others existing beyond its borders that were characterized in some way as inferior (Voltaire 1759: 119; Mitchell 1994b; Bunn 1994). It is primarily through this spatial framing of social and political organization, both within and without the nation, that the garden symbol has long been recognized as significant in the constitution of eighteenth- and nineteenth-century notions of Englishness and English identity (Drabble 1979; Lowenthal 1991, 1994; Waters 1988; Alfrey et al. 1993; Pugh 1988). In a colonial context, the garden's embodiment of intimacy in the small, well-cultivated fields and orchards of Kent operated as a defense against perceptions of an encroaching barbaric world.[8]

Cognate with the Old English *geard*, meaning yard, the word "garden" encapsulates the sense of a confined, cultivated space (Erp-Houtepan 1986: 277). A fence or wall is a necessary and basic feature of a garden; "a garden without a fence is in fact no longer a proper garden" (Erp-Houtepen 1986: 229; Crisp 1966: 49–53). Historically, fences defending against the outside world were usually made of stone, brick, or daub, and if an internal wall, were more often formed by latticework, wattle and palings, or hedges (Aldridge 1967). The bushes used for hedges were hawthorn, brier, yew, and privet (which refers to their granting of privacy).

As an allegorical narrative, garden imagery can operate as a metaphor for progress, control, order, and surveillance, masking with an aesthetic overlay power relations, as well as class, race, and gender differentiation. At the same time, the garden may function as a journey, as well as a utopian site of innocence, pleasure, and leisure. It is no coincidence that in many medieval and Renaissance illustrations of the Annunciation, the Virgin is depicted confined within the walls of a garden, an ambiguous symbol of both her purity and her impending transformation (J. D. Hunt 1992: 305–36). Whatever its foremost expression, the garden, at once imitating and espousing what is to be construed as "natural," necessarily remains distanced from any straightforward resemblance to reality. As a mode of spatial organization, the garden boundary is allusive and contradictory. The garden, above all, is

8. It is impossible to do justice to the complex historical development of English garden iconography. There is an abundance of material available on the peculiarities of the English garden and the range of experiences gardens have at various times been able to express; see, e.g., Moore et al. 1989; Francis and Hester 1990; Oelschlaeger 1991; J. D. Hunt 1992; Ross 1998; and esp. Hoyles 1994. "Getting back to the garden" and "land ethics" are tenable options for a postmodern relationship between people and the natural world, posits Max Oelschlaeger (1991: 344–46).

a fantasy. At one and the same time, it defines the limits of a perceived place and yet occupies an unfixed and ephemeral conceptual space. In its very articulation it marks, as Simon Pugh has argued, a loss or absence. The garden "is a model for everything that reality is not" (Pugh 1988: 8, 130–32).

This is precisely why conflict over the constitution and defense of the garden symbol has become a dominant issue in Kent. Concurrent with the region of Kent being essentialized in the English imagination, present-day England, as epitomized by an idealized rural Kent, has also been essentialized as an "authentic" embodiment of historical England. Adding to this dual process, and giving it even greater significance, is the fact that England has also stood, and in some cases still does today, as the historical representation of Britain. British identity was forged from the reluctant joining of English, Scottish, Welsh, and Irish nationalisms under the acts of Union in 1536, 1707, and again in 1800 (Colley 1992; Kearney 1989; Samuel 1989: xxxv). In this smoothing over of "internal differences" between pre-existing nationalisms, it was England that came to speak for and represent the rest of Britain (Hechter 1975: 164–207). Irish, Welsh, and Scottish identities were gradually co-opted and subsumed under the guise of a British—but in essence English—cultural identity (Dodd 1986: 1–28; Corrigan and Sayer 1985). People in Britain were "obliged to forget," to use Ernest Renan's terminology, that they had an identity other than that of being English (Renan 1990). Yet it was this very process of forgetting that "constitutes the *beginning* of the nation's narrative" (Bhabha 1990: 310).[9]

9. Today, ethnic and national romanticism are flourishing, as witnessed by the profusion of post-Soviet states, continuing ethnic conflicts in southeastern Europe, and older European nations experiencing similar crises of identity and a general resurgence of right-wing politics. Histories are again being dramatically rewritten. And historical narratives, in rearticulating nationalist allegiance and resistance, are providing the weaponry to justify rapid transformation and at times outrageous and terrifying events. History, notes Eric Hobsbawm, is the "raw material" upon which nationalist movements build their legitimacy and re-create their identity (Hobsbawm 1992: 3). Even the European Union is employing "cultural-building" initiatives and openly appealing to an essentialized classical "civilization" as its common European heritage (Shore 1995: 14, 21).

Homi Bhabha expands upon the theme of omission and "covering up" in his discussion of the obligation of a people to forget their past in the construction of a new national narrative. Picking up Ernest Renan's earlier and often-cited comment on the will of nationhood requiring that it forget its past (Renan 1990 [1882]), Bhabha writes: "To be obliged to forget—in the construction of the national present—is not a question of historical memory; it is the construction of a discourse on society that *performs* the problematic totalization of the national will" (Bhabha 1990: 311). Bhabha criticizes Benedict Anderson (1991) for his failure to recognize the unique and abrupt gap in synchronic time that opens up the space in which a

Throughout the eighteenth and nineteenth centuries, English historical narratives predominantly shaped the inclusive and exclusive boundaries of the modern nation with respect to both internal and external challenges.[10] This meant that the defense of England, and by extension the cherished rural Kentish landscape, in a sense came to be equated with the defense of the British people and state, despite the fact that England constitutes only part of the British nation. This conflation of symbols—Kent-England-Britain—has a long history. Since Kent is the nearest point to mainland Europe, it has always been the site of potential invasion and attack. The coast is dotted with Roman ditches, nineteenth-century Martello towers, and memorials to victims of the Battle of Britain in World War II (Rootes 1980). If one looks closely at the surface of buildings or construction site debris, there remains evidence of the destruction of Dover and the surrounding countryside that occurred in the German air raids of the 1940s. In a very symbolic sense, Kent was and remains a form of war zone and wall of defense.

FROM SMELL TO SIGHT

In the fifteenth and sixteenth centuries, medieval gardens were primarily grown for their olfactory and related medicinal qualities (Classen 1993:

---

national narrative can take form and flourish. It is this moment of "incommensurability in the midst of the everyday," of alienation and open arbitrariness in the signs of signification, that is vital for the nation to recognize itself as itself among other "contending and liberating forms of cultural identification" (ibid.: 311; and see also Chatterjee 1993, ch. 1). In short, what Bhabha recognizes is the overwhelming need for any nation to posit itself as against other nations and against other identities in order for it to be sustained as an autonomous entity. Thus, bound up with the very formation of the modern state, although not unique to it, is a knowledge of others that both unites it in opposition and, at the same time, creates a pervasive anxiety about others within that intimates a state's potential disruption.

10. The otherness of Europe, and even more so the colonial other, came to be popularized and domesticated, forming a central ideological force in smoothing over internal political and cultural divisions and shaping everyday conceptions in the production of an authentic "British" community (Bhabha 1986: 153–56). Linda Colley writes that in Britain, the "sense of a common identity here did not come into being, then, because of an integration and homogenization of disparate cultures. Instead, Britishness was superimposed over an array of internal differences in response to the contact with the Other, and above all in response to conflict with the Other" (Colley 1992: 6; for a critique of Colley, see Williams 1994). As Stuart Hall notes, the invention of Englishness "has always been negotiated against difference" (Hall 1990: 22).

22). Gardens were often located within monastery compounds or castle walls. Most important, gardens were intimate, contemplative, feminized, and above all, enclosed (Stewart 1966). This is clearly illustrated by various images of medieval gardens, irrespective of their function being primarily domestic, agricultural, or ideological. Enclosure was, in part, practical, representing the boundaries of the church or lord's secured lands. But at a more immediate level, the walled garden intensified the vegetation's perfume and fragrance. The delights perfume brought, which did not require the privileging of any one view over another, represented the sensory superiority of smell in the medieval period (Classen 1993: 15–36; Porteous 1990: 21–46).

Gradually, however, the ascendancy of sight developed as a corollary to the rise of printed documents and levels of literacy in the sixteenth and seventeenth centuries. "The sixteenth century did not see first: it heard and smelled, it sniffed the air and caught sounds" (Febvre 1982: 433, 423–42; see also Hibbitts 1992, 1994; Anderson 1991: 37–46; Ong 1967: 8; Lowe 1982: 13; Jay 1993: 83–148). As Yi-Fu Tuan has noted: "Europeans . . . have moved in the direction of the visual. In the Middle Ages, Europeans still lived for the most part in a traditional world that rewarded the senses—that was inchoate, colorful, and warmly human. From the sixteenth century onward, the world was shifting toward a cooler, larger, more deliberately conceived and precisely delineated order" (quoted in Porteous 1990: 5).

In the garden, a concern for the visual manifested itself in the increasing attention given to the pleasures of floral beauty and formal garden design (Classen 1993: 22; Tuan 1974: 140). By 1570, the Barton family, who owned a prosperous farm in Kent, gave up the pretense of growing flowers for medicinal purposes and openly admired their floral beauty and fragrance. Their garden flower beds, full of novelties such as blue primroses from the Canary Islands and marigolds from the New World via Mediterranean ports, increasingly came to represent the family's global trading prosperity and local social status (Ordish 1985: 38–39; Goody 1993: 182–205). By the time of James I in the 1620s, England had developed a formal garden style distinct from its European counterparts (Wright 1938: 231; Leslie 1993: 3–16). While the most famous garden estates were owned by the wealthy, the garden fashion was quickly copied by less well endowed families. In 1677, John Worlidge, one of the first English horticulturists, wrote: "There is scarce a cottage in most of the southern parts of England but has its proportional garden, so great a delight do most people take in it" (quoted in Wright 1938: 234). The fascination with gardens generated numerous books on the practical aspects of gardening, which, as Martin Hoyles has argued, represent, among other things, an early form of nationalist literature (Hoyles 1991, 1995).

More significant, in the course of the eighteenth century in particular, botany emerged as a serious science concerned with systems of plant classification and species grafting according to visual, not olfactory, categories. These supposedly objective explorations in botany reflect that sight had become the paramount sensory experience. Through a visual orientation, the boundaries of empirical (and valid) information could be seen, revealed, and exposed. Vision was thus privileged as the new basis of positivist truth, rationality, and cognizant modern culture as the means of scientific inquiry became integrally connected to the "eye-minding philosophy of the Enlightenment" (Classen 1993: 27; see also Rotman 1993; Gifford 1990: 17–47; Harvey 1989: 240–59). John Locke's *Essay on Human Understanding* epitomized this Cartesian philosophy. Published in 1690, by 1706 it was already being reprinted in an enlarged fifth edition, and it continued to enjoy great influence throughout the century. Locke's basic argument was that ideas were not innate, but that the mind formed complex thoughts out of the basic visual experiences registered through the eyes. This approach was espoused by Joseph Addison, who explicitly applied Locke's thesis to show how a garden landscape works upon the thoughts of its visitors. Sets of ideas derived from gazing upon the garden, Addison wrote, "awaken other Ideas of the same Sett, which immediately determine a new Dispatch of Spirits, that in the same manner open other Neighboring Traces, till at last the whole Sett of them is blown up, and the whole Prospect or Garden flourishes in the Imagination" (*Spectator* no. 417, 28 June 1712).

While sight did not completely overwhelm the other senses, it took precedence and marked an epistemological shifting that translated into how people came to *view* themselves and *recognize* others as a process of *categorizing* difference. Histories of the body, particularly the woman's body, exemplify this transition (Duden 1991: 1–49). The process of abstraction and distancing between "us" and "them" was enabled by elevating sight to a neutral form of perception, devoid of power relations and subjective interpretation (Panofsky 1991).[11] It amounted to what Jonathan Crary has

11. The translation of psychological space in the medieval period into mathematical space in the Italian Renaissance and English Enlightenment affected how people viewed the world. The shifting understanding of perspective has been interpreted from two different yet complementary positions. On the one side, geometrically derived space provided an ordering rationale and predictability to

called the "autonomization of sight" (Crary 1990: 19).[12] John Ruskin, one of the most famous of English art theorists in the 1850s, called this purified vision "the innocence of the eye" (quoted in Crary 1990: 95; see also Mitchell 1986: 38, 118). In the transfer of value from smell to sight, it was this understanding of unencumbered clarity that epitomized a cultural shift away from the immediate face-to-face remnants of a community-based feudal system and toward the rise of an abstract theoretical notion of individualism operating in a civil society (Macfarlane 1978).

Sight as the dominant sensory value is integrally linked to power dynamics in social and organizational relations (Bryson 1983: 133–62; Jay 1988).[13] As Foucault has argued, the practice of surveillance in the late eighteenth and nineteenth centuries created the conditions by which power was institutionalized as a form of discipline in schools, prisons, hospitals, and factories (Foucault 1977; Jay 1986; Darian-Smith 1993b; Hibbitts 1994; Bently 1996: 1–20). Surveillance, manifested as control, became the means through which the individual became both an object of investigation and, at the same time, an observing subject. Feminist writers have put a critical twist on this by arguing that sight is characteristically masculine and rep-

---

experience, resulting in what Erwin Panofsky calls the "objectification of the subjective" (Panofsky 1991: 41, 66; Kubovy 1986: 162–73). On the other side, people viewed perspective as distorting reality with subjective appearance and arbitrary interpretation. According to this view, perspective, despite its suggestion of scientific objectivity, is highly individualistic. But as noted by Panofsky, "this polarity is really the double face of one and the same issue, and those objections are in fact aimed at one and the same point" (Panofsky 1991: 71; Edgerton 1975: 153–58).

12. Jonathan Crary claims that the separation of the senses resulting in the dominance of sight did not occur until the first two decades of the nineteenth century, but I would suggest that it occurred somewhat earlier. According to Crary, "a new kind of observer took shape in Europe radically different from the type of observer in the seventeenth and eighteenth centuries" (Crary 1990: 6, 8–19, 67–96). This resulted in the standardization and normalization of what constituted proper sight, devoid of historical and political implications. This, Crary argues, was the necessary precondition for the mass consumption of objectified visual images essential for modern advertising and communications.

13. "Vision is the intellectual sense. It structures the universe for us, but only 'out there' and 'in front'. It is a cool, detached sense" (Porteous 1990: 7). This detachment or indifference derives from the phenomenological quality of sight, which, unlike the other senses, does not require intimate proximity or contact. Rather, sight distances the individual from other people and the particularity of one's immediate surroundings. Sight as a process of abstraction can passively observe and objectively generalize. In distinguishing or "dissecting" what are classified as differences, the gaze can valorize what appears as a timeless and systematic structure of ordering (Crary 1990: 96; see also Tuan 1995: 236–37).

resents possessive voyeurism in seeing the world as separate and distanced from oneself (Rose 1993; Taylor 1994: 268–72). Sight, writes Constance Classen, "is the particular domain of the male explorer who goes out to confront and conquer the world, while smell, taste and touch belong to the female homemaker who, her vision bounded by the walls of the house, remains behind to take care of the children and dinner" (Classen 1993: 31; see also Heidegger 1977b). It is significant that this masculine vision of the world emerged in parallel with the colonial expansions of European nation-states. The conquering, objectifying power of the gaze over family and home helped bolster and sustain, among other things, an ideological and aesthetic expansion of empire overseas. Moreover, it provided the rationale for the universalizing mythology embodied in English law and its claim to "a panoptic sovereignty in its ability to see all subjects from its vantage point" (Young and Sarat 1994: 326; and see also Fitzpatrick 1992: 111–18).

Linking this brief discussion of the history of sight back to garden metaphors highlights the power implications, and by extension the legal significance, of the transformation of garden aesthetics. By the 1730s, the English garden style quickly dropped its internal formalism as expressed in geometric paths and terraces trimmed by hedgerows, mazes, and clipped trees. This formalism is wonderfully illustrated in the frontispiece lithograph in Charles Evelyn's book *The Lady's Recreation*, reinforcing in name and form the feminine implications of the enclosed space (fig. 4). With the dropping of garden segmentation and formal borders, a new expansive and masculine vision emerged that favored the garden landscapes of Capability Brown, whose sweeping lawns merged the garden with the countryside and embodied what Alexander Pope called the romantic "picturesque" (Schama 1995: 538–45; Brownwell 1978: 103; Shepard 1967: 86–88; Martin 1984; Hoyles 1991: 38; Williamson 1995: 77–99).

No longer requiring walls to demarcate proprietorial possession, the new garden romanticism above all displayed a supreme confidence in the landowner, who took great pains to present himself as an individual identity. In eighteenth-century Britain, portraiture of the elite flourished under the artistic skill of such men as Gainsborough, Romney, and Reynolds. Partly in response to the declining centrality of the monarchy and the rise of a new entrepreneurial aristocracy, men and women were most typically illustrated walking in the grounds of their landed estates. One of the most famous portraits from this period is Thomas Gainsborough's painting of Mr. and Mrs. Andrews (1748–50). Here the landlord self-consciously adopts a casual pose, gun tucked easily under his arm, ankles

Figure 4. Frontispiece to *The Lady's Recreation*, by Charles
Evelyn (1717).

Figure 5. *Mr. and Mrs. Andrews,* by Thomas Gainsborough (1748). Oil on canvas. By kind permission of the National Gallery, London.

crossed, while beside him Mrs. Andrews sits primly on a wrought-iron garden seat (fig. 5).

Mr. and Mrs. Andrews's comfortable superiority was, in part, owing to the hardening of legal doctrine into general written principles of property law at this time (see Harwood 1993). This expansion and clarification of law touched on rules of inheritance, trespass, rights of way, easements, and access to land with respect to woodcutting, fishing, hunting, and shooting—a feature of law illustrated by Mr. Andrews's gun. An important result of this hardening and streamlining of property-related law into a national legal system was that it freed individuals from hands-on control and immediate responsibility for their land and their tenant farmers who worked and lived on it (Shepard 1967: 89–90). In the words of the late-eighteenth-century poet William Cowper, who was highly critical of wealthy landowners who sought to improve their properties, "Estates are landscapes, gaz'd upon awhile, then advertiz'd and auctioneered away" (quoted in Daniels and Seymour 1990: 501).

The fashion for romantic garden estates replete with ruined temples, quasi-Roman bridges, and ha-has (sunken fences) that granted an unfettered horizon did not last long into the nineteenth century.[14] As industrialization took hold, there was a change in English garden style to more intimate "wild" urban gardens. This represented the shift of power from the hereditary aristocracy to the entrepreneurial middle class of lesser gentry. The garden was an expression of status and a mode of fashionability emanating from London. But it was also much more than that. The garden was and remains the prerogative of those fortunate enough to own land. As an aesthetic embodiment of property, the garden exemplified, particularly after the acts of enclosure in the eighteenth century, a dynamic, highly individualized, and hierarchical social structure. Through the carving up of land on the basis of property rights to freehold estates, the garden landscape naturalized, and in a sense disguised, England's intrinsically anti-democratic and gendered system of common law. In particular, the law of perpetuities guaranteed rights in land on the basis of kinship, "bloodlines," and "family trees," creating "a landscape of exclusion," in the words of the historian Tom Williamson (1995: 100–118). This apparent injustice was very much criticized by Oliver Goldsmith, who wrote:

> Thus fares the land, by luxury betrayed;
> In nature's simplest charms at first arrayed;
> But verging to decline, its splendours rise,
> Its vistas strike, its palaces surprise;
> While scourged by famine from the smiling land,
> The mournful peasant leads his humble band—
> And while he sinks, without one arm to save,
> The country blooms—a garden, and a grave.
> (Goldsmith, *The Deserted Village* [1769],
> quoted in Hoyles 1991: 39)

Notions of the ideal garden shifted in the course of industrialization toward a smaller and more manageable private retreat (Daniels and Seymour 1990: 504; Strathern 1992: 104–5, 186). Nonetheless, the garden, as a particular feature of the landed estate, continued to operate as an aesthetic metaphor for a social elite's legal capacity to civilize, cultivate, beautify, order, naturalize, universalize, exclude, dominate, and ultimately make inequalities appear more plausible and acceptable (Pugh 1988: 11–13;

14. "The use of the ha-ha, with its military origin as a means of defense, disguised the division between garden and countryside. This ditch and rampart existing between the house and its surrounding estate provoked surprise, hence 'ha-ha' or more phonetically 'a-ha', when approached from the house. Its meaning as a barrier or fortification was, however, more apparent when it was seen from the countryside looking towards the house" (Hoyles 1991: 39–40).

Strathern 1992: 88–89). Law and its aesthetic cultural base were mutually reinforcing, keeping pace with the transition from a declining aristocracy to an economically powerful middle class.

These idealized connections between land and law were critical, as many commentators have argued (Vaughan 1993; Sugarman and Warrington 1995; Goodrich 1992; Rose 1994). Having no single founding constitution on which legal authority could draw, English law derived its legitimation from the unique doctrine of parliamentary sovereignty under a limited monarchy and with the population's voluntary acquiescence in a representative system of governance.

Today, the force sustaining England's legal imagination relies upon the image of absolute property ownership in a naturalized "old England," in which tradition, common sense, and legal precedent play significant roles. Evoking a past when the nation's economic and political stability flourished, the garden today provides an organic metaphor for a particular temporal and spatial landscape that mythically represents the imperial glory of England, the identity of Englishness, and the superior authority of English law. Beyond this, the garden symbolizes the encompassing stretch of English legal authority that once covered an enormous empire but is now more modestly contained, apart from a few remaining colonies, within its island boundaries, as dramatically illustrated around the world by Britain's returning of Hong Kong to China on 30 June 1997 (Mitchell 1994b: 20). This inward shift in spatial referencing points to the transformation of the garden's symbolism, for now, above all else, the garden demarcates a confined and cultivated space—a place of security, a guarantee of repose, a buffer zone against intrusion. And, I suggest, it is precisely nostalgia for the garden as an enduring naturalized and innocent visual representation of England's—and Britain's—legal and cultural stability that today makes it so powerful and emotive a mythology.

RAPING THE GARDEN OF ENGLAND

This sense of an untouched past articulated through Kent's garden identity is heightened by the current political and economic turbulence of Britain as a member state of the EU. The widespread resonance of the idea of the garden in Kent may well represent a popular sense of alienation and dislocation in a country very conscious of its imperial demise, revitalized Scottish, Welsh, and Irish nationalisms, dismantled local government powers, and north/south socioeconomic divides. The dim realization of the nation's internal disintegration helps intensify the need for stability and control perceived as accessible in a localized perspective. People whose expectations and dreams have been lessened as a consequence of the economic recession of the late 1980s and 1990s are more readily adopting a reflex rhetoric that speaks of a community spirit embodied in the local village, town, and region (see generally Inglehart 1990). Such sentiments are encapsulated in a few verses written (and later sung to me!) by a local rector in Rochester, Kent, which were inspired specifically by the building of the Channel Tunnel:

> So much of our county has disappeared,
> Under tarmac and concrete and brick.
> Developers and planners have all agreed, that this is the place for sacrifice.
> They called it the garden of England, but now,
> It's a wide open field, for all who can profit by rape.
>
> There's much of our county still lovely,
> They haven't spoiled all of it yet.
> The fields and the woods and the orchards remain.
> We'll fight for the County of Kent.
>
> (letter to the author, 16 Mar. 1994)

It can be argued that there is emerging an internalizing and inward-looking movement of local retreat in southern England and more generally throughout the United Kingdom as Wales, Scotland, and Northern Ireland increasingly assert their independence from London. Aiding this process of decentering are grassroots politics and a deepening commitment to green issues, especially the need to retain efficient public transport. Over the past decade, numerous environmentalists in road blockades and tree camps have demonstrated against the building of new motorways through green countryside. (The Newbury Bypass blockade is probably the best known of these.) Britain's police forces have responded with unwarranted alarm, and in 1994 the Association of Chief Police Officers decided to use the Anti-Terrorist squad to gather information on environmental activists through surveillance and bugging of phones and computers, despite there being no evidence of terrorist activity. This is not to say that the "greenies" have been entirely unsuccessful. Some hardened veterans of anti-development protests have organized themselves into groups such as the E-Team (E for environment) and make themselves available to residents campaigning against privatization of railways and the destruction of woodland. A lot more could be said about this type of disproportional police retaliation as an indication of the crisis of the British state, and about environmentalism replacing unionism as a new form of civil protest. Important for my purposes here is that through this popular investment in and mythology of an idealized countryside, new environmental movements are fueling alternative forms of citizen participation across a spectrum of socioeconomic backgrounds and promoting a rather different public sphere from that envisioned by Locke and other social theorists of the English Enlightenment.

In Kent, collective community action is, in part, generated through the garden metaphor, which helps mark out what are deemed the "natural" boundaries of the county's identity and territorial reach. This is dramatically illustrated by the many headlines in local Kent newspapers throughout the early 1990s that made use of Kent's image as the Garden of England to highlight the Tunnel's destructive capacities: "Danger of Blight in the Garden of England," "More Trouble Lurks Deep in the Garden," "Fighting Kent's Corner," and "Garden Put under Threat." The garden image offers a sense of belonging and frames a locality both distant from London and resistant to change. For instance, in a letter to a local Kent newspaper, Francisca Perrett, of Chilham, Kent, confirmed an earlier complaint about a new neighbor's "upgrading" of property that destroyed "a rambling ancient garden":

> The rich variety of plants in the borders in front of Cumberland House have been replaced with plants more commonly found in the wealthier antiseptic suburbs of London. Naturally, the new owners are free to modify the surrounding borders and gardens to meet their taste: planning law is intended only to provide control on the most critical aspects of development and then not with complete effectiveness. Nevertheless, Jenny Hill is right in her contention that what was once an open space of lawns, borders, hedges and orchards in the midst of the village has now been overlaid by concrete and order in the form of a tennis court, swimming pool, outhouses, driveways and housing. A surprising result when one considers that Chilham is a conservation area.
>
> (*Kentish Gazette*, 23 Mar. 1995: 6)

Of course, the building of roads and the Tunnel have caused irreparable damage to Kent's environment. A local resident, Edward Cookson, stressed to me how important it was to visually record the damages. This concern in fact prompted him to publish a book entitled *From Garden to Gateway: A Photographic Record of the Changing Face of Kent* (1992) (interview, October 1993). In highlighting the impact of the Tunnel and the Folkestone Terminal, there is no denying that these photographs are quite shocking. That being said, physical destruction does not explain the belief that the Tunnel will introduce pollutants and rabies into England, and other widespread anxieties, which I take up in chapter 6. Such fears are primarily linked to the Tunnel's disruption of secure spatial borders and an idealized conflation of island, nation, and defensible jurisdiction. These fears help explain the military rhetoric of "penetration," "invasion," and "rape," much used by protesters, which emphasizes the Tunnel's violent destabilizing of the received and stable history of a naturally gendered landscape (Taylor 1994: 272–74). The multiple dimensions of fear, impoverishment, and despair were brought home to me more strongly in the rather subdued but passionate demonstration against the Tunnel on the day of its inauguration by Queen Elizabeth on 6 May 1994. In fine rain and under overcast skies, about five hundred rather bedraggled spectators and protesters against the Tunnel gathered in the parking lot behind the Eurotunnel Exhibition Centre, raised their banners, and sang their chants, while international media crews looked on in open contempt (fig. 6).

In effect, the Tunnel defiles a bounded space dear to the English national imagination. By cutting across Kentish properties, orchards, hedgerows, and a dense network of public footpaths and bridle paths deemed to have existed for centuries (Wallace 1993), the Tunnel and the fast rail linking it to London metaphorically and literally undermine an established aesthetics of order that is the indispensable basis for imagining the natural authority of English law and notions of Englishness. In this way, the garden image and its multilayered iconography evoke a specific Kentish landscape and yet also justify talk about symbols dear to state-nationalist sentiment. Activists seeking to protect the environment and to reinstate what is imagined to have existed in the past are also prone to assimilate reactionary tendencies, jingoism, right-wing conservatism, and blatant parochialism (see Gray 1993). Nature's presumed femininity and impartial universality imbues those who fight for its defense with a militaristic sense of righteous purity, supposedly free of any nationalist impulse. This becomes important in the wider context of England's and Britain's relationships with the EU. For none of this discussion can be divorced from the supranational political scene or from the notion of a larger European legal entity, which strikes at the heart of national legal identity—of Englishness (Goodrich 1992: 16).

The current political climate between Britain and the European Union helps explain why the Tunnel has caused such enduring bitterness. As a symbol of European intervention, the Tunnel and related plans for a fast-rail link between London, Paris, and Brussels have dramatically polarized public opinion (see Appendix 2). Despite enthusiasm for the project among

Figure 6. Banner protesting against "Raping the Garden of England" at a public demonstration outside the Eurotunnel Exhibition Centre, Folkestone, on the day of the Tunnel's inauguration on 6 May 1994. Author's photograph.

many Londoners and people in Wales, Scotland, and Ireland, a large percentage of the English population remains firmly against the Tunnel and relies heavily on the notion of the debasement of the countryside as justification for its objections. It is within this extended European context that the garden, as proprietorial product and symbolic metaphor for the rule of law, assumes heightened meaning. Analogous to the way the garden historically served the English nobility by masking disparities of legal, social, and economic power, the Kentish garden bolsters a pretense that the nation's central institutions in London are stable and in control. After all, there can be no garden without there being a home.[15] Moreover, the association of the garden with English identity sustains the illusion of Britain's ethnic homogeneity, despite the rising presence of minority peoples. In this way, the garden ideology in its present form continues to mask Britain's history of class and cultural inequalities. Kent's garden imagery provides comforting reassurance that the British remain culturally and ethnically identifiable, and that London remains the controlling center (the landowner and gardener) of a significant world power.

MARKETING THE GARDEN OF ENGLAND

"The walls around the garden are the rules, the frame, which define the possible, the permissible," Simon Pugh writes (1988: 10). Given the value of a garden image, it is hardly surprising that there now exist strict rules governing the responsibility of owners to maintain so-called heritage gardens throughout England (Goulty 1993). Kent itself has 254 parks and gardens considered of historical interest to the county. Kent County Council imposes its own planning restrictions on home and countryside development in by-laws and in the Kent Structure Plan. It also supports the campaigns of groups such as the Kent Gardens Trust, the Countryside Commission, and the Council for the Protection of Rural England on behalf of new laws, such as the 1995 Environmental Bill, which sought to introduce, among other things, regulations to protect "natural" hedgerows, significantly depleted since World War II.[16]

Yet while Kent County Council supports the conservation of heritage gardens on behalf of the wider nation, it also expediently uses the powerful garden imagery to sell itself and its role in integrating a future Europe. Kentish gardens are touted as a major tourist drawing card and so function as an explicit form of commodity (Mitchell 1994b: 14). A tourist brochure put out by the Kent County Council Economic Development Department,

15. The idea of home has many meanings, but above all it functions as a territorial core, supplying both unity and security (Porteous 1976: 383–90; on the myth of home in Britain, see Warner 1994, ch. 6).

16. This protection of an invented "natural" landscape struck me as rather peculiar, highlighting that what we think of "nature" is intimately connected to how long we think it has existed in time. In a conversation on this point with Bill Maurer, he made an interesting connection with William Cronon's book *Changes in the Land: Indians, Colonists and the Ecology of New England* (1983), which argues that early English colonists in New England did not have the capacity to "see" how native American peoples had cultivated the land, and that many landscape features they thought "natural" were in fact not.

Figure 7. *Off the Motorway*. A Kent County Council tourist brochure that can be picked up at either of the Channel Tunnel terminals (1994). By kind permission of Kent County Council.

Figure 8. Untitled cartoon by Steve Bell. *Guardian*, 31 January 1995. This cartoon refers to the intense demonstrations along the southeast coast of England protesting the export of live animals, and in particular sheep, to France. In alluding to the supreme confidence of eighteenth-century English gentry (see fig. 5), the cartoon mocks the British government's ineffectual pretense at controlling its own landscaped garden estate. It also indicates the extent to which such eighteenth-century representations of class and hierarchy continue to resonate. A vicious, "wolf-like" France stands by ready to attack. © Steve Bell 1995. By kind permission of Steve Bell.

which you can pick up at the French Terminal, displays romanticized images of Kent, complete with old touring car, small village, church steeple, and oast houses (fig. 7). These images are deliberately reminiscent of the early-twentieth-century postcards designed to sell Kent to Londoners, mentioned above. Kent County Council has also established links with the county of Bács-Kiskun to the south of Budapest, bringing together "the Garden of England together with the Garden of Hungary." The beauty of this link with Hungary, according to Stephen Barber, head of European operations at Kent County Council, "is that we have attracted £200,000 through national and Community funds, and it hasn't cost KCC a penny . . . we get a tremendous amount of kudos for this," as well as the possibility of establishing future links with Germany (interview, 19 Nov. 1993). Kent County Council's promotion of itself as a "builder of bridges" between regions and nations was further underscored at the time of the Channel Tunnel's inauguration in May 1994. The festivities organized by

Eurotunnel (and Kent County Council) to celebrate the event included "A Garden Alliance" promoting a unique opportunity to visit ten beautiful gardens in Kent and Nord–Pas de Calais. Here, the innocent beauty of the garden was still functioning to smooth over political differences and supposedly provide a neutral site on which to forge transnational exchanges. The intention was admirable. Yet I was told discreetly by one of the Eurotunnel employees that they had a hard time finding French "gardens of quality."

Still, where Kent County Council may see opportunities for business and commercial expansion, for many people in Kent and among the wider English population, the building of the Tunnel undermines the Channel's capacity to function as a physical buffer against the outside world. In this context, the public's clinging to an essentialized symbol of Kent as the garden of England inadvertently, and somewhat ironically, draws attention to the vulnerability and indeterminacy of the garden's perceived boundaries. The extent to which this overlapping imagery articulates popular sensibilities is illustrated in a political cartoon that appeared in the national newspaper the *Guardian* on 31 Jan. 1995 (fig. 8). Alluding to the supreme confidence of eighteenth-century English gentry, and underscoring how accessible this imagery remains in the popular imagination, the cartoon mocks the then Tory government's ineffectual pretense at controlling its landscaped garden estate. A vicious "wolf-like" France stands by ready to attack.

With the building of the Tunnel, no longer can the sea stand in for the British nation's isolationist status. No longer can the "naturalness" of English law shut out the expanding presence of the New Europe. With the breaking down of its landscaped boundaries, the garden image of England is being pulled apart, revealing and confirming the country's lack of spatial cohesion and judicial sovereignty. And without its garden, the grandeur of the English home is being dismantled, suggesting that England—and by implication Britain—is in a sense becoming a sublot or periphery of the European mainland.

3 Napoleon's Long Shadow, 1802–1985

The Conflation of Territory, Identity, and Nationalism

Shake hands with union, O thou mighty state!
Now thou art all Great Britain and no more;
No Scot, no English now, nor no debate:
No borders but the ocean and the shore.
Samuel Daniel on the accession of
James I in 1603

THE IMPORTANCE OF TERRITORY

Historically, territoriality has been linked to statehood and been one of its defining features (Weber 1946: 77–83; Foucault 1991: 93–94; Baldwin 1992: 207–30; Sack 1986). Modern nation-state building is grounded in the idea that a particular "people" is necessarily tied to and defined by a specific geopolitical place (Agnew 1987). All modern states have had to rationalize and naturalize the spatial limits of their jurisdictional boundaries as part of the ongoing process of defining their managed populations. Today, this conflation of territory and national identity is no less pertinent (Slowe 1990; Sharpe 1987; Cheshire and Gordon 1995). Evidence of control over a bounded, identifiable space remains a prerequisite for international recognition and for any new country to join the United Nations. "Spatial control and spatial expansion are the conditions of the invisible hand extending its grasp: in a sense they also *are* the state," writes Teresa Brennan (1993: 152). This echoes an earlier analysis of the state as being, not the mere owner of its territory, but actually that territory (Parry 1968: 18).

Not all states have used the same vision in their rationalizing and naturalizing of state boundaries, nor are such visions in any way fixed over time. The historian Peter Sahlins has written about the historical conceptualizing of the "frontier" and "boundary" as "natural" phenomena and noted the linguistic differences between the two words—*frontière* and *limite*—in French. A frontier is a zone of expansion and defense, in contrast to a boundary, which is more like a linear line of demarcation representing the "*limites* of two jurisdictions or territories" (Sahlins 1990: 1426; 1989; see also Mellor 1989: 74–103; Gottman 1973: 123–60; Prescott 1987). This distinction is important in understanding French history, for only in the late eighteenth and early nineteenth centuries did France become a territorial nation with fixed, internationally recognized boundaries. Up until that time, frontiers described the peripheral reaches of France and came to be associated with features such as mountains and rivers. These physical characteristics were interpreted as representing natural political divisions, and even when nonexistent, they were often drawn in by cartographers in the service of the king (Konvitz 1990: 4). Mountains, rivers, valleys, and coasts underpinned strategies of state policy by becoming objects to be conquered and barriers to be broken (Sahlins 1990: 1433). However, this relationship to nature as historically determining political entities slowly shifted in the context of emerging modern state-building, whereby nature came to be interpreted as a justification for preordained boundaries. By 1714:

> France had acquired much of its contemporary shape—minus the provinces of Lorraine and Savoy. At the same time, that shape had gained coherence as a unified territorial domain. The movement toward a territorial state, however, was far from complete: not only did the idea of territorial sovereignty remain undeveloped, in theory as in practice, but the political boundary in the north and east was largely undelimited. France's frontiers were riddled with enclaves, exclaves, overlapping and contested jurisdictions, and other administrative nightmares. The eighteenth-century state was to rationalize its administration and to rectify its limits, shifting the orientation of its policy from natural frontiers to natural boundaries.
>
> (Sahlins 1990: 1435)

In France, the modern state was mapped out according to a highly sophisticated system of centralized control and regional governments. It was a belief in democracy and its embodiment in the bureaucratic infrastructure that provided the modern rationalizing and naturalizing of spatial divisions and political boundaries (Weber 1979; Konvitz 1990). By contrast, geographical features remained a more enduringly significant component in understanding English identity (Urwin 1982: 21; Bulpitt 1983). Throughout the eighteenth century, the island space gradually came to be articulated through and equated with the emerging British state, and as the British empire pushed the nation's peripheral boundaries further afield, the state core hardened and consolidated its central authority (Anderson 1992).

By the mid eighteenth century, David Hume, Montesquieu, and Jean-Jacques Rousseau in their various treatises on the moral and proper limits of a state were united on the doctrine of natural boundaries as the containing and restraining bounds of statehood. In the words of Rousseau, "The lie of the mountains, seas, and rivers [in Europe], which serve as boundaries of the various nations which people it, seems to have fixed forever their number and size. We may fairly say that the political order of the Continent is in some sense the work of nature" (quoted in Sahlins 1990: 1436, see n. 46). On this basis, state governments could claim justification for defending natural borders and a national culture since, in a fundamental sense, these had been preordained by Mother Nature.

It is no coincidence that in conjunction with modern state-building in the eighteenth and nineteenth centuries, symbols of national identity were increasingly represented by female figures such as Britain's Britannia and France's Marianne. Womanly icons of nationhood conflated a feminized chaste nature with a naturalized, virtuous, and hence legitimate, landscaped territory (see Mosse 1985: 1–23). James Thomson's famous song "Rule Britannia," first published in 1740, was revived in the French Revolutionary wars of the 1790s. It spoke rousingly of Britannia who ruled the seas, relying upon her rightful and natural claim to conquer and possess, which had originated in antiquity, as illustrated by her armor, shield, and classical dress (Mosse 1985: 97–98).

> When Britain first, at Heaven's command,
> Arose out from the azure main,
> This was the character of her land,
> And guardian angels sung the strain:
> Rule, Britannia! Rule the waves!
> Britons never will be slaves!

> The nations not so blest as thee,
> Must in their turn to tyrants fall;
> Whilst thou shall flourish, great and free,
> The dread and envy of them all.

The conflation of territory, identity, and nationalism helps explain why the English rejected Tunnel plans in Britain's general retreat from Europe in the aftermath of the French Revolution at the beginning of the nineteenth century. One consequence of this attitude of withdrawal, according to Jacques Darras, is that it resulted in locking "England up in its own home-made brand of insularity" (Darras 1990: 52). The Channel was central to maintaining isolation, sharply defining the country's national boundaries and marking "a sort of void," or "in-between" frontier (Certeau 1984: 127). As a "middle place, composed of interactions and interviews" between France and England, the Channel spatially fixed the national limits.[1] It aligned state with territory, and foreign policy defending the interests of the island with national identity. At the same time as the coastlines and the 21-mile expanse of open sea operated as markers of difference and distance, they also helped generate popular desire for the Tunnel and the establishing of a new point of contact between England and France (Certeau 1984: 127). This complex interaction of difference and desire characterizes the ebb and flow of tensions between governmental and popular support for the Tunnel scheme throughout its 200-year history. The Tunnel, now and in the past, embodies a new space of both hope and fear in the national imaginary, simultaneously offering opportunities for connections between the two countries while reinforcing their separation.

Martin Heidegger has discussed how bridges, like tunnels, bring into existence a location and a space that did not exist before: "Before the bridge stands, there are of course many spots along the stream that can be occupied by something. One of them proves to be a location, and does so *because of the bridge*. The bridge does not first come to a location to stand in it; rather, a location comes into existence only by virtue of the bridge" (Heidegger 1977a: 332).

In a similar vein, the Tunnel brings into existence many of the differences and similarities existing between England and France. The Tunnel in itself was never necessary to confirm the locations of England and France in the nineteenth and twentieth centuries, although it certainly redefined the strategic locations and meaning of the coastal towns of Dover and Calais. But with respect to the national context, what various tunnel schemes did do was activate, rearticulate, and consolidate periodic debates about the two states' differences and, particularly as allies during the first and second world wars, their similarities. The idea of the Tunnel operated as a spatial metaphor and testament to the ideological viability and strength of the modern nation-state as an autonomous and sovereign (island) entity. Hence various responses to the Tunnel over time can be interpreted as a historical gauge, measuring the rise and fall of the British government's

1. Yet as Homi Bhabha notes, no signification of nation is ever total or complete, so boundaries and borders are turned into *"in-between* spaces through which the cultural and political authority are negotiated" (Bhabha 1990: 4).

optimism and fears, which were inseparable from the history of the nation's naval strength, legal and political stability, international and domestic relations, and vast imperial economic power. In reinforcing the Channel coast as the limit of the nation's homeland, Tunnel debates sustained the naturalness of Britain's island borders at the same time as naturalizing the economic imperative for colonial expansion and much-needed sources of raw materials.

Today, territorial circumscription has assumed heightened import. This is precisely because state territory—the spaces of central power and jurisdictional authority—can no longer be taken for granted as the primary contextual frame in a world of postcolonialism, reterritorialization, and an escalating politics over the meanings of small-scale locations (Keith and Pile 1993; Carter and Squires 1993; Keating 1988; Pred 1990; Massey 1991, 1993). With the free movement of ideas, goods, and peoples defining the essential character of a new borderless Europe, the rising salience of territorial control emerges to oppose this characterization, particularly in the security and transportation areas. Over the past decade, perhaps nowhere have issues of territoriality, sovereignty, and the boundaries of authority been so explicitly and passionately debated as they have been with respect to the building of the Channel Tunnel. Symbolic of the new borderless Europe, the Tunnel has been a focus of contention. Among other objections, the Tunnel is a vital branch of the Trans-European Transport Network, a Brussels scheme proposing to break up state insularity by linking up all major European cities. As discussed in chapter 6, in its centralizing intent, this scheme curiously echoes nineteenth-century railway imperialism by the British and French governments in India and Africa (Schibelbusch 1986: 33–44).

In an interview by the French newspaper *Libération*, published in Britain's *Guardian* newspaper on the day of the Channel Tunnel's inauguration, 6 May 1994, the then British Prime Minister John Major and French President Édouard Balladur were asked what the Tunnel represented for their respective countries:

Major: It is a potent symbol of Britain's new role in Europe. . . . The tunnel links Great Britain with the Continent for the first time in many thousands of years. It will bring us nearer still to the French people, with whom our ties have grown closer over past years.

Balladur: The Channel Tunnel will bring our two countries closer in many ways, not just economically. It will help strengthen economic cohesion within the European Union.

Major: It is certainly true that the British have never been accustomed to the idea of getting into a train and arriving in another country. The sea crossing, however short, has represented a barrier. But countries such as France, which has always had land boundaries, are clearly sovereign and have distinct identities. Britain is no different in that respect.

Balladur: The main feature of British civilization has undoubtedly been its extraordinary expansion throughout the world. I cannot believe that the great British people, in order to protect their identity, would now be cowering on the very island from which they set sail to travel the world. On the contrary, I am convinced that Britain has a major role in the building of Europe, not least in the originality of its contribution to the overall structure.

While the language in this exchange points to tense undercurrents between these national leaders such as Major's use of "Continent" and "barrier," and Balladur's use of "cowering" and what could be viewed as a tongue-in-cheek description of the "great British people," overall the rhetoric represents the British government's and the English people's reluctant but increasing involvement in the European Union. The complexity of this transition, merging and dividing old loyalties and new political allegiances across national, regional, and local arenas, builds upon a long history of physical and mental boundaries between the two countries.

OVERCOMING PHYSICAL BOUNDARIES

Britain has not historically experienced the same amount of spatial ambiguity with respect to its national borders as its western European neighbors. This is not to say that Britain has always been contained within the island frame. Hard as it is to imagine today, the Channel has not always unequivocally represented, as it does now, the limits of British and French territories.[2] The British have enjoyed complex exchanges with the French for many centuries, which imbricated land ownership, family genealogies, commercial ventures, legal controls, and monarchies across the Channel region (Harrison 1986). One of the more explicit instances of this indeterminacy of English and French territorial boundaries occurred when the

2. For a wonderful analysis of the complex relations between England and France, and why there is no inherent reason why the Channel must be the boundary between them, see Norbert Elias's "On the Sociogenesis of the State" (1982: 91–200).

Port of Calais surrendered to Edward III in 1347 and became an English colony until 1558. Calais was taken by the English for its commercial advantages, and a garrison was established there to protect the heavy sea trade. In 1362, the Staple, or supply base, was established at Calais, making it the center for collecting English customs and excise and storing English merchandise (Sandeman 1908: 57–83). The Venetian ambassador Michele noted in his report on his return to England in 1587, a year before Calais was once again appropriated by the French, that if the English were to lose the port "they would not only be shut out from the continent, but also from the commerce and intercourse of the world" (quoted in Nichols 1846: xxv).

England managed to retain a minimal influence in Calais until sovereignty was formally returned to Napoleon at the Peace of Amiens in 1802.[3] This event is important in the history of the Channel Tunnel. It was at this moment of official territorial separation between the nations that the first serious plans to spatially link France and England by a tunnel were proposed. As one of those nice ironies of history, it was only after Britain renounced its claim to Calais that a "bridging" Tunnel was envisaged.[4] The idea of a fixed link in the form of a channel tunnel was first properly broached by a Frenchman, Albert Mathieu. His design was for horse-drawn carriages under the sea, lit with oil lamps and ventilated by intermittent mid-Channel air shafts. Today, this scheme appears quaint and comical. But when Mathieu presented his plan to Napoleon Bonaparte during the brief interlude of calm at the Peace of Amiens, Napoleon was, according to historical accounts, excited by the idea (Hunt 1994: 17). He shared his enthusiasm with the English statesman Charles James Fox, who was in Paris doing research on the French Revolution and generally taking advantage of the respite offered by peace. The two leaders envisaged that the Tunnel project would further unite their countries.

This vision was thwarted, however, when war resumed a year later in 1803. As France prepared to invade England, doubts arose in England as

3. As to the physical presence of England in France, the exact boundaries of the Pale of Calais are apparently difficult to determine at any given time because of the swampy land and vast network of canals and waterways (Sandeman 1908: 114–15).

4. Earlier, in 1785, a hot air balloon had been launched from Dover to cross the Channel and had caused quite a sensation. However, the turmoil of the French Revolution and renewed war between Britain and France in 1793 interrupted any planning developments and tainted them with unpatriotic sentiment. For a fuller account of the building of the Channel Tunnel, see Wilson 1994; Hunt 1994; and see Appendix 1 for a list of major dates in the Tunnel's history.

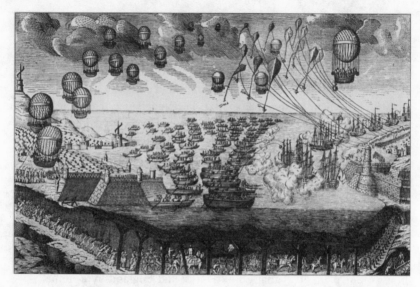

Figure 9. Invasion of England by France using an undersea tunnel. Anonymous drawing, ca. 1804. By kind permission of Eurotunnel.

to Napoleon's real intentions in supporting the Tunnel (fig. 9). After much indecision and general panic at the news of Napoleon's marshaling 15,000 soldiers and 2,000 huge barges along the French coast packed with munitions in readiness to invade on a "foggy night," England responded by strengthening its Kentish coastal defenses (Bloomfield 1987: 1–56; Vine 1972: 19–33). In 1804, William Pitt came out of retirement to lead the British government and quickly sanctioned the building of the Royal Military Canal and the Martello tower fortifications along the coast. Supported by strategically placed gun batteries, these were intended as a defense against Napoleon's landing on the nearest and most accessible strip of coast to France. But by the time the canal was completed in 1809, the invasion scare was over and Pitt dead.

Today, the canal is owned by the National Trust and provides a constant historical reminder both of the proximity and hostility of the French and the vulnerability of the Kentish coast. More dramatic in terms of their impact upon the landscape are the remaining Martello towers, of which a chain of seventy-four were originally built along the seashore (fig. 10).[5] These were in effect small forts, circular in plan and known as Martello

5. One of these homes is famously described in the opening chapter of James Joyce's *Ulysses*, albeit the tower is in Dublin and not Kent.

Figure 10. Martello tower, southeast Kent. Author's photograph.

towers because they were based on the fort at Cape Mortella in Corsica. The most easterly of the Martello towers in Kent is at Copt Point, near Folkestone, and they extend west to Romney Marsh and eventually into Sussex. The two-story towers were usually about 30 feet high and 25 feet in diameter, with walls about 6 feet thick, and designed to hold about twenty-five soldiers (Bloomfield 1987: 34–36). Today, many of these towers have been pulled down, blown over by storms, or appropriated as posts for birdwatchers, coastguards, and geologists. Despite their rather forlorn and stark appearance, a few have been auctioned and converted into homes, museums, and cafes (Vine 1972: 213–14). Like the Royal Military Canal and the numerous Roman ditches and castles along the Kentish coast, the Martello towers mark the southern English landscape as essentially vulnerable and requiring protection against foreign attack.

The defeat of the French by the British at the Battle of Trafalgar in 1805 prevented Napoleon reaching the shores of Britain. However, it did not end Napoleon's ambitions to conquer Europe, and he refocused his attention on other targets, such as Russia and Austria. But Napoleon's relatively short-lived invasion scheme produced a long and complicated history with respect to the Tunnel's genealogy as a historically significant national symbol. From its very first conception, the English have associated it with images of invasion and a cynical reading of France's overtures of peaceful cooperation. The French, in contrast, have generally considered

"Le Tunnel" primarily as a grand and inspiring public work, and thus an opportunity to display to the world their engineering genius and national might.

It was some years after the Battle of Waterloo in 1815, and the return of relatively stable relations between France and Britain, that tunnel plans were again renewed. However, from the 1820s on, the tunnel was no longer envisaged as a carriageway for horse-drawn vehicles, but rather as a form of submarine railway. This switch from horse to train reflected England's first "Railway Mania" of 1824, in which, "in just over one month, forty-nine separate companies were formed for making about 3,000 miles of railway involving some £23 million in capital" (Thomas 1972: 11). The Kentish Railway Company was one of these new enterprises and immediately put forward a shareholder's prospectus to build a railway line from London to Dover, passing through towns such as Greenwich, Rochester, Chartham, and Canterbury. However, this visionary scheme never materialized. In 1826, the Kentish Railway Bill failed for lack of funds, and the line was never completed (Thomas 1972: 14; White 1970). Nonetheless, it helped establish the idea of a rail passage under the sea to eventually connect up with existing tracks on either side of the Channel. This scheme was most extravagantly adopted by a Dr. Payerne, who in 1869 suggested a crossing by underwater steam locomotive. Despite this and some other rather crazy plans, including a square tunnel, a floating road tunnel, and a tunnel made of ice, the idea of an underwater rail persisted (Hunt 1994: 257–60). It was strengthened and romanticized in the second half of the nineteenth century when railways promoted cross-Channel traffic by fostering seaside holidays along the Kentish coast and packaged continental tours on such famous luxury trains as the Golden Arrow (White 1970: 5–6).

In contrast to an underground rail route, the fixed link has also been imagined as a great bridge. The first overwater scheme is attributed to a Frenchman, Aimé Thomé de Gamond, known as the "father of the tunnel" for his long and courageous devotion to its conception. Studying civil engineering and geology in Paris in the early 1830s, Gamond became a friend of Prince Louis Bonaparte, the future Napoleon III, and convinced him of the feasibility of his plans. Gamond began his career studying the possibility of cutting what was later known as the Suez Canal, but soon turned his sights closer to home and became fascinated with the idea of "communication between England and the Continent" (Hunt 1994: 21). In 1833, he returned to Mathieu's earlier plans and carried out extensive geological studies on the seabed between Dover and Calais. In 1855, at the age of 48,

Gamond undertook pioneering undersea research by descending to 100-foot depths weighted down by bags of flint, and wearing only head bandages against conger eel attacks (Haining 1989: 23). These studies established the feasibility of a number of viaduct and bored tunnel schemes put forward over the years, including one in 1836 for an elevated platform bridge.

Other bridge plans were proposed, such as M. Ferdinand's floating surface tube, which unfortunately ignored the navigational needs of the Channel. Moreover, as one critic noted disdainfully, "his tunnel would be exposed to the full action of storms, not merely of the wind against its sides, but the swelling of the sea under the vessels upon which it was borne" (Haining 1989: 46). Steel suspension bridges presented a viable alternative. The French engineers M. Schneider and M. Hersent proposed a splendid bridge design stretching 24 miles, and requiring 120 piers to stand 180 feet above the sea (Haining 1989: 52). This idea was reworked by Willem Frischmann, who proposed a mid-Channel island linked by two steel-tubing bridges suspended 230 feet above sea level (Hunt 1994: 259–260).

The fascination with the idea of a Channel bridge has endured. As recently as 1985, two of the four projects selected for further consideration by Margaret Thatcher and François Mitterrand involved bridges. These were the "Eurobridge," a 70-meter-high construction, and the "Euroroute," a complicated combination of a bridge-tunnel and railway tunnel. Needless to say, neither of these plans were adopted. "[T]here was no question of a bridge being chosen by the British Government as I knew from my meetings with British Ministers," writes chair of the rival and finally successful Channel Tunnel Group, Nicholas Henderson (1987: 26–27). Arguably, a bridge design could be more easily dismissed on the grounds of security and safety. However, what the British government perhaps did not anticipate was the extent to which the building of a tunnel has raised more symbolic and emotional anxieties with its unsettling invisibility.

CONSOLIDATING MENTAL BOUNDARIES

In a recent history of the political debates surrounding the building of the Channel Tunnel, a mere ten pages are devoted at the end of the text to the "intangible and psychological factors" that blocked the building of the link (Wilson 1994). In contrast, I suggest that these factors were the most significant and disabling barriers preventing the Tunnel's realization for almost two hundred years. The engineering and technological debates surrounding the viability of a cross-Channel tunnel or bridge were of considerably less importance than the mental anxieties and competing moral dilemmas that the Tunnel has over time symbolized.

Gamond was well aware of these mental barriers. In 1867, near the end of his long career devising tunnel schemes, he stated that if any plan were to succeed, the English would have to "take the initiative" (Haining 1989: 25). Gamond himself had been enterprising in his attempts to sell the Tunnel to the English. He had easily managed to get the support of Isambard Kingdom Brunel, who had, alongside his father, built a tunnel under the Thames in 1827, and of Joseph Locke and Robert Stephenson, both men involved in the introduction of railways into England. (Stephenson, in particular, was widely known for his famous locomotive the Rocket.) The greater difficulty for Gamond was convincing the queen, prime minister, and British government of the project's value. Gamond recalled his efforts in an account written for the Exposition Universelle of 1867 in Paris:

> The first time we had the opportunity of talking to Lord Palmerston on the subject of the Submarine Tunnel, we found him at first rather close: What! you pretend to ask us to contribute to a work the object of which is to shorten a distance which we find already too short! We expressed to him our wish to talk of it to Prince Albert in his presence, and to this he very kindly consented.
>
> The prince consort had supported this project with truly enthusiastic sympathy. His reception was therefore most kind. He entered into conversation, in which the Prince unfolded all the advantages which his elevated mind foresaw for England in the creation of a road to the Continent. Lord Palmerston, without losing that perfectly courteous tone which was habitual with him, made, however, a remark to the Prince which was very rude at bottom: You would think quite differently if you had been born on this island!
>
> We were ourselves perfectly stupefied with his unexpected apostrophe. To make Prince Albert, whose love of the country of his adoption was well known, feel that he was a foreigner, was shocking to us, and we felt deeply hurt. Some days after we went to excuse ourselves with the Prince. The Prince appeared not to have been offended, and told us that he had received this innocent dart as one of the frequent sallies in which Pam dealt. Then he added that he had said a few words about the Submarine Tunnel to the Queen, and Her Majesty had been graciously pleased to answer him in these good words: "You may tell the French engineer that if he can accomplish it, I will give him my bless-

ing in my own name, and in the names of all the good ladies of England."

(Aimé Thomé de Gamond quoted in Hunt 1994: 28)

The queen's delicate reference to the seasickness that often resulted from traveling by boat across the Channel was the source of many cartoons and jokes, particularly in *Punch* (see Pimlott 1947). While it was a factor not to be discounted, the more forceful argument enhancing the Tunnel's appeal was that once in place, it would be instrumental in establishing peace with France. In fact, this was what motivated Gamond's lifelong study of the Tunnel's feasibility throughout the mid nineteenth century. Peace, however, was a sentiment that proved the biggest psychological barrier for the English. In acknowledging the peace-inducing feature of a fixed link between the two nations, the countries' imminent warring was also admitted, accepted, and presented as a real threat.

More immediately appealing to the English, and a real enticement to participate in the Tunnel scheme, was its potential for improving communications with the British empire in the East. Gamond wrote:

> The construction of a road link between England and France, an idea conceived before the end of the last century, has become the object of renewed interest, especially since the introduction of the railways gave such great impetus to transport in these two countries. If one takes a look at the map of those new roads, abruptly intercepted by the sea, one grows convinced that their heads, at both sides of the Straits, are no more than half posts destined to be joined in a common and continuous transport system. . . . The creation of such a route is not an isolated concept; it is the complementary link of a great current of traffic among the nations, a current which extends across Europe in parallel branches, converging on the Mediterranean and then turning towards the Orient to penetrate into India, thus extending towards the two poles of England's possessions.
>
> (Aimé Thomé de Gamond, *étude pour l'avant-project d'un tunnel sous-marin entre l'Angleterre et la France* [1857], quoted in Hunt 1994: 24–25)

Gamond's proposal was extremely attractive to many Britons and was returned to again and again over the years. The appeal of such dramatic schemes seems to have increased in inverse proportion to the decreasing predominance of Britain as an industrial world power toward the end of the nineteenth century. Perhaps the most spectacular of these plans was one for a Trans-Alaska-Siberian Railway, linking Europe, Asia, and America. Put forward by an American syndicate, this fantastical 1902 scheme envisaged linking up the existing Trans-Siberian railway with the transcontinental line from San Francisco to New York. As one contemporary commentator grandly noted, this would enable rail carriages to bear the romantic inscription "Through Carriage Aberdeen, London, Dover Channel Tunnel, for Paris, Berlin, St. Petersburg, Alaska, Canada" (Channel Tunnel Archives 1/44).

A MONSTROUS BORE

Despite the glamorous associations of international train travel and the fantasies it conjured up of world transport links and overreaching state power, the history of the Channel Tunnel is remarkably repetitive and in many ways rather dull. It seems that as early as 1825, arguments for and against the Tunnel were already commonplace in England as summed up in a popular ditty of the time:

> A tunnel underneath the sea, from Calais Strait to Dover, Sir,
> That qualmish folks may cross by land from shore to shore,
> With sluices made to drown the French, if e'er they will come over,
> Sir,
> Has long been talked of till at length 'tis thought a monstrous bore.
> (quoted in Thomas 1972: 12)

In examining governmental debates, newspapers, cartoons, jokes, novels, and popular discourse throughout the nineteenth and the first half of the twentieth century, it becomes apparent that the arguments for and against the Tunnel are very repetitive. Recurring again and again throughout the 1870s, 1930s, and 1960s—times of political upheaval in Europe and the threat of imminent war—is an underlying fear that England might lose control of the Tunnel and that an invasion from the European mainland would result. This sentiment was encapsulated rather vulgarly, but memorably, by Lord Randolph Churchill when he told the Commons on 12 May 1885, in the course of throwing out the Channel Tunnel (Experimental Works) Bill, "England's reputation depends on her remaining, as it were, *virgo intacta*."

When public talk about the Tunnel again flared up in 1906, the director of military operations, Major-General John Spencer Ewart, and two other military men represented the army at the Committee of Imperial Defence. Ewart wrote a "hostile paper" against any plans for a Tunnel link. The project was thrown out after the prime minister told the House of Commons that apart from military concerns, there were strong policy reasons that made such a scheme insupportable. And indeed, foreign policy did come into play, with a growing concern expressed about the potential rise of crime with an influx of illegal immigrants. So, too, was concern declared for the particular qualities of the English race. As Ewart noted with respect to the Tunnel, "I am prepared to admit that with France friendly or in alliance it might be a Military advantage—but its completion will Europeanize us" (quoted in Wilson 1994: 68). Yet it is Ewart's private and very frank diaries that manage to encapsulate a public sentiment that has reappeared again and again throughout the century, with slightly different emphases and slants, but basically in the same form:

> Great Britain has always been an island. To its insularity it probably owes its peculiar institutions. It has always been able to adopt so much of Continental civilization as it thought wise and desirable. In fact, however it has adapted rather than adopted. The result is something quite unique. British civilization, as American and Canadian travellers often point out, is much more different from Continental civilizations than is one Continental country from another. Thus British characteristics have developed themselves in partial isolation from the rest of the world and have, indeed, made a contribution which is perhaps greater than that of any other country to the civilization of the world. . . .
>
> This historical sense of insularity, this pride in the distinctive features of British civilization, this belief in the influence of the sea upon British character, is a factor which ought not to be overlooked in any examination of the problem of the Channel Tunnel.
>
> (Ewart quoted in Wilson 1994: 192)

The themes of war, invasion, sea, racial insularity, and its connection to a "naturally" existing English "civilization" recur, much as they did in 1906, in today's English newspapers, under headlines such as "No Longer an Island" (*Guardian*, 6 May 1994). There is, as the 1825 ditty quoted above proclaimed, a certain tediousness to the political rhetoric and repetitive refrain about the Tunnel and its likely impact. What is different now, of course, is that the Tunnel is complete. And since the island issue was historically the central objection to the Tunnel, it might be assumed that the whole controversy and debate would no longer be of any public relevance. But in a way the building of the Tunnel is only the beginning of a new story, because no one can really anticipate what impact it will produce, despite the vast number of scientific and not-so-scientific projections.

The Tunnel is certainly the logical extension of a great range of exchanges between Kent and Calais and England and France in the past, as well as promoting and giving justification to new forms of association. By officially endorsing these exchanges and openly acknowledging that the two sides of the Channel are complementary, however, it gives rise to a more interesting question. Georg Simmel noted that a bridge not only connects a former separation, but part of making the bridge also requires the construction of new divisions: "In the immediate as well as the symbolic sense, in the physical as well as the intellectual sense, we are at any moment those who separate the connected, or connect the separate" (Simmel 1994: 5). If the Channel and Channel Tunnel now ostensibly operate as a bridge and not divider, what are emerging as the new symbols and practices through which these communities of complementary opposition draw their necessary difference?

RESURFACING 1066

From the above discussion, it becomes clear that the history of the building of the Channel Tunnel is first and foremost a history of English anxiety about the possibility of invasion and war and moral values linked to ideas of nationalism and civilization. The English Channel—which the Tunnel undermines—is thought of as a battle-torn sea separating England from the rest of the world. Clearly, the threat of foreign invasion of English soil is not illusory, but the last successful invasion of England was in 1066 by William the Conqueror and his band of Norman warriors. Since that mythic moment, English history has been punctuated by famous sea battles in defense of the island nation. But as Derek Urwin has argued, the sea did not really function as a barrier until the rise of reasonably strong nation-states and the building of effective naval fleets (Urwin 1982: 21). So while the sea came to define Britain's national borders, it has not always been construed as the natural barrier to foreign attack that current history presents it as being.

Today, France and Europe pose a new threat of invasion to England, and anyone who has lived in Britain in recent years will be aware of the constant references to 1066 in political rhetoric, national newspapers, and throughout the general media. Unlike other European nations, whose borders have in many cases geographically shifted over time, the threat of potential invasion carries intense and particular meaning in England that integrally challenges essentialized (and racialized) images of what it means to be English and, more generally, British (MacDougall 1982). This is wonderfully illustrated in a cartoon by David Simonds in the *Guardian* (14 Feb. 1994) depicting Britain as a castle in the sea and lampooning, yet again, the isolationist policies of Thatcherism (fig. 11).

Figure 11. "Yours—Ours." Cartoon by David Simonds. *Guardian*, 14 February 1994. By kind permission of the *Guardian* and David Simonds.

The French remain scornful of this English sensibility of invasion. Many of the French residents I talked to on the Calais side could not understand what the English were making a fuss about. "The British are only concerned with keeping themselves to themselves," a French construction worker said. "In France the whole country is keen. My sister's kids in the Dordogne have been pestering me for all the local newspaper reports and photos—they are all doing projects on it at school" (*Independent on Sunday*, 8 May 1994, p. 2). Unlike the English, to a majority of the French, the Tunnel does not represent the demise of their cultural integrity. It does not follow from this line of argument that the French, in the past, any more so than today, are less insular or nationalistic than the English. However, most of France is defined by its land borders with Belgium, Germany, Italy, Luxembourg, Spain, and Switzerland. And as a consequence, French people have historically had to deal with constant border friction and shifting borderlines. The French people and French government are clearly more comfortable with the idea of physically connected boundaries and read its significance differently than the island-bound English. And typically, the English are happy to accommodate these historical differences to mark themselves as patronizingly superior in the enduring "purity" of their institutional customs and laws, and by implication their national identity. "They [the French] have to be part of a bigger community, and we never have been," said one person I talked to in Kent. "This country's institutions have gone on uninterrupted for eight hundred years, you know. France has chopped and changed over that time a lot. Therefore they will accept new institutions. After all, they were occupied by Germany for some years, which must affect one's attitudes" (interview, 25 Feb. 1994).

The threat of invasion repeatedly enabled the British government to block schemes for the building of a Channel tunnel. Short periods of peace, when the British nation-state was relatively stable and confident, coincided with rising enthusiasm about the possibility of a tunnel and more open communications with France, but social and political unrest led to the prompt throwing out by the government of tunnel plans. Public debates about a tunnel, which always came down to issues of defense, underscored the extent to which the threat of war was needed in the consolidation of the British state.

The threat of external warfare consolidated internal conflict within Great Britain. Linda Colley's 1992 study *Britons: Forging the Nation, 1707–1837* points to the irony of the forging of British identity out of the Scots joining the English and Welsh under the Act of Union in 1707. Beginning with the establishment of Protestantism, she argues, Scottish Presbyterianism co-partnered English anti-Catholicism in the defeat of the Jacobite challenge (Colley 1992; and see also Urwin 1982: 23–40; Kearney 1989; Bryant 1967). This religious certainty served to create a sense of righteousness through which Britons came to regard themselves as exceptional. More important, it provided the moral and ethical justification for England's colonization of its Celtic periphery, which, the historian Michael Hechter argues, was prompted by the threat of foreign invasion: "[E]ach of the Celtic regions became politically incorporated at a critical juncture in English history. Largely out of *raisons d'état* England desired to insure its territorial integrity at all costs, rather than suffer the threat of invasion by hostile Continental neighbors" (Hechter 1975: 69).

In her analysis, Colley relies on Anderson's loose definition of a nation as an "imagined political community" superimposed on older alignments and loyalties in acknowledging the constant presence of dissenting voices, particularly in Scotland, and the juxtaposition of multiple nationalisms (Colley 1992: 5, 373; Anderson 1991). While Raymond Williams may be correct in his argument that Colley goes too far in suggesting a "univocal nation of Britons" (Williams 1994: 326), it was nonetheless the case that

Britain's relatively stable internal affairs enabled the government to spend more public money on external warfare and colonial investment than it did at home (Mann 1988: 73–123). Regional and local governments were largely left to cope alone, reflecting the absence of state concern for a uniform welfare policy and cohesive social unity.

For most of the nineteenth century, Britain can be characterized as primarily an economic and commercial venture, with fluid, vulnerable, and contested borders both in its colonial hinterland and within its state frame. The "protective shield of empire" had cultural repercussions in that pressures for class, gender, and national social hegemony were promoted and extended by Britain's imperial superiority. The otherness of Europe, and even more so the colonial other, came to be popularized and domesticated or exoticized and denigrated, forming a central ideological force in smoothing over internal political and cultural divisions and shaping everyday conceptions in the production of a subject (not citizen) of the authentic "British" community (Bhabha 1986: 153–56; Said 1979: 211, 216).[6] Modern English identity is, above all, about inclusion and exclusion, which was intricately mapped onto the British state's spatial expression as an isolated island-nation. In turn this necessitated and confirmed the need for constant military defense of what was constructed as a naturalized cultural space.

IN SEARCH OF BATTLE

In analyzing Britain within the European Union today, it is not surprising that the historian Stephen George characterizes the country as Europe's "awkward partner" (George 1990). British foreign policies cannot be divorced from the dramatic changes now occurring within the nation with respect to older ethnic and regional nationalisms in Scotland and Wales as these regional entities reinvent and reconstitute themselves in tandem with a broader loss of a collective British identity. Colley points to the deep historical roots of Britain's nationalist movements, now no longer able to be united against the other in the shape of militant Catholicism, a hostile continental Europe, or a colonized people. In fact, one of the major reasons for the creation of the EU in the wake of World War II was pre-

6. This distinction between subject and citizen refers to the principle of parliamentary sovereignty. "Though modern constitutions typically locate the source of sovereignty in 'the people,' in Britain, it is the crown in Parliament that is sovereign. Nor is this merely a technical point. The political culture of democratic Britain assigns to ordinary people the role, not of citizens, but of subjects" (McKenzie and Silver quoted in Nairn 1981: 40).

cisely to extinguish the threat of war, which, as recently as the Falklands war, has been so central to the consolidation of a British identity. As former Prime Minister Margaret Thatcher ominously pronounced in the wake of military victory over Argentina in 1982, "The lesson of the Falklands is that Britain has not changed" (quoted in Chambers 1990: 14). So while the Germans and the French, who have more confidence in their own unique identities, view plans for a borderless Europe (which the Channel Tunnel symbolizes) mostly in terms of opportunity, the English are inclined to see it as a threat. "Consciously or unconsciously, [Britons] fear assuming a new identity in case it obliterates entirely the already insecure identity they currently possess" (Colley 1992: 375).

The loss of a British identity is central to understanding the appeal and power behind Thatcher's Conservative political program of the 1970s. As Stuart Hall has noted, Thatcherism as an ideology addressed fears, anxieties, and lost identities by inviting people to think about politics in terms of images and social imaginary, addressing "our collective fantasies" (Hall 1990: 167). Thatcherism was a project that strove to break the spell of the welfare state, transforming it in order to restructure society by appealing to the trappings of an imagined modernity (Hall 1990: 163). This was imaginary, for despite Karl Marx's assessment of England as the classic representative of capitalist production (Marx 1976: 90), historians such as Tom Nairn, Stuart Hall, and Perry Anderson argue that the British state never made the full transition to what Antonio Gramsci identified as industrialized Fordism. By "exporting its industrial revolution" overseas, the country never made the transfer to a modernity as expressed through self-improving domestic economies, ideologies, and integration. Britain did not experience a national "corporate reorganization" of the kind that in very different ways, and at great social costs, characterized nineteenth-century forms of modernity in Germany, the United States, Russia, and Japan (Hall 1990: 164; Chambers 1990: 17; Nairn 1977: 22).

Today, the mythological sense of "Britishness" has lost its vitality. Decolonialization throughout the first half of this century began the structural breakdown of Britain's peculiar form of modernity, and Germany's and Japan's distinct forms of post–World War II modernization challenged its industrial prominence. Moreover, at a cultural level, Britons can no longer pretend to be homogeneous.[7] Despite official measures to restrict

7. Until the 1960s "the United Kingdom was accepted as a text-book example of a homogenous society where influences and characteristics were equally significant and effective throughout the whole territory," notes Derek Urwin (1982: 19).

immigration in the 1950s and 1960s, multiple ethnic groups are now an important element of the total population, and today racism is acknowledged to be a central social dilemma. This influx of colonial subjects has been instrumental in developing two general versions of "Britishness," which in a way reflect two different trajectories of modernity: the first, regressive, conservative, and falsely based on the idea of a stable unified culture; the second, motivated by the tense, and at times bloody, overlapping of cultural histories and traditions further linked to class and ethnicity, which challenge the very notion of British homogeneity (Chambers 1990: 27). Although the repeated success of the Conservative party throughout the 1980s and into the mid 1990s suggests the dominance of the "regressive" type of British identity, the May 1997 general election and the dramatic victory of Tony Blair's new Labour party demonstrates that it is also somewhat vulnerable.

One response by the Conservative British government to increasing European "penetration" was its refusal to sign the Social Charter in October 1989.[8] The other eleven member-states, which had approved the Social Charter, publicly condemned this refusal, which in many ways was a last-ditch measure by the government to consolidate British identity against a European other. With Britain no longer able to engage in actual military war, as Thatcher had done in the Falklands, the conflict was staged at the level of high politics. Revealingly, the French prime minister, Pierre Beregovoy, responded to John Major's battle cry, "They can have the Social Chapter. We will have the jobs," by saying, "[L]et us stop this little war to work all together" (*European*, 4 Mar. 1993, pp. 8, 14). The problem is that without a public war—without imaginary battles—the need to justify the myth of Britain as an autonomous economic, cultural, and political

8. The Social Charter is a document that sets out in greater detail the European Community's commitment to social policy as enshrined in the Single European Act (1986). In broadening the terms of European social policy formally laid down in the Treaty of Rome, Britain, while a signatory to the Single European Act, was the only member-state to refuse to accept the final version of the charter at the Strasbourg summit in December 1989. Britain's singular position was further highlighted when its Conservative government refused to accept the Social Charter of the Maastricht Treaty in 1992, causing it to be attached as a protocol to the treaty. Under the protocol, Britain was excluded from making social policy legislation and so from voting in the Council of Ministers. In May 1997, in Amsterdam, Britain did finally become a signatory. However, much ambiguity still remains as to the future progress of social policy, its methods of implementation, its legal status, and the perceived advantages Britain has gained by not being subject to strict labor controls governing such things as sex equality and improved worker-employee relations (for a brief summary, see Moxon-Browne 1993).

Figure 12. "The Island Race Is No More." Full-page advertisement, *Guardian*, 29 October 1993. By kind permission of Eurotunnel.

nation grows weak, and the myth itself becomes distorted. This floundering of purpose was evidenced in the hue and cry raised by veterans over the "frivolous" fiftieth anniversary celebrations of D-Day planned by the British government for June 1994. Confusion over what the day represented underscored implicit recognition that in "retrospect D-Day appears more as the defining moment at which [Britain's] geopolitical greatness came to an end" (*Guardian Weekly,* 12 June 1994, p. 12).

It is in this context of increasing desperation about what Britain stands for as a modern western nation that Margaret Thatcher finally agreed to meet François Mitterrand to sign the Channel Tunnel Treaty in 1986. The signing of the treaty culminated two centuries of public debate about a symbol that epitomized the rise of the modern nation-state and identifiable—and for that reason contestable—national identities. The building of the Tunnel heralds, to refer back to Homi Bhabha, that the "obligation to forget" is symbolically over. Or in the words of Philip Abrams, that the "secret of the non-existence of the state" is out (Abrams 1988: 77). Poignantly marking this transition were the full-page advertisements in national newspapers commemorating the Channel Tunnel's 1994 opening by declaring "The Island Race Is No More" (fig. 12). Present but unspoken in these declarations lies an acknowledgment that it never was.

4 Penetrating Britannia, 1986–1994
The Continuing Significance of Sovereignty

In examining governmental negotiations between Britain and France leading up to the building of the Tunnel and their local impact in the county of Kent, this chapter's analysis moves between local, regional, national, and EU levels. Somewhat as a juggling act, my aim is to highlight the interrelated dynamics of these various political and legal arenas. Local reactions to the Channel Tunnel must be understood and contextualized within wider popular opinions, as well as national economic interests and legal and political conflicts between Britain and the European Union.

I begin with an interview with Hazel McCabe, former Conservative mayor of Canterbury, Kent, who talked to me about the events surrounding her office at the time of the signing of the Channel Tunnel Treaty in 1986. As representative of a local community, she encapsulates the sense of betrayal many local people felt toward the Tory party, which had seemingly sold out their small-town interests in the name of greater state economic and political gains. I then give a brief history of the British/French state negotiations about the Tunnel to illustrate how much their respective governments' final agreement to build it represented—at least symbolically—a form of reconciliation, despite the fact that the British government refused to finance any part of the project. This half-hearted commitment on behalf of the British had an impact on the speed with which the Tunnel project progressed in England. Apathy and disinterest were also well demonstrated in the inaugural celebration of the Tunnel's completion in 1994.

The second part of the chapter turns explicitly to the cultural anxiety expressed by the presence of Europe on English soil. This cultural anxiety is evident in the much publicized debates in the media and popular culture about the Tunnel being a focus of terrorist attack. It also prompted Kent County Council to take its own initiative in the creation of a new transborder police force with French gendarmes. Ironically, Kent's local police force is forging new political opportunities that extend its legal horizons beyond that of the sovereign state's jurisdiction at the very moment that it seeks to maintain strict border controls. This exploration of Kent's transborder police returns the final discussion to the local Kent responses to the signing of the Channel Tunnel Treaty with which the chapter begins. The anti-French chants against then French President Mitterrand by a local Canterbury crowd, I argue, mask the complex overlapping of both abating and emerging local, regional, national, and transnational discourses about the physical and symbolic penetration of the nation's island borders.

LOCAL POLITICS IN INTERNATIONAL CONTEXTS

"I knew it was going to be a bit of a rough ride. Oh yes, very anti-French, and I knew there was going to be that sort of trouble. There were eggs thrown and all sorts of things, which doesn't normally happen in an English crowd in a little town like Canterbury," Hazel McCabe, a former Conservative mayor of Canterbury, said of the signing on 12 February 1986 of the Channel Tunnel Treaty by Prime Minister Margaret Thatcher and President François Mitterrand (interview, 20 Jan. 1994).

I remember being slightly amazed by our conversation, which covered topics ranging from frantic communications with the Foreign Office over the organizing of the signing of the treaty, the intricacies of high-level government and international politics, police security, and racism to Canterbury Cathedral—images that did not seem to go with the cozy farmhouse and large pot of tea that accompanied our conversation, as the rural quiet set over the fast-fading light of a mid January afternoon. Hazel went on:

> I remember discussing the impact of the Tunnel and its impact on Canterbury at a policy meeting. By a vote of forty-five to four councilors, across all political parties, they were against the Tunnel as being damaging to the city and district, and for its general impact on Kent.
>
> The Tunnel was not going to be applied for in the normal way as a planning application, which would have led to a public inquiry about the Tunnel link to London—all that was kept very quiet when the Tunnel was announced, because I think if Kent had really known about that, it would have risen as one against it. The gut reaction of

all was against it—the WI [Women's Institute], Men of Kent people, the NFU [National Farmers Union]—everyone.

So I was somewhat surprised when about two or three weeks before the signing of the treaty, I was coming out of one of the new shops in Canterbury, wearing my [mayoral] chain and so on, when a canon from the Cathedral [who was] in the gents underwear section said to me, "Oh, hello, Hazel, do you know they're coming over here to sign the Channel Tunnel Treaty in the Cathedral?" And I said, "Oh no, pull the other one."[1] You see, I didn't know, and you could have knocked me over with a feather!

(interview, 20 Jan. 1994)

The signing took place in Canterbury Cathedral's Chapter House, a highly symbolic setting. The cathedral is one of the most beautiful and well-known in the country, as well as being its religious center as the seat of the primate of England and the Anglican church. As such, the cathedral represents Henry VIII's break with Catholicism and the spiritual independence of England from mainland Europe. It is hardly surprising that many residents of Canterbury and Kent in general felt that using the Chapter House for the signing of a civic and intergovernmental treaty was inappropriate, a reaction further exacerbated by the fact that 12 February was Ash Wednesday. Hazel McCabe continued her story:

> Come Monday morning, I made some inquiries. It seemed everyone was keeping their heads down. Apparently the Foreign Office was arranging all this, and we all thought Leeds Castle was better for security reasons and so on—it would take two days to clear the Cathedral area. . . . The final straw was they chose Ash Wednesday to do it. Now this good soul rang me from the Foreign Office and assured me I would receive an invitation to the luncheon. Of course, I said, that is not quite the point, I'm not concerned about the luncheon, but more about the venue and the fact that you are doing it on Ash Wednesday. I don't think this had ever crossed their minds.
>
> Margaret Thatcher was keen to show Mitterrand something special and it made a good background for the media. The Deanery was empty, so they moved in furniture and carpets and so on.
>
> I did not attend the signing. My duty was to greet them as guests of Canterbury, but I'd made it clear to everyone I wouldn't attend the signing of the treaty for two reasons. I was chairman of a council who had voted democratically forty-five to four against it, therefore at no time would I be seen to be supporting it, otherwise that would be thoroughly cynical. The second reason was, shall I say more personal,

1. "Pull the other one!" = "You've got to be kidding!"

and this was the use of the premier Anglican cathedral on Ash Wednesday for what was entirely inappropriate and really just a civic bun fight.[2]

(interview, 20 Jan. 1994)

THE UNCERTAIN STATUS OF A PRIVATE AND INTERNATIONAL PROJECT

The feeling that the Tunnel had very little to do with the interests of Kent communities and was, in effect, a bargaining chip between hostile national governments permeated local anti-Tunnel reactions. While this charge could be leveled throughout the Tunnel's history, it was a sentiment particularly pertinent to the events of the 1980s leading up to the signing of the treaty. In 1979, Margaret Thatcher was elected Britain's new Conservative prime minister, and a year later, François Mitterrand was swept to power with an overwhelming majority as the first Socialist president of the Fifth Republic. In September 1981, the two leaders met for the first time in London to discuss, among other things, the Channel Tunnel. The outcome was surprisingly enthusiastic and an agreement in principle was made for a fixed link that would benefit both countries. Negotiations were again commenced among the newly formed European Channel Tunnel Study Group, British Rail, its French equivalent, the Société Nationale des Chemins de Fer (SNCF), finance companies, banks, private and governmental committees, transport ministers, and engineering and technical experts. But once again external events interfered and the project was delayed for another two years owing to the outbreak in 1982 of the Falklands war with Argentina.

The resumption of interest in the Tunnel in 1984 was symbolic of a reconciliation between Britain and France. This was marked by the joint statement of support for the Tunnel by Thatcher and Mitterrand issued at the annual Franco-British economic summit in late November. According to many historians, it represented a new beginning for Britain in terms of its relations both with France and with Europe (George 1990: 166). Throughout the early 1980s, recession, high inflation, further oil crises, and unprecedented levels of unemployment and bankruptcy had plagued Thatcher's government and contributed to her unpopularity before the Falklands war. Internal economic depression also colored all of the country's external affairs. Nowhere is this clearer than in Thatcher's tough stand on a settlement claim for Britain's contributions to the European

---

2. "Bun fight" is a metaphor for general confusion and unbefitting behavior, literally referring to a food fight with bread buns.

Monetary Co-operation Fund. Thatcher demanded £1 billion of her "own money back" at the European Council in 1979. France and Germany flatly refused, with the French indicating that they would accept at most a return of £350 million (George 1990: 148). Tensions escalated as negotiations throughout 1981 and 1982 tried to establish a formula for reductions in budgetary contributions acceptable to all member-states. In March 1983, conflict came to a head at the Brussels European Council meeting. Hours of heated discussions ended with Thatcher threatening to withhold Britain's contribution to the 1984 budget. Serious talk began of dropping Britain from the European Economic Council (EEC), as it was then called (George 1990: 148–66). So it was a surprise and relief to many that three months later, Britain came to the Fontainebleau European Council with a discussion paper in hand entitled "Europe—the Future" and a willingness to accept a rebate of one billion ecus (European currency units, now called euros). The immediate crisis over England's relations with Europe had been averted. It is in this highly charged political context that the conclusion of the Tunnel agreement between Britain and France in 1984, and the subsequent signing of the Channel Tunnel Treaty in 1986, should be interpreted (see Holliday et al. 1991: 13–14).

The big media extravaganza at Canterbury Cathedral was the culminating event in a long history that linked plans for the Tunnel with the evolving development of the EU throughout the last half of this century. This history parallels the British government's ongoing and turbulent relations with leaders of the original EEC member-states. France's President Charles de Gaulle vetoed Britain's first application to join the EEC in 1963, for example, but he was an ardent supporter of the Tunnel scheme. It was said that this was no surprise, given that de Gaulle's brother-in-law was the mayor of Calais, and that the deprived Nord–Pas de Calais industrial region would benefit greatly from Tunnel traffic. In any case, both de Gaulle and his successor Georges Pompidou openly declared themselves *tunnelists* (Hunt 1994: 108). The social unrest in Paris of May 1968 did not alter popular opinion. French citizens, particularly in the northwestern corner of France, who anticipated that the Tunnel would be a great financial advantage, were enthusiastic about the project.

In England in the 1960s, Prime Minister Harold Wilson had also declared himself an active supporter of the Tunnel. Since Wilson considered the Tunnel a symbolic gesture of commitment to the idea of a united Europe, it became instrumental in the drive for getting Britain into the EEC after its initial rejection in 1963. But Wilson's plans were held up owing to a combination of internal party politics, debates over private and government financing, continuing fears about defense, interventions from the Channel Tunnel Study Group, and a reluctant wider population. In the late 1960s, there were endless parliamentary committees, confused findings, and constant delays with respect to the Tunnel's progress. The Tunnel project resembled a "soporific TV soap opera; anything dramatic, or decisive, always seems as far off as ever," said the *Financial Times* (28 July 1969). By 1970, "five years had been wasted in a tedious repetitive spectacle—the consequence of indecision, indifference, and procrastination—coupled with a total lack of imagination" (Hunt 1994: 118).

A breakthrough came on 15 July 1970, when the French and British governments issued a statement about establishing a new international financial group that would join up with the Channel Tunnel Study Group. The Channel Tunnel Study Group was a private syndicate that had been in operation since 1957. It was an independent body joining French and English supporters of the Tunnel scheme, including shareholders of the 1872 Channel Tunnel Company. Over the years, it had poured over £1 million into extensive engineering and technical research and had acquired extensive knowledge of the requirements of the Tunnel. In 1971, the Channel Tunnel Study Group, the new financial consortium, and the governments of Britain and France signed an agreement covering the construction program. Tenders were offered, financing arrangements discussed, and inquiries made about the Tunnel's impact.

But there were again delays, despite the impetus given to the Tunnel project by Britain's formal acceptance into the EEC in January 1973, the passing of the Channel Tunnel (Initial Finance) Bill, and the signing of a treaty by the British and French foreign secretaries in November of that year. In late 1973, war broke out in the Middle East between Israel and Egypt and Syria and quickly escalated into a world oil crisis. Preparatory works, which had expanded upon the earlier 1880 Beaumont Tunnel at Shakespeare Cliff, Dover, Kent, and Sangatte in Calais, were halted. The British government had miscalculated its legislative timing and could not ratify the Anglo-French treaty without the prior enactment of a bill. In addition, the estimated cost of building the Tunnel rose steadily, and investors voiced their concern. To the dismay of many, in January 1975, the Wilson government unilaterally abandoned the Channel Tunnel project on grounds of economic uncertainty that related to internal politics, the appeasing of trade unions, and its overcommitment to the Concorde airplane project (Hunt 1994: 152). It was not until the early 1980s that the Tunnel idea was again revived.

PROPOSED TUNNEL SCHEMES

In July 1985 a French company, France-Manche, signed a cooperation agreement with the English Channel Tunnel Group, and upon their full merger, a new company, Transmanche-Link, was established. By 31 October of that year, Transmanche-Link and nine other bidders each tendered a proposed Tunnel plan under the "Invitation to Promoters" issued jointly by the British and French governments. Five of these proposals failed to meet the four basic criteria set out in the invitation: entries had to be technically feasible, financially viable, Anglo-French, and accompanied by an Environmental Assessment Impact Study (Holliday et al. 1991: 14). Of those proposals remaining, four were seriously considered. These were Euroroute (a submerged rail tunnel joining up two islands and bridges), the Europont project (a suspension bridge and rail tunnel), Channel Expressway (two underground rail and road tunnels), and finally the Transmanche-Link project (two underground rail tunnels plus a central service and ventilation tunnel). Thatcher favored a cross-Channel motorway, since for her the car represented true independence. The alternative of loading your car onto a train that then carried you across seemed to epitomize state interventionism, but not surprisingly was favored by Mitterrand. After much discussion and behind-the-scenes negotiations, Mitterrand's preference for rail won the day. At the Canterbury signing of the Channel Tunnel Treaty in February 1986, a 55-year concession was awarded to Transmanche-Link (Holliday et al. 1991: 15–21; Hunt 1994: 168–98). Transmanche-Link then signed an agreement with Eurotunnel as its appointed administrative parent company in August of that year.

While François Mitterrand's backing of a dual rail system overrode Margaret Thatcher's preference for a tunnel motorway, she did manage to ensure, in article 1 (1) of the 1986 Treaty, that absolutely no government money, not even state guarantees, would support the project. This conflicted with the earlier 1974 Tunnel scheme and the enduring French notion that financial risks should be shared across private and public funds. This explicit absence of state participation was viewed skeptically by the French government and many financiers, who foresaw difficulty in raising capital without state backing. And indeed lack of state support proved a central stumbling block in Eurotunnel's dealing with banks regarding overspending throughout the late 1980s, making ineffective decisions about Waterloo station with state-run British Rail, implementing a variety of environmental plans that involved the state, and in the first instance, in the drawing up of workable legislation.

THE CHANNEL TUNNEL'S OFFICIAL INAUGURATION ON 6 MAY 1994

The British government's nonparticipation in the Tunnel project was widely supported among segments of the general English population throughout the late 1980s. Interpreting the Tunnel as a symbol of European intrusion on English soil may help explain one of the more offensive gestures in recent British history. On 1 November 1990, a month before the Tunnel's official opening, the *Sun* newspaper invited its 12 million readers to travel the twenty-three miles to Dover, stand on Shakespeare Cliff (beneath which the Channel Tunnel runs), and curl their fists in a rude gesture toward France, shouting in unison "UP YOURS DELORS" (fig. 13). Apparently, there was a high turnout for the event.[3]

It is hardly surprising that the Tunnel's inauguration itself was a dreary, lackluster event, despite the pomp and ceremony that accompanied the exchange between Queen Elizabeth II and President Mitterrand. The heavy symbolism of two trains, each carrying a head of state, slowly advancing until their noses nearly touched in Calais, was accompanied by a loud fanfare and the national anthems, followed by the EU theme, Beethoven's *Ode to Joy.*

> Then President Mitterrand, as host, hopped from his carriage first and waited on the platform for the various high British dignitaries to disembark: Her Majesty in a vivid fuchsia ensemble (clashing horribly with the sodden red carpet underfoot), John Major (clashing horribly with current electoral opinion), and Baroness Thatcher (clashing horribly with the whole idea of European fraternity).
>
> (Barnes 1995: 312–13)

After the requisite cutting of the tape and French reception, the British and French dignitaries then all traveled back along the track to an exclusive luncheon reception in the bowels of the Cheriton Terminal at Folkestone, Kent. The queen and Mitterrand rode in her special Rolls-Royce, a Phantom VI, which was according to many journalists the highlight of the day. It did not have a license plate and had to get special clearance from the French police when driven over by ferry earlier by the queen's chauffeur,

---

3. The target of this abuse was, of course, Jacques Delors, président de la Commission européenne. A remark by George Orwell about English patriotism comes to mind: "[T]here can be moments when the whole nation suddenly swings together and does the same thing, like a herd of cattle facing a wolf" (quoted in Mander 1963: 200).

Figure 13. "Up Yours Delors." *The Sun*, 7 November 1990. Courtesy of *The Sun*.

who then caused further hilarity (much to the pleasure of a bored media crew) when a packet of 200 duty-free Benson & Hedges cigarettes was found in the trunk of the Rolls-Royce.

The main difference between the respective state welcomes in England and France lay in the accompanying receptions for onlooking citizens. The local population in Calais had been celebrating for a week before the actual inauguration with street parties, fireworks, and much enthusiasm. From all accounts, there was much drinking in the bars and general festivities. By contrast, in Kent, the official party of state dignitaries and business-people was spirited away under high security, leaving a small, wet, be-draggled crowd of about 500 people in the carpark of the Eurotunnel Exhibition Center looking at an enormous but very poor quality video screen of official events about a mile away. In the Eurotunnel parking lot, I watched some journalists trying to drum up a bit of pizzazz for the evening news. A group of three or four children waving British flags provided a much-needed visual highlight, and reporters took lots of pictures of the kids. Even the protesters from the Campaign for an Independent Britain were rather pathetic. In their attempt to burn an EU flag they had brought along, they could not find matches and had to ask watching reporters for a light (fig. 14). When they finally did manage to ignite the flag, its cheap synthetic material melted rather than flared. As the meager crowd cheered, I was not sure whether it was in support of the symbolic burning or as encouragement to a good-natured group of "radicals" who clearly needed all the help they could get.

The Tunnel's newsworthiness was summed up in the English national newspaper headlines the following day. Across a variety of papers, commentary on the Tunnel was largely dwarfed by the dramatic defeat of the Conservative party in the local government elections on 5 May, the day prior to the inauguration. The Labour party gained 4 councils and 88 seats, the Liberal Democrats 9 councils and 388 seats, and the Conservatives lost 18 councils and 429 seats. This shift of support represented a real challenge to the Tories and predicted (correctly) bad results for the party in the upcoming European elections only a month away on 6 June 1994. Once again, anything to do with England's relations to the European mainland took second place to the country's domestic politics. The *Guardian* did devote a third of its front page to a wide-angle photograph of the dignitaries marching en masse away from the Tunnel platform, with the Eurotunnel trains just glimpsed above their heads. Nonetheless, the event was presented with an eye-catching yet somewhat ambiguous headline: "Major Pledges Fight to the End" (*Guardian*, 7 May 1994).

English reactions to the Channel Tunnel—which largely amount to pretending it doesn't exist—dramatically illustrate a certain myopic vision. As a population characteristically uncomfortable with accepting change, the English have historically viewed the idea of a Channel tunnel or bridge with suspicion. The reasons for this are both obvious and complex. Any bridge "alternately welds together and opposes insularities. It distinguishes between them and threatens them. It liberates from enclosure and destroys autonomy," notes Michel de Certeau (1984: 128–29). At the ceremonial opening of the first bridge built by the Native Affairs Department in Zululand in 1938, according to the anthropologist Max Gluckman, the bridge provided a common interest around and through which groups and individuals of different races mingled together on the banks of the river and cooperated in a moment of "temporary equilibrium" (Gluckman 1958:

Figure 14. Demonstrators from the "Campaign for Independent Britain" outside Eurotunnel's Visitor's Centre, Folkestone, Kent, burning an EU flag in protest against the Tunnel's inauguration on 6 May 1994. Note the "No Euro State" banner, as well as the huge boring machinery in the far distance that was used to dig the tunnels. Author's photograph.

25). Homi Bhabha also discusses the bridging of social spaces. In his discussion of national culture, he talks about the "turning of boundaries and limits into the *in-between* spaces through which the meanings of cultural and political authority are negotiated" (Bhabha 1990: 4, 299). As discussed above in chapter 3, the Channel can be interpreted as an in-between space; the Tunnel marks its inability to fully signify the division of national boundaries and national cultures.

Yet the Channel is more than an in-between space between two national populations, delimiting the line between what Bhabha loosely calls "nation-spaces" (Bhabha 1990: 297–302). In addition to space, the Tunnel also bridges time. This was underscored by the queen in her opening statement at the Calais opening, "To rejoin what nature separated some 40 million years ago has been a recurring dream of statesmen and engineers for several centuries" (*Kent Today,* 7 May 1994, p. 6). You do not have to go that far back in time to get a sense of the temporal complexities, continuities, and conflation the Tunnel has generated. This was brought home to me standing atop of Castle Hill (sometimes known as Caesar's Camp), where a Norman defense had once stood. From here, looking down on the

Folkestone terminal, you can see a new road cutting sharply into the hill face, underneath grass-covered trenches built against Napoleon's possible invasion and later fortified during World War I. The landscape is deeply layered with historical associations. And this in part is what the English fear about the Tunnel—that their autonomous and distinguishable national consciousness, both spanning and conflating centuries into the present, will be undermined by it.

LEGISLATING AGAINST TERROR(ISM)

The bookseller at Dillon's laughed with me when I marveled that James Adams's novel *Taking the Tunnel* (1993) was so popular that it had been reprinted in paperback. The book is about a terrorist attack by a Chinese mafia on the Tunnel. In its subject of a Channel Tunnel disaster, it joins a genre of fiction that has enjoyed long popularity. But whereas nineteenth-century fiction like Grip's *How John Bull Lost London or the Capture of the Channel Tunnel* (1852) tended to focus on the sneaky French emerging suddenly on English soil, terrorism has now emerged as a new form of horror very much emblematic of the post–Cold War period and contemporary forms of violent warfare (Clutterbuck 1990). By building upon the English public's recognition of foreign invasion as a well-established subject matter, *Taking the Tunnel* draws its power by adding a new twist of realism, substituting Chinese and the IRA for the French, and missiles and nuclear bombs for cannon fire. Writing on global terrorism, Joseba Zulaika argues:

> There is a historical sequel to the present discourse of terrorism. The figure of the "Terrorist" seems heir to the frightening and lawless attributes of the figures of the "Barbarian" during the classical Greek period and the "Wild Man" during the Middle Ages. . . . That the second part of the twentieth century has added a new type—the "Terrorist"—to this old myth testifies to its enduring power. . . . The terrorist poses a frontal assault on any type of norm, whether tactical, political, legal or moral. It is antinomy in its pure form. The terrorist enemy, identified as international in scope and in a symbiotic relationship with the nuclear predicament, falls outside the ordinary realm of humanity.
> (Zulaika 1998: 101)

As a "remythification of the Wild Man," a fear of terrorists and terrorism greatly preoccupies the English imagination (ibid.: 101). Alongside rabies, it endures as a much-touted argument against the Tunnel. In the passing of the Channel Tunnel Treaty and Channel Tunnel Bill in the second half of the 1980s, fear of terrorism was officially articulated as a central concern across all political parties, classes and socioeconomic backgrounds. And, it should be added, this fear was not entirely unjustified, given the record of terrorism in Britain. In the House of Lords, Lord Moran spoke for many when he stated:

> Even the most stringent precautions are not always effective. You will remember that last April the effort to put a bomb on an El Al aircraft by the terrorist Hindawi very nearly succeeded. The bomb was taken through all security measures at Heathrow and was only discovered by the vigilance of an El Al guard. We have our own terrorist problems in this country and it is the same in France. In France there were 13 bombs in 1986, resulting in 10 deaths and 243 injured. As we all know terrorists seek publicity and they look for spectacular targets— for example, Harrods, the Household Cavalry and the Cabinet at a party conference. What could be more spectacular than the Channel Tunnel? It will be an obvious target for them.
>
> (Channel Tunnel Bill, *Parliamentary Debates*, vol. 484, no. 40 [1987], col. 932)

In 1998, fear of the Tunnel being a target of terrorism escalated rather than diminished. The World Trade Center bombings in New York in 1993, the Tokyo subway gas attack on 20 March 1995, which killed 12 people and injured 5,500 commuters, and the bombing of the Alfred P. Murrah Federal Office Building in Oklahoma City on 19 April 1995—have all conveyed a general sense of panic with respect to spectacular acts of terrorism and fear of the "enemy within." President Clinton has declared that U.S. security forces will stockpile antidotes and vaccine against chemical and biological weapons. In England, terrorism is very much a widespread topic of concern, especially with the current fluctuations of relations between the British government and Irish republicans, and a widespread alarm at the increasing presence of Islamic fundamentalists seen to be mustering across the Channel in France. In September 1998, Tony Blair's government rushed through Parliament a new anti-terrorism law called the Criminal Justice (Terrorism and Conspiracy) Act. This comes in the wake of a spate of bomb attacks, including a bomb explosion in a regional subway station in central Paris on 25 July 1995, a car bomb that injured fourteen people outside a Jewish school in Lyon on 7 September 1995, the 1998 bombing in Omagh in Northern Ireland, and the two bomb attacks on the U.S. embassies in Nairobi, Kenya, and Dar es Salaam, Tanzania, on 7 August 1998, which have increased anxiety about terrorism both across Europe and in the rest of the world. The testing of nuclear weapons by

India and Pakistan in 1998, despite widespread condemnation, has enhanced fears of nontraditional warfare and terrorism occurring at local and international levels.

Up to now, the British government has purported to make Eurotunnel comply with the same level of security as that found at international airports. This governmental responsibility is clearly stated in the Channel Tunnel (Security) Order, which was introduced in late 1993 and came into force in February 1994. The order establishes a binational agreement between the British and French governments to ensure that electronic screening of all carry-on and stowed luggage and surveillance of passengers is carried out at the Waterloo International Station and the Gare du Nord. In the Channel Tunnel (Security) Order debate it was noted that a number of new offenses, including hijacking, seizing control of the Tunnel system, destroying or damaging trains, and the making of threats likely to endanger safety would all be punishable by life sentences (*Kent Messenger*, 5 May 1994, p. 40). But despite the risks involved, and no doubt good intentions on behalf of Eurotunnel to enforce security measures, if only for commercial reasons, in many instances the scanning of cars and especially lorries is very difficult. According to one driver, his truck was simply too long. "They have tried to put me through the scanner, but it's impossible," he said (*Observer*, 29 Jan. 1995, p. 3). One of the most publicized recent security transgressions occurred in August 1997, when it was discovered that illegal immigrants from France were regularly boarding trains in Paris and traveling unchallenged to the outskirts of London. In the words of John Tincey, an immigration inspector and spokesman for Britain's immigration workers' union, "Every criminal gang in Europe knows that Eurostar is an open door to London. It is the only way to get into Britain without a document" (*Los Angeles Times*, 25 August 1997, p. 1).

Despite widespread fears of infiltration and the tightening of border security legislation designed to fight terrorism, the lack of general security aboard the Eurostar trains speaks to wider issues of cross-border policing and maintenance of safety. Set out in the Channel Tunnel Act (1987) are arrangements for Tunnel policing and the Intergovernmental Safety Authority. Section 14 briefly states that all policing on the English side is to be carried out under the direction of Kent's chief constable. Moreover, Eurotunnel finances the Kent Police and provides them with accommodation and facilities. In early 1994, the Longport Police Station, situated about a mile from the mouth of the Tunnel, was officially opened, at a cost to Eurotunnel of £2.4 million, to serve as a base for 100 officers responsible for the Tunnel's policing. Remarkably, the British government did not make any contribution to the expenses involved, despite the operation involving the control of a national border. This lack of financial support is in keeping with the government's refusal to pay for any part of the Tunnel's construction and maintenance, including, it seems, the country's long-term security.

The absence of government participation in border policing was somewhat modified by the introduction of the Sangatte Protocol in November 1991, signed by the British and French governments. This protocol is derivative of the Schengen trans-European policing agreement, of which France is a signatory but Britain is not (see Appendix 3). Article 5 of the protocol sets out its aims to simplify and speed up formalities for those using the Tunnel. At the same time, the protocol aims to harmonize security and safety measures so that in the event of an emergency or threat, action can be taken immediately without being hampered by disputes involving issues of state sovereignty. The protocol also gives extraterritorial powers to British and French police officers in specially designated control zones at the international passenger terminals at Waterloo, Ashford, and the Gare du Nord, and at shuttle terminals at Folkestone and Calais. It is in these special zones that French gendarmes can be seen carrying pistols on English soil, in contrast to English police, who are generally prohibited from carrying firearms. Article 10 of the protocol states:

> The officers of the adjoining State shall, in exercise of their national powers, be permitted in the control zone situated in the host State to detain or arrest persons in accordance with the laws and regulations relating to frontier controls of the adjoining state or persons sought by the authorities of the adjoining state.

What is significant about the Protocol is that it involves Kent police in activities beyond the experience of many of their police colleagues (see Birch 1989, 1991). The protocol streamlines law in accordance to the Schengen Agreement, which came into force in May 1995. Thus Kent police operate as if the Channel were, for all intents and purposes, an "Internal Frontier" according to the definition in article 1 of Schengen Agreement II (1990) (Fijnaut 1993; Hunnings 1991: 39–40). This is despite Britain refusing to be a signatory to the original Schengen Agreement of 1985, signed by Belgium, France, Germany, Luxembourg, and the Netherlands, and later joined by Italy, Spain, Portugal, and Greece (see Appendix 3). In other words, while Britain officially treats the Channel crossing as an external national frontier and is adamant about maintaining it despite the open borders policy enshrined in the EU, for practical purposes, Kent police approach the Channel somewhat differently in working together with French police in a cooperative system of surveillance.

POLICESPEAK AND KENT'S BOYS IN *BLEU*

Police cooperation between Kent and Calais is most clearly evidenced in the establishing of a European Liaison Unit in Dover by the Kent Police force in 1991. This unit works with the Police Nationale in Nord–Pas de Calais, the Belgian police in West Flanders, and the Dutch police in Zeeland, Rijnmond, and Haaglanden to create a cooperative team of police investigation and procedure. This cooperation is formalized in the PoliceSpeak Project, which operates out of the European Liaison Unit, and a comparable setup in Calais, the Brigade Frontalière Mobile. The PoliceSpeak Project is locally based yet transnational in vision. It was begun in 1990, after the Kent Constabulary launched a major review of communication needs presented by policing the Tunnel. Under the guidance of a working group of professionals drawn from police, ambulance, and fire emergency services, research was conducted by a team of linguistic experts from Cambridge University. The academic team analyzed a vast database of police communications, and on the basis of its recommendations a PoliceSpeak lexicon or handbook was produced, intended for Kent and Calais Police in their cross-Channel operations (fig. 15). The handbook is in effect an English-French dictionary of police terminology, and begins with the explanation: "The PoliceSpeak project aims to standardize and refine the language of police operations, thereby improving communicative efficiency and speeding the flow of information, with the ultimate objective of increasing inter-agency cooperation across national and linguistic frontiers" (PoliceSpeak 1993).

The PoliceSpeak handbook contains 5,000 lexical items (words and phrases) that are meant to streamline English and French translations. This lexicon is intended as a tool for translators and interpreters, as a source of specialist vocabulary for training purposes, and as the basis for the development of automatic translation systems. The link established in 1993 was a basic e-mail loop between Kent and Calais police, which had two language access codes. At this time, the long-term plan was to install automatic translation software that would supposedly allow full communications across nations unhampered by the fact that a Kent constable may not know a word of French. For the English this represented a dream come true!

In 1994, I went to visit Inspector John Gledhil, head of the PoliceSpeak Office at Maidstone, Kent. In a rather cramped but neat set of office

Figure 15. PoliceSpeak brochures. By kind permission of Prolingua Ltd., Cambridge
Research Laboratories, 1998.

PoliceSpeak

COMMUNICATIONS AND LANGUAGE.....

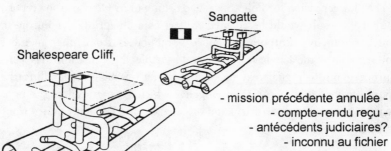

Sangatte

Shakespeare Cliff,

- mission précédente annulée -
- compte-rendu reçu -
- antécédents judiciaires?
- inconnu au fichier

Calling Papa Sierra One
<u>VETO</u> Do not approach
the scene....

On file as
Chrysler Alpine GLS. Colour....

Priority caller: Transmit. Over.

Priority <u>SITREP</u>
Location: M20 Coast-bound A229 exit.
<u>Incident:</u> Serious injury.
RTA Require Ambulance

.....AND THE CHANNEL TUNNEL

buildings, the inspector leaned back in his chair and put his hands behind his head, assuring me that while it was impossible to achieve zero ambiguities: "[W]hat we've found already is if people use the protocols, transmissions get shorter, you get less of them, less requests for repetition, and far less confusion about who is talking to who" (interview, 31 Mar. 1994).

The longer vision for PoliceSpeak, according to its October 1993 report, is that its results could be adapted to "act as a blueprint" for European collaboration by incorporating police vocabularies from other member countries into the database. This would enable the "creation of a pan-European multi-lingual text messaging system capable of handling the speedy exchange of accurate intelligence which is so crucial to the fight against international terrorism and organized crime" (Kent County Constabulary 1993).[4]

4. While PoliceSpeak and LinguaNet sought to standardize words through an amalgamation and, in effect, corruption of conventional English and French grammar and sentence structure, another reemerging antagonism between the two countries over the issue of "dominant languages" arose in 1994 (see Grillo 1989). France's then culture minister, Jacques Toubon, proposed a draft bill in March 1994 to protect the French language from an "Anglo-Saxon cultural invasion." Toubon's bill, which won the support of the French cabinet, extended an original French law passed in 1975 and sought to toughen up existing restrictions. Toubon proposed making it a criminal offense to use foreign languages—even individual foreign words—in any official communication if a French term or expression with the same meaning existed. For noncompliance, the French language police were to impose a fine equivalent to $8,500 and imprisonment of up to six months. A spokesman from the Ministry of Culture said:

> French will be obligatory for all communications by public bodies such as the civil service, government departments and public services. As far as commercial advertising is concerned the use of a foreign language is not prohibited in written text, such as on advertisements, but the French translation must appear in letters of the same size. There has been a growing abuse of the law during the past few years and the proposed law is not only to protect cultural aspects, but also for consumers' benefits. (*European: élan*, 4–10 March 1994, p. 7)

Toubon's language defense bill drew heavy criticism, especially from socialists who viewed Prime Minister Édouard Balladur's support of Toubon as a means of courting the xenophobic votes of Jean-Marie Le Pen's Front National. While debate raged in France between the Académie Française and the French Academy of Sciences about the appropriateness of language controls, Toubon went ahead. He renamed *Jurassic Park* on billboards *Le Parc jurassique* and complained that the name of the trains carrying cars through the Channel Tunnel, "Le Shuttle," was a bastardization of the language, saying that they should have been called "La Navette."

In early July, the language defense bill was heard by the French Parliament and was accepted despite the abstention of all socialist members of the National Assembly and some socialist members of the Senate. No longer is it true that "[a]n

This long-term planning took on a measure of reality in October 1995 when the EU gave the LinguaNet initiative a grant of 1.5 million ecus to implement a purpose-built multilingual telematic network specifically designed to improve international police and emergency service cooperation. LinguaNet, centered in Cambridge and run by Edward Johnson, involves a consortium of commercial, academic, and professional organizations in five countries, including the Kent County Constabulary, Philips Communications BV, Prolingua Ltd, Leuven University, Bordeaux University, Cambridge University, and Copenhagen Business School (LinguaNet 1996). According to a phone conversation I had with Edward Johnson in May 1998, the new system is working very effectively, linking up police forces in Britain, France, Belgium, and the Netherlands, with plans to institutionalize ties between twenty-three different police forces in seven EU countries over the next few years.

The mechanics of the system are quite complicated. From what I understand, the software component is configured to run English, French,

---

honorable fact about France is that she has never sought to win unity of language by coercive measures" (Renan 1990 [1882]: 16; and see Weber 1979). For as a result of the bill passing, 3,500 foreign words, including "cheeseburger," "chewing gum," "computer," "marketing," and "fast food," are now banned from official documents. Under the law, an advertisement produced in a foreign language must be accompanied by a French translation. All products sold must have French instructions. And broadcasters on television and radio must not use foreign words when French equivalents exist. The terror of invading foreign words had been effectively legislated against.

The law was somewhat modified in August 1994 when an appeal was made to the Constitutional Council, which ruled as unconstitutional a paragraph in the legislation ruling that the use of "any foreign term or expression" is banned when there is a French term or expression of the same meaning. The council ruled that this was an infringement of "freedom of thought and expression" (*Guardian Weekly*, 7 August 1994, p. 15). But even with the council's modification, the inviolability of the French language has been firmly reasserted under the new legislation. In celebration, Toubon organized an eight-day athletic event that involved three thousand participants and forty-five nations in the Jeux de la Francophonie, which roughly translates as "Games of the French-speaking Community"—a sort of French equivalent to the British Commonwealth Games. Here the government was asserting that athletes, as much as artists, are making a contribution to the sustaining of French culture and a pure French language. According to French authorities, the French language is the natural vehicle for justice. "French is first of all by its nature, the language of human rights," Toubon explained. "What better than our language to express fully, truly, the essence of the human message: All men are equal" (*Times*, 9 July 1994, p. 12). What Toubon presumably meant was "all men are equal if they speak French." One wonders what he would think of the modest efforts of the Kent and Calais police to break down national linguistic barriers through their use of PoliceSpeak.

Dutch/Flemish, Danish, Spanish, and German versions of a series of templated messages that relate to matters of common concern, such as missing persons, credit card checks, prison record checks, and so on (LinguaNet 1998). These messages are translated into all the languages available. There is also the capacity to transfer "free-text" communications, which are outside the automatic translation modules and so not translatable. The overriding purpose of the LinguaNet system is to facilitate basic operational demands and not provide a full free-form translation service, which, according to one of its brochures, would be rejected, because, "Ease of learning and operation, reliability and security, compatibility and ease of maintenance, together with cost, are the overriding practical constraints" (LinguaNet 1998).

Precisely because the translation system is limited to prefigured templates with standardized forms of information and communication, what I find fascinating is the extent to which software technology is defining the parameters of cross-border police communications in the New Europe. As the LinguaNet brochures note, there are different rules and regulations for interrogation and dealing with suspects across different countries, and while organizations such as Interpol exist, they do not generally respond to problems in "real time." In order to overcome the complexities and incompatibilities of various national jurisdictions, the LinguaNet system has streamlined the relay of certain types of information that satisfy various different legal requirements. Specific types of activity, which may or may not constitute illegal action in a particular country, are being standardized and collectively defined across jurisdictions as issues of concern. In short, within the EU, the LinguaNet technology is helping to universalize particular legal categories and a particular format of how and what information related to a given category of activity is deemed pertinent. Ironically, the extreme difficulties of communication across eighteen different languages in the EU is helping to promote a transnational, albeit crude, police vernacular that will potentially play a part in shaping future legal codes and regulations within national jurisdictions.

LOCAL REACTIONS AGAIN

This brief history of some of the legal and political implications surrounding the building and managing of the Tunnel underscores how local perceptions of it in the late 1980s and first half of the 1990s were intimately connected with French and British internal politics, and further contextualized by each nation's wider transnational relations within a developing European Union.

By 1986, Canterbury's Mayor Hazel McCabe and other Kent residents were justified in thinking that the signing of the Treaty amounted to little more than a political "bun fight." The Tunnel was a bargaining chip among European leaders primarily interested in their respective national economic interests. So despite McCabe's own Conservative party allegiances, as the representative of Canterbury, she felt entirely justified in denouncing Thatcher's actions. When the official reception began, she retreated to her car, which sat parked outside the Cathedral. An article in a local paper, headlined "Non! The Mayor Sits It Out," read: "Canterbury's own Iron Lady stuck to her principles on Wednesday. Explaining her decision to stay away from the ceremony, the Mayor said she had received many letters and phone calls urging her not to go at all" (*Kentish Gazette*, 14 Feb. 1986).

What should have been one of the most significant days in the recent history of Kent turned into a fiasco as local leaders rejected the signing, their head of state, and their own political party. Eggs and tomatoes were thrown, and demonstrators chanted, "Froggy, Froggy, Go Home!" Thatcher was accused of ending the nation and, according to one local resident, "assassinating" Kent. As discussed further in the next chapter, throughout the 1980s, public opinion in Kent was very antagonistic to the Tunnel scheme. At this time, many locals would not have conceived it possible that the future of the county lay in residents strengthening their immediate French connections and local politicians and businesspeople increasing their transnational relations with Brussels.

However, since the change of British leadership from John Major to the Labour party's Tony Blair in 1997, there has been a new enthusiasm for cooperation with the EU. Ironically, at the same time that Britain is now supposedly entering an era of support for Brussels, France, the long-time champion of European integration, is demonstrating hesitation. By calling for an early general election in late May 1997, President Jacques Chirac ushered in a government of the Socialist party, much to the nation's surprise. Under the new prime minister, Lionel Jospin, the immediate result has been a much more cautious approach by France to the conditions necessary to establish a common European currency. This hesitation was publicly displayed at the EU summit on 2 May 1998, where the fifteen member states agreed to the conditions to set in motion the establishing of the euro by 1999 only after France's demands that its candidate head the new European Central Bank were in part met.[5] No one can say how these changes in leadership both in Britain and France will eventually affect the shaping of the New Europe. Yet what these shifts in national policies toward the EU illustrate is the extent to which international relations are intimately linked to domestic state and regional politics, as well as to the more nebulous cultural anxieties emerging as a result of the blurring of state borders and the challenging of central state systems.

5. That being said, France along with ten other member-states (Austria, Belgium, Finland, France, Germany, Holland, Ireland, Italy, Luxembourg, Spain, and Portugal) are geared up to participate in the establishing of a common monetary unit, with Britain, Denmark, and Sweden choosing not to join, and Greece currently not meeting the technical requirements. In January 1999, the ecu was replaced by the euro, and currency rates were locked in with each participating nation. It is planned that a new currency will be issued and in use across the EU by 2002. Visit http://www.ecb.int/ to read a 1998 report by the European Monetary Institute (EMI).

5 "The Assassination of Kent"
Local Politics, Environmental Concerns, and Rethinking the Centrality of British Law

The Tunnel Link may help us prosper
Europe now is close to hand
Trans-Manche in one fell swoop becomes
The modern Conqueror of our land!

Kent resident

SIGNING AWAY THE KINGDOM

On 12 February 1986, the actual day of the signing of the Channel Tunnel Treaty, an estimated three thousand people turned out to line the streets of Northgate and the Borough in Canterbury (fig. 16). As the official cars arrived, eggs were thrown, and one hit Mitterrand's Rolls-Royce, while the crowd shouted, "Froggy, Froggy, Froggy, Out, Out, Out" (*Times*, 13 Feb. 1986). Students, union members, Labour party supporters, activists, and villagers also joined in the chant "Maggie Out" as the motorcades, flanked by police motorcycle outriders, approached the cathedral (*Kentish Gazette*, 14 Feb. 1986). Small skirmishes broke out, a policeman received a cut on the chin, and two arrests were made, although both people were released without being charged. Security was on a mammoth scale, and the cathedral precincts had been under surveillance for the preceding two weeks. In anticipation of expected trouble on the day, police officers from all over the county were drafted to help. As the English and French parties arrived, Cathy Methven, chairman of ACTS (Against Channel Tunnel Schemes), greeted dignitaries seated on a horse bedecked with "No Fixed Link" stickers.

On arrival, Thatcher and Mitterrand proceeded inside the cathedral's Chapter House accompanied by a Royal Marine band, which drowned out the protests. Christopher Gay, chief executive of Canterbury, noted in his

Figure 16. Local protesters in the streets of Canterbury as François Mitterrand and Margaret Thatcher arrived to sign the Channel Tunnel Treaty Act in the Canterbury Cathedral Chapter House on 12 February 1986. The crowd responded by throwing tomatoes and shouting, "Froggy, Froggy, Froggy, Out, Out, Out!" By kind permission of the *Kentish Gazette*.

retelling of events to me that the mayor's decision to sit outside in her car:

> was quite a striking venture at the time . . . and as the mayor didn't go, I myself went to the signing ceremony at the Chapter House. There were a number of toffs of one sort or another there—all rather

a fascinating performance and media event really. The vast majority of people there were media, and there were a few sort of local representatives of councils from the area to give it some sort of local flavor as well.

(interview, 21 Dec. 1993)

Once inside, Thatcher rose to deliver her speech, which included a special declaration to Kent residents:

As we meet today, in this ancient city in the very heart of the region of Britain most affected by the link, I should like to address a few words to the people of Kent. Many of you are concerned about the consequences the link will have for the local environment and for employment in the area. Let me assure you: the Government is alive to your concerns. Environmental impact was one of the factors which we took particularly into account.

(*Kentish Gazette*, 14 Feb. 1986)

Thatcher concluded with references to Napoleon and an "illustrious predecessor" who was also a Channel Tunnel supporter, Sir Winston Churchill. She struck all the right notes, including, according to the *Times*:

ten sentences in studied French, telling M. Mitterrand that the treaty marked a new chapter in industrial collaboration and was a significant event for the whole of Europe. M. Mitterrand, in an expansive speech entirely in French and replete with Gallic hand gestures, rehearsed historic references of his own. They included St. Thomas Becket, the Entente Cordiale, and surprise, surprise, Joan of Arc.

(*Times*, 13 Feb. 1986)

After much handshaking and a signing of the cathedral visitor's books, the party retreated to the master's common room at the Deanery for a traditional English meal of roast beef with carrots and new potatoes and an iced confection called Swans of the Lake. According to those with whom I talked, after the departure of Thatcher and Mitterrand, the dignitaries quickly dispersed, the crowds disbanded, and the streets were cleaned. After the buildup of excitement over the previous weeks, the actual day of the signing was a bit of an anticlimax—probably as much as the luncheon fare!

What the event punctuated for many people living in Canterbury and Kent more broadly was a strong sentiment opposed to the Tunnel and particularly the use of the cathedral for the signing of the treaty. Labour's parliamentary candidate for Canterbury, Councilor Linda Keen, said that the visit was "like adding insult to injury" and urged people to demonstrate against Thatcher and Mitterrand. Councilor John Purchese said Thatcher's presence in Kent gave "people a chance to express their revulsion at the invasion of their territory" (*Kentish Gazette*, 7 Feb. 1986). "We won't forgive Mrs. Thatcher for the contempt she has shown towards local democracy by riding roughshod over the opinion of the people of Kent," said another county councilor (*Kentish Gazette*, 21 Jan. 1986). And according to an angry protester, "The last great act of treachery in Canterbury was in 1170, when Becket was murdered in the Cathedral. Perhaps it is fitting that the signing will take place only yards from the martyrdom. Undoubtedly, 1986 will be remembered for all time as the year a Prime Minister assassinated Kent" (*Kentish Gazette*, 7 Feb. 1986). According to Christopher Gay, there was "a real sense of fear that was an unstated thing—a more visceral thing—that some people call the 'garlic factor.' This is the idea that thousands of Frenchmen we didn't like would come pouring across into East Kent" (interview, 21 Dec. 1993).

Of course, not all residents were against the Tunnel. Some people I talked to claimed that they had ignored the whole event, in the belief that it would make no difference to their lives or futures. Others, such as David Crouch, a longtime Conservative member of Parliament, argued openly and consistently that the Tunnel was vital for both Britain's and Kent's future economic prosperity. Letters to local newspapers also indicate that some thought the Tunnel was worthwhile and represented a realistic and visionary approach toward communications with Europe. "[I]f East Kent persists in such negative thinking, then it will deserve all it gets from the new transport scene," observed P. D. Smith, a resident of Canterbury (*Kentish Gazette*, 31 Jan. 1986). This view was shared by Christopher Gay, who told me:

> After the ceremony, my council passed a resolution instructing me to write to the prime minister and express their feeling that it had been insensitive to have signed the treaty in Canterbury when it was known that there were strong feelings here against the project. I did not write the letter overenthusiastically, as I recall it. Certainly those of us working in local government had no strong love for Margaret Thatcher, because she was perceived as somebody who very much looked down on local government. But this was one issue that I remember I agreed most strongly with her about. Anyway, I wrote this letter. There was silence for some time. I think one or two people from Whitehall wrote me a briefing, and I realized they were working on a reply. Anyway, I finally got this reply that I treasure. It was a

sort of "Dear Mr. Gay yours sincerely" letter, I mean there was a personal flavor to it. And I liked the way it started off with "I noticed Mr. Gay that you were one of the fortunate ones present when we signed this treaty, and doubtless you heard my speech outlining what a wonderful project it was, and if you had paid attention, and taken it in, and reported it properly to your council, they would not have passed a damn silly resolution!" I treasure that particular memory.

(interview, 21 Dec. 1993)

Whether residents were for or against the Tunnel when the Channel Tunnel treaty was concluded, there was a sense in which most people sided together against the British government regardless of party allegiance. In conversations about the Tunnel, local Canterbury people repeatedly told me things like: "We weren't going to be pushed around!"; "They couldn't tell us what to do!"; and "Who did she [Thatcher] think she was?" Many locals remembered the day as one on which they had stood proudly independent as representatives of Canterbury and, indeed, as representatives of historic Kent. These people were, according to the repetitive claims of the Kent newspapers, fighting the "invasion of their territory." But in the end, the day was a bit of a disappointment and came and went with only cursory official acknowledgment of local objections. National media attention chose not to explore the angle of Kent's resistance to the Tunnel scheme. Somewhat overdramatically and despondently, a local newspaper headline declared a few days later, "The Deed Is Done" (*Kentish Gazette*, 14 Feb. 1986).

THE CHANNEL TUNNEL HYBRID BILL

This section builds on the emotional distress experienced by many Kent residents that accompanied the signing of the Channel Tunnel treaty. Specifically, I examine Kent residents' subsequent interaction with the British legal system when thousands of locals submitted their objections to the proposed Tunnel under the Channel Tunnel Hybrid Bill, and the government chose to ignore them. I argue that this failure to listen to local objections has over time helped foster the feeling that London, the embodiment of the central British legal structure, is failing ordinary people, and that its dominant concerns are now transnational European politics and global economic activities.

After the emotional events surrounding the signing in Canterbury in 1986, the British government declared that it was prepared to listen to Kent residents' objections to the Tunnel, but officials made only token efforts to do so. Arguing that Britain could not afford a delay like the four-year holdup that had resulted from the public inquiry into the nuclear power station at Sizewell in the mid 1980s, the British government decided to quickly push through the Channel Tunnel Act. In order to expedite proceedings, it was declared that the hybrid bill procedure would be adopted, on the basis that the Tunnel project involved both public and private law in its impact on individuals (Read 1989: 82–83). This meant that the usual public inquiry held for all major planning applications was circumvented. Instead, individuals could petition a House of Commons select committee, which would hear and evaluate all objections and then make amendments to the proposed legislation before its final approval by Parliament. While the hybrid bill procedure is theoretically much quicker and provides greater bargaining power to petitioners, who can directly negotiate concessions from the select committee, it was widely perceived by the public as a shirking of responsibilities by the government to listen and pay heed to local objections.

For many Kent residents, one of the most frustrating aspects about the Channel Tunnel Hybrid Bill was that once the bill had been formally accepted by the government in principle, objections could not be raised as to the actual need for a fixed-link Tunnel. Only the contents of the bill itself could be debated. This prevented Kent residents from having a full say in the first place, since by the time they were allowed to voice their opinions, the decision to go ahead with the project had already been made.

The Commons select committee was appointed on 16 June 1986. By 27 June, the closing date for petitions, the committee had received a record 4,845 requests, and most of these were from individuals. Many of these petitions were never heard, because they involved objections to the Tunnel or to the hybrid bill procedure itself, and so were outside the committee's jurisdiction. This angered many, who interpreted this as suppression of legitimate dissent (Holliday et al. 1991: 39–41; Hunt 1994: 182–84). Public reaction was strong. In a press release entitled "Breakdown of British Democracy," ACTS declared: "As Mrs. Thatcher becomes progressively like Hitler, her bullies become like the Gestapo" (*Kentish Gazette*, 10 Oct. 1986). Arthur Percival, a local Kent resident, wrote to the newspaper expressing a sentiment many shared: "The Select Committee is in danger of going down in history as a monument of flagrant injustice" (*Kentish Gazette*, 3 Oct. 1986). The Dover Chamber of Commerce offered free legal representation to residents in an action before the European Court of Human Rights against what it believed was an irresponsible British government (*Times*, 16 Sept. 1986).

Many of the 4,845 petitions were particularly concerned about protecting Kent's flora, fauna, and landscape aesthetics, but the select committee's seventy amendments made only minor adjustments with respect to the environment and tended not to formally incorporate regulations protecting the environment into the Channel Tunnel Bill itself. Instead, private assurances from Eurotunnel and the government were invoked to persuade the public that the environment would be properly safeguarded (see Anderson 1987). Concerning the statutory and administrative framework that would apply to environmental issues, the committee reported:

> The Petitioners made several requests relating to the statutory framework for the project and the formal machinery for consultation relating to it. The first was a requirement in the Bill for an additional clause requiring those authorized to carry out works to pay special regard to wildlife. The Government acknowledged the importance of the Channel Tunnel works being carried out with due regard to these matters. . . . [but] argued that a continuing duty of this kind was inappropriate. . . . The Petitioners accepted these points subject to a formal undertaking being made by the Concessionaires to consult the Kent Trust for Nature Conservation and to the need for the Memorandum to be an obligation on the Concessionaires to further the interests of conservation.
>
> Another matter relating to the statutory framework is the Petitioners' contention that the Bill should provide for the Concessionaires to set up a capital fund to give financial assistance in cases where there are unforeseen environmental and social effects arising from the Channel Tunnel in view of the scale of those impacts. The Government argued that there was no precedent for a statutory obligation of the kind proposed by the Petitioners. . . . The Committee do not support the Petitioners' proposal.
>
> (*Special Report from the Select Committee on the Channel Tunnel Bill:* xxxi–xxxii)

As it turned out, Eurotunnel appears to have taken good care of Kent's environment, considering the scale of the terminal's construction and the near total lack of any government support. What I want to stress is that at the time of the passing of the Channel Tunnel legislation, the absence of amendments to incorporate environmental protection clauses into the Channel Tunnel Act underscored a general sense that the public was not being listened to by the government.

Eurotunnel sought to compensate for the government's lack of concern by commissioning the Canterbury Archaeological Trust to survey the Folkestone terminal site before building began. This survey unearthed over

15,000 archaeological finds, including Roman jewelry and remains from Bronze Age, Iron Age, and Roman settlements (Channel Tunnel Group 1991). Moreover, two buildings classified by the National Trust, Stone Farm and Mill House, were carefully dismantled and catalogued for reassembling elsewhere. And perhaps most amazing of all was the transfer of soil and saplings from Biggins Wood, a small 5-hectare (12.35 acres) area of ancient woodland, to a "new Biggins Wood" on the northern periphery of the terminal buildings. When I went to speak to Sir Donald Murray, the Channel Tunnel complaints commissioner, he proudly asked me, "But you do know about Biggins Wood don't you, and the pond and the newts?" I said no. "Well," recalled Sir Donald with evident pleasure, leaning back from his desk, "the wood was moved and replanted with the same vegetation, but what was the real problem, no, part of the problem, was that the pond was the habitat of a protected species of newt, and so one evening after dark the entire office staff of Transmanche-Link went out with fishing nets and jam jars and caught these newts and transferred them to a new pond" (interview, 10 Jan. 1994).

The Channel Tunnel Bill was put before the House of Lords for a second reading on 16 February 1987. Discussion went on for hours, finally adjourning at 11:34 P.M. Lord Tordoff was the third speaker to comment and raised various concerns that were returned to throughout the evening's debate, one of these being the environment and its relationship to popular attitudes both in Kent and across the nation:

> We cannot, one realizes, have a major engineering enterprise of this size without considerable impact on the community and on the environment. The first criticism that I have is that the Government were very slow to consider the views of the people of Kent. They have gone some way to repairing that damage but unfortunately a very sour taste was left. . . . The Select Committee of your Lordships' House must therefore take this matter very seriously and do what it can to repair that damage and to ensure that the genuine views of genuine people from real communities are taken very carefully into consideration, even if that means doing things which are not necessarily of themselves commercially viable.
>
> (Channel Tunnel Bill, *Parliamentary Debates*, vol. 484, no. 40 [1987], col. 907)

Lord Tordoff was correct in pointing to the general sense of alienation amongst many people in Kent. The appointment of a complaints commissioner to hear protests about actual site construction no doubt played a role in providing advice and help to local residents affected by noise, pollution, road blocks, land damage, and so on. According to the complaints commissioner, "in our experience as soon as any new construction activity starts, public anxiety goes up just like that, and if they can be reassured that somebody knows about it, and that above all that their complaints will be listened to, the angst goes down" (interview, 10 Jan. 1994). But the powers of the complaints commissioner's office were severely limited, in that it was able to deal only with objections relating to the direct effects of construction. Less direct destruction of woodland and landscape on crown property was beyond its ambit. Moreover, the complaints mechanism could not assuage a wider and more pervasive local sense of having been treated irresponsibly by the government.

A sense of injustice permeated a variety of actions begun by local people in Kent throughout the later 1980s protesting the Tunnel and the fast train's proposed track. As an issue of democratic principle, this perception helped unite both local Tunnel supporters and objectors. Many people told me that these injustices made them seriously question their political party allegiances. For others, it motivated them sufficiently to get involved in local politics for the first time in their lives. Despair and outrage comes through in a variety of town and village community actions in response to the Tunnel project. Notable is the Halling Rail Action Group, which explicitly evoked World War I recruiting posters, declaring with an aggressively pointing fist, "Your Village Needs You!" (Newsletter No. 3, June 1990). Three years after the publication of the poster, I asked one of the Halling Rail Action organizers about the use of war symbolism that deliberately replaced state with village nationalism. According to this middle-aged gentleman, it was highly appropriate, since "Kent was at war with Thatcher."

Another outlet for local anger was a highly successful opera production called *Dreamdragons*, put on by Ashford locals in collaboration with the Glyndebourne Company in 1993. This involved hundreds of Ashford residents of all ages and degrees of acting skills. In talking to some of the children that had been involved, they considered it was the best thing that they had ever done, primarily because it united everyone in a collective event. "We showed them that the Tunnel is both good and bad," one young man told me. "It's changing a lot of things, but that is OK." Of course, Ashford, which supports a population of 55,000, has materially benefited from the Tunnel's International Passenger Terminal being built in its rather uninteresting and dreary environs. It is now the first passenger stop by the fast train in England, making it less than two hours travel time from Paris and only one hour from Lille. Because of its proximity, it has attracted a lot of interest by French businesspeople who are tired of the higher taxes and greater bureaucratic control in France. Now, in the late 1990s, Ashford is enjoying a boom in the development of its retail and service industries, which seems to have effectively silenced its initially very vocal opposition to the Tunnel scheme, as depicted in *Dreamdragons*.

Dreamdragons was relatively restrained, but outrage and indignation against the Channel Tunnel also fueled a musical production curiously entitled *Joan of Kent*. This production toured around regional towns and when I saw it in May 1994, it was playing at Deal in a local hall. The production's "Joan of Arc" theme ironically adopted a French icon of freedom and resistance against English oppression to explore one Kentish woman's attempts to rally local support and contest government intervention.[1] The night I went, the musical played to a full audience of about sixty people, mostly under the age of fifty, who sat on rickety folding wooden chairs and clapped and hummed loudly to the singing of the theme song, "Battle of Kent" by Henry Lewis. Tapes of the production's musical score were available for sale, and about fifteen orders were placed after the show. Lewis's theme song speaks of residents being left with no alternative but to stand and fight for what they believe is reasonable and right. The many verses, of which I reproduce only a few, are highly provocative and clearly struck a chord with the receptive audience. At the back of the hall, a low murmuring developed as people began to hum along to the words of the chorus.

> You've left us no alternative
> Except to stand and fight
> For what we think is reasonable,
> For what we know is right.
>
> I'm not some red hot activist,
> I pay my tax on time,
> My biggest misdemeanor has
> Been one small parking fine.
>
> We're fighting for our countryside
> For every hedge and tree,

1. Joan of Arc, or the maid of Orléans, was born in 1412 in a small peasant community. At the age of sixteen and dressed as a man, she persuaded the dauphin of France that divine voices had informed her that her mission was to help him recover the throne. She gallantly led French troops into battle against the English at Patay in 1429, which resulted in the crowning of the dauphin. Unfortunately, she was captured in 1430, handed over to the English, and tried for heresy and witchcraft. After torture and an exhausting trial, she was condemned to death on 30 May 1431, aged nineteen.

We're fighting your incompetence
And your bureaucracy.
(Lyrics by Henry Lewis from
the song "Battle of Kent,"
Joan of Kent, 1989)

With all these local events, what becomes clear is that the Tunnel, emblematic of European intervention, mobilized a new sense of resistance and purpose focused against high-level politics. The Tunnel, in short, was instrumental in underscoring for many ordinary Kent residents the distortion—even corruption—of British and more essentially English legal processes. And the fact that the majority of these people were long-standing supporters of the Conservative government, the party that had pushed through the Channel Tunnel Hybrid Bill and essentially ignored their objections, only made such a revelation more difficult and embarrassing.

The EU's part in disrupting conventional attitudes in Kent to law and order and government does not necessarily mean that people automatically began to think of the EU as an attractive legal alternative. Important is that the EU intruded upon domestic sensibilities and was seen to be the cause of much confusion. And London, the embodiment of the central British legal structure, was (and is) seen to be failing ordinary people in its wider participation in transnational European politics and global economic activities. In this context, David Engel's analysis of law seems apt:

> The law has an alien, intrusive character when it is used to change power relationships and to assert norms and invoke procedures that have no antecedents within the domain. In such situations it contributes to a sense of disharmony between internal and external realms. It creates a feeling on the part of some, at least, that the state or large-scale institutions of mass society are "taking over" and the traditional authority figures within the domain (and the traditional values and practices associated with them) are under attack.
>
> (Engel 1993: 169)

These sentiments of confusion and disharmony became apparent in a conversation I had with a resident of Kent aboard a train, coming home to Canterbury from Wye College, where we had both been attending a meeting about the impact of the Channel Tunnel called "Garden?—or Gridlock!" in October 1993. It was my first experience of the emotional intensity surrounding the Tunnel project and how it affected people's very identity and sense of who they are. As we rattled along, looking out on the gathering afternoon dark, the sprightly but elderly woman declared passionately and sadly that she had voted Tory all her life, but now didn't care what political party a person stood for because the former days of long-term party allegiance were over. Law and government had got out of hand. Things were changing, she said, nodding her head slowly in time to the motion of the train.

ALL ABOARD! TRANSPORT NETWORKS AND CITY-STATIONS

The Channel Tunnel is part of the Trans-European Transport Network, which links major EU cities and expressly aims at breaking down national borders and the centralizing authority of national city capitals (map 2). The system is illustrative of a wide range of new functions that are being assumed by London in its new capacity as a global city center, which, I suggest, challenge its historical role as the national capital (see Williams 1989b: 227; 1973: 1–8). Global cities, as strategic sites in what is commonly referred to as the global economy, have attracted much interest as an emerging phenomenon related to internationalization and transnationalism. "Cities are strategic to economic globalization because they are command points, global marketplaces and production sites for the information economy," Saskia Sassen observes (1994c: 28). In binding together such places as London, Sydney, Hong Kong, Zurich, Tokyo, New York, and Paris, as well as São Paulo and Mexico City, it is argued, global cities constitute "new geographies of centrality" that are not necessarily defined through and by the legitimating authority of the state (ibid.: 4–5; Castells 1994).

As part of the Trans-European Transport Network, the Tunnel is a crucial link in the EU's general plan to establish transport corridors for fast trains linking up major European cities. So far, the cities targeted by the EU tend to be, but are not limited to, capital cities, which are likely to be the most economically significant cities. Under this scheme, cities are regarded, not so much as final destinations, but more as "city-stations" along a circuitous route—a plan with obvious implications for the movement of peoples across national borders and the general deepening of European integration and a sense of fortress Europe.

The Trans-European Transport Network now confronting major European metropoles is indicative of the many more nebulous administrative, electronic, and technological links that characterize global cities (see Bianchini 1993; Harding et al. 1994). The fast train linking London to places beyond Britain's borders via the Channel Tunnel, and thus reinforcing its

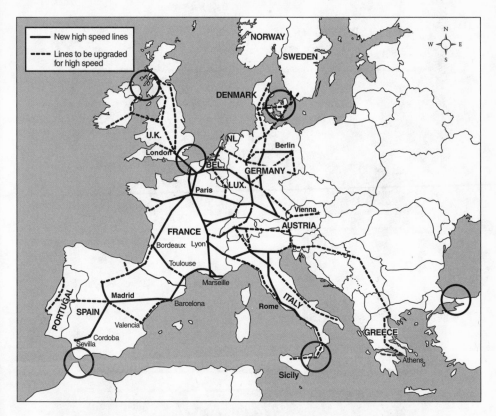

Map 2. The projected Trans-European Transport Network, planned to link up major cities across the EU by the year 2010. To this end, there are additional plans to build a tunnel under the Strait of Gibraltar and to link Sicily to mainland Italy, with talk also of a bridge or tunnel linking Scotland and Northern Ireland. Courtesy of Dirk Brandts.

character as a global city, simultaneously also alters its political and spatial relations within the British state itself.

Accompanying the intervention of high technology and a European presence on English soil has been the partial destruction of the Kentish "south country" and a perceived anxiety about its possible disappearance altogether. As travelers race at an anticipated 180 mph through Kent's countryside, residents fear that a sense of local identity, formerly determined by Kent's peripheral isolation from London, will be destroyed. And Eurotunnel exacerbates this fear by promotional advertising depicting Kent as a void between the global cities of London and Paris (fig. 17). For

Figure 17. One of numerous full-page advertisements in national newspapers for Eurostar trains traveling between London and Paris, represented by Big Ben and the Eiffel Tower. Note the spatial void between the two cities. *Guardian*, 28 November 1994. By kind permission of Eurotunnel.

many locals, the most dreaded consequence of the fast-rail link is that the perceived distinction between city and country will be blurred, Kent's garden country obliterated, and with that will come a drop in tourist spending.[2] In the words of one resident of Rye, in a poem called "Chunnel Vision":

> Out of the void and we're into the light.
> Piercing the air with a rhythmic song,
> Sleek and swish, gliding along.
>
> Passports and tickets ready to hand;
> Enroute from Paris, still on dry land.
> Oast houses and hopfields come into view.
> Must get to London so much to do . . .
>
> Bright yellow fields of rape fly by,
> Steeples and oak trees reach for the sky.
> The refreshment trolley comes rolling through,
> Snacks, tea and coffee, one lump or two?
>
> London approaches, sprawling ahead,
> The Garden of England has all but fled.
> Gone are the green fields and sands of gold,
> Replaced by tall buildings and miles of road.
>
> Couldn't we have stopped for a breath of fresh air?
> Oh why did we rush; was there no time to spare?
> To enjoy the scenery and to make the most
> Of a walk in the fields and a swim at the coast.
>   (Phil Lyons quoted in Purdy 1993: 167)

The fast train's destruction of the southern country landscape typifies the widespread altering of the relations between periphery and center, country and city, that in the past have underpinned the idea of London as the nation's center (Williams 1973; 1989b). The increasing power of the EU, of which the Trans-European Transport Network is indicative, suggests that the physical countryside and its symbolic imagery have in effect become a new focus of contestation between spheres of English and European governance. Of course, the countryside has long been a battleground over which different conceptions of rurality compete (Wright 1994: 31; Simmons 1993). But what is often overlooked is how such battles also involve, and in fact may be generated from, competing notions of what constitutes the city, through

2. Images hover of the seedy and depressed Isle of Thanet on the Kent coast as a constant reminder of the importance of tourist spending. Hence there are real concerns that tourism, vital in the reproduction and survival of Kent's symbolic garden landscape, will be diverted elsewhere (see Vickerman 1991).

which the countryside is defined, mediated, and renegotiated. The country-side, in short, is to a large extent an urban construction, and so it is to new forms of urbanization that attention should be directed.

One such form of urbanization is the construction of an International Terminal in Ashford, which, as mentioned above, is rather a small, insig-nificant and unattractive town in the center of Kent. The initial developers predicted that this International Train Terminal would change the eco-nomic and social character of Ashford, creating a vast commercial complex and trading center in the terminal's environs. And to an extent, these predictions are promising to come true. Ashford is attracting a growing number of young French citizens keen to take advantage of Britain's more moderate taxes and employment laws, which make it easier to start a busi-ness. According to the chief executive of a marketing organization that encourages foreign investment in Kent, of the fourteen Asian businesses that came to England in 1997, five relocated in Kent. And he anticipates that about fifteen more will relocate to the area in 1998 (*New York Times*, 9 Mar. 1998, p. 4).

Just as Ashford is becoming a new location for European business, it is also a new site for customs controls, export and import duties, and general passport inspections. The International Rail Terminal is altering existing ideas of what constitutes the countryside. Perhaps more significant, the very presence of an international train terminal at Ashford helps to un-dermine the status of London as the countryside's central focus. At the same time, it suggests a redrawing of English territory by pushing inland an important aspect of the legal relevance of the national border.[3] Thus Ashford may be coming to represent—if only perceptually—a relocation of control within the state, modifying both the nation's center and the nation's boundaries. Among other things, it is a site overlaid by EU au-thority, replete with large international shopping malls and marked by the presence of French police carrying guns on British soil.

LONDON AS NATIONAL CAPITAL AND GLOBAL CITY?

As the national capital, London has played a particular historical role in consolidating modern Britain and centering the national and imperial

---

3. The fast train's redrawing of state borders raises parallels with Le Corbusier's discussion of the impact of the railway in the nineteenth century. Cities, which were conventionally entered from the outside via gates and walls, suddenly found the city's gates—reinscribed as the railway station—now in its center (Le Cor-busier 1929: 109; Schivelbusch 1986: 171–77).

processes of capitalism throughout the eighteenth and nineteenth centuries (Williams 1973: 142–52; Urwin 1982: 34). London was the first occidental city to develop at the rate it did, and to come so powerfully to symbolize the nation and the controlling authority of the state metropolis over both the surrounding countryside and the extended empire. London, in short, epitomized the conventional model of a hierarchically structured, center-periphery government (Rokkan and Urwin 1982: 5; Rokkan et al. 1987).

As Raymond Williams has convincingly shown in his famous book *The Country and the City* (1973), the country and city cannot be conceived of without each other and share complex social histories. Yet under nineteenth century capitalism, the city—particularly the capital city—became the dominant social form. Henceforth, there was "unequal interaction" between country and city, Williams remarks (1973: 147). The capital city, by definition a place of decision-making, was the site from which modern power flowed (Gottmann 1990: 63–82). It housed the institutions of authority, embodied in the courts, Parliament, stock exchange, jails, and police headquarters, as well as such things as state libraries, theaters, and museums, and the palaces of the monarchy. From the city, both civilization and order emanated (Gurr and King 1987: 30–33). Thus it was the capital that ultimately governed the shape and practices of the countryside through its controlling of interrelated elements such as labor markets, transport, education, export prices, and private and public property rights.

Of course, the concept of the country, like that of the city, is a moving and multifaceted symbol with both positive and negative implications (Pugh 1990). But as Keith Thomas has noted, town-dwellers started to idealize the country cottage and project a presumption of health and morality on its farming inhabitants in contrast to the vices supposedly found in cities (Thomas 1983: 248). In Kent, this communal imagery was strongly linked to hop-picking when groups of itinerant workers from the city descended upon the county in late summer to pick the crop and supposedly enjoy the bounty of the region. By the end of the nineteenth century, when London, with its swollen middle classes and imperial economic dominance, consolidated the modern British nation, this idealization of rural life had crystallized. In fact, it was London's expanding imperial plans (paralleling the emerging concerns of anthropology in "primitive" oral customs and cultures) that provided the impetus for the nostalgic, inward-looking movement known as English Folk Revival, which glorified the "quaint" customs and rituals of rural people, suggesting extensive popular anxiety over who and what could be identified as authentically English (see Boyes 1993; Fernandez 1985). Robert Colls claims that this revival "represented a flight away from external threats deep into the nation's racial and rural essence" (Colls 1986: 47).

During this late-nineteenth-century surge of interest in England's interior, the countryside surrounding London became a yardstick of "rurality" by which the rest of the national landscape came to be measured (Howkins 1986: 54). This "south country" was essentially a fantasized landscape of quasi-Tudor thatched cottages, village greens, church spires, cottage gardens, small cultivated fields, and manicured hedgerows, in which the wilderness of the Yorkshire moors or the flint cottages of Cornwall had no place (Howkins 1986: 54). Variations on this landscape contextualized a dominant Anglo-Saxon racial type perceived as living in the south of England close to London.[4]

One reason for this apparent fixation on a mythologized countryside is raised by Raymond Williams in his discussion of the village ideal as a "knowable community." The village epitomizes direct relations and face-to-face communication in contrast to the alienating qualities of the industrial metropolis (Williams 1973: 165–81; see also Spengler 1928: 85–186; Simmel 1950: 409–24; Mingay 1989b). The village supposedly speaks of mutual responsibility and a sense of community duty, values that historically served to veil great economic disparities between the landed gentry and the majority of feudally based tenant farmers. For above all, Williams argues, the imagined village represents a certain consciousness about social hierarchies, gender representations, class divisions, morality, and order (Williams 1973: 165–66; Thomas 1983: 243–53).[5]

Today, such community ideals are invoked and recreated as part of a political program seeking to tap into the mythology of England's glorious past. It appears in public debate, such as Prince Charles's reflections on architecture and landscape and his declaration that "man seems to function

4. Between 1875 and 1883, the British Association for the Advancement of Science established a program known as the "Racial Committee" with the aim of investigating, through photographs, "the national or local types of race prevailing in different parts of the United Kingdom." Photographs of people from Scotland and Wales were measured against those representing residents of southern England and invariably considered inferior (Poignant 1992: 58–61; Urry 1984: 83–85).

5. By the early twentieth century, this consciousness curiously appealed both to the possibility of return to a golden paternal age and to an advance toward a classless community whose members share equally in the burdens and benefits of "back to the land" agricultural programs (Howkins 1986: 75–76; Marsh 1982).

best in small, recognizable units—hence the village—where he is part of a community of people to which he can relate" (Jencks 1988).[6] And it appears in public policy, such as the former Prime Minister John Major's "back to basics" campaign, which advocated returning to an archaic image of the family and neighborly values. Moreover, it filters through into the country's approach to the New Europe in public declarations that Britain, even within the European Union, will remain a nation of stereotyped images of small villages, green commons, local shops, and warm beer (*Guardian*, 23 Apr. 1993; Dodd 1995: 8). In this context, it is hardly a coincidence that in 1992, in the midst of talk over the devaluation of British currency and its replacement by the new European currency unit, the English £10 note was redesigned. The illustration of Florence Nightingale was replaced by a scene from Charles Dickens's *Pickwick Papers* showing a cricket match played on a village green in the heart of Kent, framed by a marquee and parish church steeple—an image "quintessentially English" (although not very Dickensian!) (Andrews 1992). As has been noted, in contrast to soccer, which is essentially an urban street game, cricket stands for ancient agricultural seasons, where, after harvesting, a "field" would become vacant for the community (Bale 1994: 27; Klinck 1994: 44). In a wider context, cricket also symbolizes Britain's imperial past rather than its postcolonial and European present (Bale 1994: 153–65; Appadurai 1996: 89–113).[7]

Throughout political rhetoric about the value of the countryside and its moral fiber, what often goes unremarked is that the government's withdrawal of finances, transport, and local services throughout the 1980s has seriously undermined the power of local government and so the future of many villages (Rhodes 1985: 62–75). A survey by the Rural Development Commission in 1994 found that 93 percent of rural parishes had no rail

6. The prince has translated this sentiment of idyllic ruralism into building model village communities that supposedly provide a classless countryside. Despite open criticism, few home buyers, and, ironically, much protest from the Campaign for the Preservation of Rural England about Poundbury, the Prince's first village, four more model villages are planned on Duchy of Cornwall land. Like Poundbury, these are envisaged as houses around a common village green, "where rich and poor can gather to admire their classically designed chimney pots and stone-clad gable ends" (*Guardian*, 5 March 1995, p. 15).

7. In May 1998, the Centre for Sport Development on behalf of the London Community Cricket Association issued a 57-page report, called *Anyone for Cricket*, alleging that racism is rife in the cricket world and that apartheid exists in local community cricket games, with white teams refusing to play black and Asian teams (*Guardian*, 15 May 1998, p. 15).

service, 83 percent no permanent doctor's surgery, 80 percent no pharmacy, 43 percent no post office, and 41 percent no permanent corner-store (*Guardian*, 14 Apr. 1995, p. 6). According to one Kent resident: "We like living in the country, we wouldn't want to go into the town, but if you don't have a motor you're stranded. There's no facilities at all, we haven't even got a village shop now and there's only three buses a day" (quoted in Alison and Lardinois 1994: 42).

It comes as no surprise that even in remote areas, such as the wilds of Romney Marsh on the Kent coast, small villages like Lydd are plagued by problems common to urban living, including vandalism, drugs, violence, and high unemployment. When I visited some of these areas, I was struck by how bleak and depressing they seemed. Men and youths were hanging about, appearing bored and hopeless, against a backdrop of low scrubland and concrete public housing. The pretty orchards and picture postcard scenery that attract both national and international tourists to Canterbury were nowhere in evidence. It seems that what remains of the idealized village existence is largely a "green tranquillity buoyed up by Sainsbury's [supermarket] and the property market" (*Guardian*, 18 Aug. 1994, p. 16). Still, the idealized image of the village is clung to by locals as much as by those commodifying it for economic purposes.

Just as the reality of the countryside does not match its projected idealized and essentialized imagery, so too the ideal of the nation's state capital is being reconfigured and redefined in the public imagination (Robins 1993). As public reaction to the government's handling of the Tunnel's construction attests, London may be changing in terms of how it is perceived and received by ordinary people as the symbolic representative center of the nation. The Tunnel, in generating widespread feelings of violation, penetration, alienation, and "assassination" among local residents, has also in the process altered people's horizons in terms of forcing individuals to acknowledge new, alternative forms of political and legal authority and rethink the limits of each individual's own political participation.

Large cities such as London, in refusing "to submit their perceived interests to the nation-state interest," become new locations of political activity and may be an alternative to the nation-state as seats of political power, Raymond Williams has suggested (1989a: 238; 1973: 287), an observation that remains remarkably salient today. However, talk of global cities too often veils events at the other end of the economic scale, among immigrants, illegal refugees, women, and the poor—the others who supply the basic services and labor that keep the metropolis in operation (Sassen

1994b: 40; Massey 1984). Even as cities forge new transnational links, they are relatively bounded spaces, in which new social boundaries emerge. Globalization has an impact upon a range of issues from immigration and labor segmentation to the homeless and the unemployed, all relating to the creation of particular neighborhoods, marginal associations, ghettos, and spatial divisions of inclusion and exclusion—in short a new configuration of intercity inequalities and economic division (Cooke 1988: 487–89; Ford 1994: 1878).[8] More analytically, new spatial configurations raise the dilemma of how transnational, national, and subnational processes can be talked about without using a simplistic and reductionist global/local model.

In the reproduction of the postmodern city, these tensions between more nebulous global/international networks, on the one hand, and locally grounded community responses, on the other, situate this brief characterization of shifting public perceptions of the capital London. Today, the

8. Race riots, such as those in Brixton in 1981, at Broadwater Farm in 1985, and again in Brixton in 1991, have highlighted both English racism and minority retaliation against the poor economic standing in which many nonwhite English disproportionately find themselves (Gurr and King 1987: 163–65). Although these problems are not confined to London, 40% of the country's ethnic minorities do live in Greater London, and especially in the East End (Kyle 1994: 58). This concentration increases conflict, creating the perception of social disintegration in London. Friction between nonwhites and whites, which has steadily escalated since the first West Indian migrations to Britain in the 1950s and the Notting Hill riots in 1958, dramatically marks postcolonial England, illustrating the challenges alternative cultures and histories pose to the very notion of British homogeneity (Gilroy 1991; Chambers 1994: 76; Jones 1990: 189–90; McLeod 1994).

One consequence of this form of social unrest is that lawlessness and the dangers of the "concrete jungle," images usually associated with large American cities, are more readily applicable to the conditions within which London's ethnic and economic minorities live (Kasinitz 1995: 387; Shapiro 1992: 86–103). A growing underclass is seen to be creating and sustaining urban frontiers (such as Waterloo Bridge), in turn promoting an idea that flourished around the end of the nineteenth century of capitalist pioneers braving out the perils of the city (Jones 1990: 82; Davis 1995: 355, 365). Events such as Muslim attacks on Hindu temples, the stabbing of a Kashmiri taxi driver as a result of a clan dispute, and the death of an African student precipitated by conflict over a separate prayer room for Islamic militants at Newham College of Further Education in East London now dominate public discussions, however. Long gone is the preoccupation with health, housing, and sewerage of the late nineteenth and early twentieth centuries, as recorded by Charles Booth in his massive surveys of poverty (Jones 1990: 78–84). With the decline of the manufacturing sector in England, disease and corruption, which at the turn of the century were regarded as an inevitable consequence of poor labor conditions and overcrowded factories, are now more readily linked to foreign immigrants and perceived as an introduced cultural import. As discussed in chapter 6, the association of foreignness with pollution and disease informs much of the anxiety about the Tunnel's long-term impact.

ready conflation of capital city with nation-state is increasingly open to challenge, and perhaps nowhere is this more dramatic than in Britain, as Scotland and Wales increasingly carve out a sense of independence from England with the devolution of power and the creating, at least in Scotland, of a theoretically autonomous parliament. In this climate of London's diminishing status as the country's center, it is perhaps no coincidence that the city's politicians have been preoccupied with establishing the new position of mayor of London in a bid to give the city back to its people.[9] How effective or not these measures will be does not detract from the necessity to "rethink traditionally held views of cities as subunits of their nation states" (Sassen 1994a: xiv). This raises numerous questions, such as, what are the ways in which cities express challenges to both the legitimacy and effectiveness of the modern state? (MacGregor 1994: 228). How may the material and iconographic symbolism of London be shifting to accommodate more complex relationships that are not perceptually framed or necessarily constituted in the national context, such as those institutionalized by the EU? To what extent are London's global economic and political networks, as aesthetically represented by the Tunnel on British soil, forcing English people to rethink the assumed central authority of the country's rule of law?

CONCLUDING COMMENTS

Amid all the bulldozing, transporting, building, and development surrounding the Tunnel and fast train, issues of center and periphery are raised and materialized through the shifting relations between the capital city and its surrounding countryside. London poses a new definition of "capital" and "city" within Britain. At the same time, London's participation in transnational projects such as the Trans-European Transport Network linking it by fast train to Paris and Brussels helps dissolve a spatial

9. On 7 May 1998, a referendum was held in London on whether the city should have an elected mayor along the lines of Paris, New York, and Rio de Janeiro. This was a deliberate bid by Prime Minister Tony Blair and the new Labour party to increase grassroots participation in local government institutions, rethink the running of the capital, and rejuvenate public morale. While the referendum was passed, there was much disappointment about the lack of voter turnout and absence of popular enthusiasm for such an office. In any case, in the year 2000, five million voters in thirty-two boroughs will vote for a mayor and twenty-five elected officials to form the Greater London Authority, harking back to the Greater London Council abolished by Margaret Thatcher in 1986.

perception held by many that London is encircled by an idealized countryside, and so contests the construction of "country."[10]

These definitional ambiguities are further provoked from within England by a growing postcolonial population that implicitly challenges the heritage industry, forcing the question, "Whose tradition is being conserved and whose conception of a rural landscape?" As John Urry has argued, the countryside is largely constructed as "white" (Urry 1990: 142; Walsh 1992: 128). Blacks and Asians do not regularly adopt the particularly English tradition of country walking as epitomized by the Ramblers' Associations (Taylor 1994: 274–76). And I can attest that in the many times that I walked back roads and fields in southern England, I never once saw anyone other than a very white English-looking person walking too. Furthermore, blacks and Asians are not very responsive to billboard invitations such as that by English Heritage to board weekend getaway trains and find in the nation's country periphery a "Place in History." What is unappealing about these advertisements is that they underscore a singular, fixed, and official historical narrative of the past. They make no room for minority and ethnic groups to assert their own historical and cultural narratives, build up an identity with a particular place, and perhaps one day call the country home. A startling image that visually affirms the implicit racism in romanticized imagery of the English countryside is a photograph taken by Simone Canetty-Clarke, a photographer sponsored by the Cross Channel Photographic Mission. In black and white, the photographer depicts turbaned Indian migrants sitting straight-backed and cross-legged in a rural orchard (Alison and Lardinois 1994: 53). Through deliberate dislocation, what the image asserts is the Indians' right to be present in a very traditional and idealized English landscape, and the necessity of their

10. It is here that critiques of Raymond Williams, while often caricaturing and simplifying his argument, nonetheless provide insights relevant to this discussion. In general, these critiques highlight limitations in Williams's country/city thesis with respect to its implicit presumption of Eurocentrism. Specifically, the argument is made that Williams's inadequately takes into account the historical role of the colonies in shaping English culture, primarily because of his Marxist-based concern with economics, thus ultimately treating the history of colonized peripheries as derivative of the west (Viswanathan 1993: 220; Skurski and Coronil 1993: 234). With respect to thinking about the relations between city and country, it is argued that Williams too readily assumes it to be a model of universal application (Williams 1973: 286). This underlines his failure to discuss the extent to which this model itself is shaped and constituted through the influential impulses of England's imperial frontiers playing back on the assumed center.

working as itinerant laborers in a job that conventionally employed poor whites.

I have argued in this chapter that through global and postcolonial forces, and more specifically the reconceptualizing of state sovereignty within the European Union, London may be losing its hold on the institutions and symbols that have historically identified it as the state capital at the very moment when Kent residents (and others) are increasingly being pulled into the orbit of the EU. The Channel Tunnel has brought to the fore the authority of British law, both in the manner in which the government dealt directly with the people of Kent in the 1980s, and more surreptitiously, in the recent challenge to modernity's country/city dichotomy. In the process, it has also called into question the liberal presumption that in modern nation-states, legal and political power necessarily emanate from a capital center.

6 Rabies Rides the Fast Train

Transnational Interactions in Postcolonial Times

Why is the Channel Tunnel like a mosquito?
Because it bites you when unaware, injects a great tube into you,
sucks out your life blood, and is likely to introduce infections!
Kent resident, 26 February 1994

ELECTRIFIED BARRIERS UNDER THE SEA

The high-speed railway link, and the Channel Tunnel through which it rushes under the sea, have been declared at the forefront of technological progress and engineering expertise. As part of the Trans-European Network of transport, they dramatically encapsulate hopes of a new era of European economic integration and transnational political cooperation (see Viegas and Blum 1993). In the words of President François Mitterrand, "the Channel Tunnel . . . is nothing less than a revolution in habits and practices; . . . the whole of Community Europe will have one nervous system and no one country will be able indefinitely to run its economy, its society, its infrastructural development independently from the others" (quoted in Holliday et al. 1991: 191).

Despite these positive speculations, as discussed in earlier chapters, the Channel Tunnel dramatically highlights England's popular anxiety about being a member of the European Union. Although the Channel Tunnel was officially inaugurated on 6 May 1994 and is a fait accompli, information about the Tunnel, and the high-speed rail link joining London to Paris and Brussels, continues to pervade the media. Such publicity excites popular reactions that are by any standards out of proportion to the problems with the railway's actual route through Kent and its effects on the county's people and rural environment. While the disruption caused is certainly not trivial, it does not fully explain the widespread and seemingly irrational unease that embellishes the Channel Tunnel's impact with forecasts of terrorism, apocalyptic fires, and most dramatic of all, a sudden influx of rabies. "It was as if, lining up behind Mitterrand and the Queen as they cut the tricolor ribbons at Calais, were packs of swivel-eyed dogs, fizzing foxes, and slavering squirrels, all waiting to jump on the first boxcar to Folkestone and sink their teeth into some Kentish flesh," Julian Barnes writes of the Tunnel's inauguration (Barnes 1995: 318).

In the first section of this chapter, I interpret the English fear of rabies as a metaphor embodying distinct cultural meanings and messages. Understanding the rabies phenomenon in this way is helpful in unraveling contradictory English reactions to the EU. For the national excitement and apprehension about rabies and the fast train on which it supposedly rides are, I argue, inextricably linked to England's imperial history. Such imagery recalls both the glory of nineteenth-century Britain and the twentieth-century dissolution of the empire. Situating talk about rabies (and railways) in a historical context is one of many possible ways to locate a postcolonial legacy that lives on in the construction of English attitudes and identities. What I hope to show is how this legacy is also implicitly present in Britain's relations with other western nations and hence significant in the shaping of England's European future.

In the second section of this chapter, I examine the meaning of transnationalism, further exploring the salient, but often unremarked, overlapping connections between postcolonialism and the forms of Europe's unfolding. Taking what Homi Bhabha calls "a post-colonial perspective" as my cue, I argue that it is not surprising that England is caught between both acclaiming and fearing the intervention of Europe. The postcolonial perspective, according to Bhabha, emerges from "the colonial testimony of Third World countries and the discourse of 'minorities'" (Bhabha 1994: 171). What this perspective does is recognize the modern nation-state's pretensions to universalism and its people's need to see the state as a rational, sovereign entity in contrast to external others. Being part of a European superstate expands England's economic and political opportunities. At the same time, England's postcolonial experiences counter this imagined amalgamation by positing multiple discourses and critical revisions that challenge the presumption of England's universal "hegemonic 'normality'" (ibid.). In other words, locating postcolonial experiences occurring within the nation in a larger transnational landscape suggests that many English people perceive their country's very identity as an enduring, singular state to be at stake.

In the construction of the English national identity, law is, as discussed in chapter 1, a particularly important dimension. Here I explore how EU law may be presenting alternative legal avenues and, inadvertently, sanctioning competing legal voices not contained by the British state. This discussion, then, seeks to go beyond the more visible negotiations between people and law in order to probe how transnational activities may be calling into question how law, as embodied in the nation-state, continues to represent a credible narrative of impartiality (Fitzpatrick 1992). In turning to local-level responses to the Channel Tunnel, what is fascinating is the extent to which these could be interpreted as responding to the breaking down of national narratives by and through the EU's "colonization." I suggest that as a result of the Channel Tunnel, there may be emerging in Kent, to borrow again from Bhabha, the conditions by which to establish a "hybrid location of cultural value." This refers to the porous quality of state entities and the transformative potential in the crossing of cultural and political borders within a given location (Bhabha 1994: 173). Fundamental to this emergent "hybridity," I argue, are the legal infrastructures through which Kent is being reimagined as part of a primary European region, rather than, as discussed in chapter 2, a peripheral "garden" county of England.

RABIES IN ENGLAND?

Rabies, in French *la rage*, has a unique and long history. For many people living in England today, rabies conjures up images of other deadly diseases such as cancer and AIDS, as well as of the medieval terror of the bubonic plague. In some interesting ways the exaggerated response of the English to the threat of rabies tunneling under the Channel echoes the prescientific or premodern response to the Black Death. In medieval times, it was believed that one of the only effective defenses against the Black Death was to isolate the community from all outside contact. In the years since 1902, when rabies was eradicated from England, there have been periodic outbreaks, such as when 328 infected French dogs were brought back to England by returning soldiers after World War I. The last major rabies scare occurred in 1969. According to official records, there have been no deaths from rabies in Britain for over sixty years. Any animal coming into the country has to be isolated for six months.[1] As a result, Britain can claim

1. The EU has somewhat modified these regulations by allowing dogs that have been vaccinated against rabies before entering England to forgo the six months' quarantine requirement, so long as the dog has come from a registered commercial breeder. In contrast, British customs officials have stood firm against implementing the vaccination system rather than the six months' quarantine. In a recent twist to this tale, there has been a backlash against these strict regulations. A BBC program that aired on 5 May 1998, called "Inside Quarantine," reported on animal

to be one of the few countries in the world today to be rabies-free. This is achieved through rigorous customs controls and quarantine laws by the government, justifying its deploying twenty-eight rabies vans and a rabies crew bus, as revealed in late 1997 by the British Treasury (fig. 18).

Rabies is indeed a terrifying disease. It is transmitted to humans by bites and scratches from rabid foxes, rats, bats, and, more insidiously, domestic dogs and cats. The disease attacks the central nervous system and salivary glands, leading to lunacy and seizures. "Once clinical signs of the disease develop (convulsions, frothing at the mouth, hydrophobia[,] or fear of water[,] and hallucinations) there is no known cure and death is inevitable," notes a Eurotunnel publication, *Rabies and the Channel Tunnel* (Channel Tunnel Group 1990: 1). For an animal-loving population such as the English claim to be, images of warm and cuddly creatures being the carriers of death are potent and captivating. At the Eurotunnel Exhibition Center in Folkestone, which sells a vast range of gimmicks and promotional information about the Tunnel, one of the salespeople told me that *Rabies and the Channel Tunnel* is one of the biggest sellers. As seems to be the case with most things to do with death, people are fascinated.

The British government has not been able to ignore the media hype about a possible rabies outbreak in the wake of the Tunnel's construction. This is hardly surprising, considering that it has for years been responsible for "sometimes horrendous anti-rabies propaganda," according to Bradley Viner, a well-known English veterinarian (*Los Angeles Times*, 10 Nov. 1996, p. 23). According to Mark Jones, a representative of the London and Essex International Quarantine Pound, the "main worry is that animals

---

holding facilities and presented strong evidence that the quarantine procedure was both unnecessary and ineffective. Moreover, campaigners for legal reform argue that these severe laws violate EU standards and must be modified. According to Lady Mary Fretwell, a leader of an anti-quarantine group called Passport for Pets, "It is a monstrously archaic system, totally xenophobic and fanned by hysteria. It must go" (*Los Angeles Times*, 10 Nov. 1996, p. 22). In evoking the lesser EU standards as an argument for legislative reform in Britain, these campaigners are appealing to the authority of Brussels and in the process challenging the legitimacy of Britain's rule of law. In March 1998, the Quarantine Abolition Fighting Fund was granted leave to challenge Britain's quarantine law in the European High Court. And in September 1998, a ten-person panel of independent government advisors suggested that the laws on quarantine should be replaced with a system of electronic surveillance that would monitor dogs imported into the country. However, the panel also advised that strict quarantine laws should remain in place for foreign dogs coming from "problem countries" where the risk of rabies is perceived to be high. These countries are in east Europe, east Asia, Africa, and north and south America.

Figure 18. This poster visualizes the threat of rabies by linking it to domestic pets, evoking the disease's targeting of "innocent," "cuddly" animals. Note that Britain is shown as white against a black background, emphasizing both its island status and its (ethnic) purity in contrast to the tainted gray of France and mainland Europe. By kind permission of Eurotunnel.

will slip in through that bloody tunnel or past lazy customs officials, although no one at the Ministry of Agriculture is admitting it" (*London Student*, 24 Feb. 1994, p. 10). Eurotunnel, not surprisingly, denies these risks. Its claim is that the Channel Tunnel is just one more form of transport among many, and is no more likely to be used by animal smugglers than the enormous number of ferries, hovercraft, and planes that cross the Channel daily. This view was supported by Christopher Gay, chief executive of the Canterbury City Council, who stated that those fearful of a mass influx of rabid foxes were a "lunatic fringe" (interview, 21 Dec. 1993). Yet despite much evidence that no animal would travel many kilometers along a dark, cold, and foodless tunnel (Crowley 1981; Channel Tunnel Group 1985), the British government was not satisfied with this argument, and in 1987 it made Eurotunnel incorporate measures to defend against rabies into the construction of the Tunnel. In the House of Lords debates about the Channel Tunnel Bill, Lord Pennock, former chair of Eurotunnel, remarked,

> I should like to dismiss the point concerning rabies very quickly. Last year I went to Japan and went into eight of the 18 tunnels that the Japanese have. Every engineer in charge of every tunnel independently said to me, "no rats, no rodents, no dogs, no cats, no foxes, no animals of any kind ever come into a tunnel, for the simple reason there is no food there and they know it. They never never come near it." However, because of the sensibilities of the great British public, noble Lords can rest assured that we shall have deep pits, electrified fences, electronic sensor devices and everything known to man to make sure that there are no foxes running through the 50 kilometers at whatever miles per hour they care to make it.
>
> (Channel Tunnel Bill, *Parliamentary Debates*, vol. 484, no. 40 [1987], col. 923)

As a result, a complex electronic system has been installed to catch adventurous animals. According to a Eurotunnel document, this consists of:

> a *security/perimeter fence*, with animal proof mesh buried below ground, surrounding the terminals. There will be surveillance to detect the passage of animals at terminal entrances.

> a *high-security fence* around the tunnel portals, with animal-proof mesh buried below ground, and an environment at the portals which will be hostile to animals. In addition, there will be *round-the-clock surveillance*.

electrified barriers at each end of the undersea sections of all three tunnels, preventing the passage of animals in the unlikely event that they have passed through the first two *lines of defence*.

(Channel Tunnel Group 1992: 1; emphases added)

Despite conflicting reports about the Tunnel's involvement in a rabies epidemic, it is clear that the fast train will not pose a significant new threat. Animal smugglers can cross the Channel by sea and air too. And even the most daring, cunning, and determined foxes and rats will find it difficult to travel underground, avoiding the "round-the-clock surveillance" and a "high-security" electrified fence. Ultimately, the scare is unsubstantiated and speculative. However, I suggest, lying beneath the surface of the rabies debate, in a political climate that makes open xenophobic attitudes intolerable and nostalgia for the "lost" empire repugnant, there is a profounder logic to the English public obsession with rabies.

Rabies, for many English people, represents a form of invasion.[2] As the Conservative MP Norman Tebitt noted in 1990, "The blessing of insularity has long protected us against rabid dogs and dictators alike" (quoted in Walsh 1992: 87). More recently, Raymond Seitz, the U.S. ambassador to Britain, and a dog fancier himself, noted: "It's about sanctuary and the invulnerability of Britain. It has a strong psychological hold" (*Los Angeles Times*, 10 Nov. 1996, p. 23). Britain's current freedom from rabies reinforces a sense of the nation's unique superiority in both military and cultural respects. This absence of disease upholds the virtues of a rational and law-abiding citizenry, as well as the country's ability to control its ports and borders. Sovereign law, an essential ingredient in the makeup of the English identity, is sustained. And it is law that allows Britain to structure its defensive stand against a deadly disease that, according to media publicity, is being spread by unrestrained "third world" migrations into Europe, and particularly into France, and is now creeping westwards toward England. In the words of the official Eurotunnel publication on rabies, the disease runs "virtually unchecked" in foreign (postcolonial) countries (Channel Tunnel Group 1990: 3). In India alone, an estimated 20,000 people die annually from rabies. In Europe over the past twelve years, 36 people have died (although 10 of these people contracted the disease in

2. As discussed in chapter 3, Britain's historical independence is constantly evoked in the national imagination (Walsh 1992: 90), and unlike in other European nations, whose borders have been the subject of constant friction and in many cases have changed, the thought of potential invasion carries intense and particular meaning in England.

Africa or the Far East). The implicit message is that rabies is associated with "developing" countries and nonwhite peoples. And despite an EU scheme to stamp out the disease, it is unlikely rabies will ever be fully eradicated.

This imagery has been strengthened by the outbreak of bubonic plague in New Delhi in October 1994, which resulted in newspaper headlines such as "The Return of Ancient Enemies Which Modern Science Cannot Defeat" (*Guardian*, 1 Oct. 1994, p. 12). This outbreak resulted in panic across England and elsewhere, and in the monitoring and "disinfecting" at Heathrow airport of passengers arriving from India. According to a member from the Department of Health, "There have been so many rumors breaking out it's an epidemic in itself. I've been trying to tell people there's no cause for alarm" (*Guardian*, 1 Oct. 1994, p. 12). Then in May 1995, the deadly Ebola virus broke out in a remote village in Zaire, heightening a general sense of horror. This had been further fueled by Hollywood movies such as *Outbreak*, which describes the transmission to the United States of a deadly microbe carried by a monkey from the Congo. A more recent headline sums it up: "Europe Faces Disease Invasion from the East" (*Guardian Weekly*, 13 Apr. 1997). In all this hype about microbes and viruses, what I want to stress is that, like AIDS, these deadly, mysterious foreign diseases seem to emerge suddenly out of developing third world countries or that abstraction still known as the East. To put it crudely, from the perspective of the English, these diseases are tainted with racial characteristics.

ENEMIES WITHOUT AND WITHIN

What the threat of rabies excites, then, is the sense that Britain must remain vigilant. Round-the-clock surveillance and electric fences cannot be deployed against incoming "foreigners," but rabies provides an acceptably neutral explanation for the maintenance and reinforcement of border controls. Rabies makes customs enforcement critical and spatial boundaries of inclusion and exclusion essential. In this context, Stuart Hall's analysis of the Falklands war as representing the need to fight for a meaning of Englishness seems apt: "If we cannot defend it [England] in reality, we will defend it in mime" (Hall 1991: 25–26; Kirby 1993: 125). The threat of rabies sustains the logic that the pure political and social body of England, visually manifested as a feminine Britannia, requires protection against intruding infection *and* the imposition of an alternative European "nervous system," as described by Mitterrand (Martin 1990: 414–19;

1992). By implication, a temporal rationale operates, suggesting that society should stay as it is in order to withstand the invasion of a contagious, anomalous, and lawless force. Implicitly, Britain should remain steadfast as a united, homogenous, "white" nation. Change—at least in the direction of a more open and borderless Europe—is denounced, notwithstanding that the EU claims such change as the basis for its existence.

What makes rabies a particularly powerful metaphor is its difference from all other viruses. Unlike AIDS, which is peculiar to contemporary society, rabies represents the return of a premodern disease, often linked to images of the Black Death, that alienates and dehumanizes by physically transforming the victim into raving, frothing lunacy (Sontag 1989: 45). Still, there are connections between the diseases. According to a local rector in Rochester, Kent, rabies presents real concerns, but, he says, these are exaggerated. Rather: "The Channel Tunnel is a violation of our island integrity—a rape. Building it was a triumph of power and money over ordinary people and the English countryside. People think it might give us rabies in the same way as a rape victim might catch AIDS. I suspect something like this is happening at the psychological level" (interview, 16 Mar. 1994).

Rabies and AIDS, unlike cancer, are both caused by an "infectious agent that comes from the outside," Susan Sontag notes (Sontag 1989: 17, 47–50), and descriptions of epidemics are thus conflated with ideas of otherness, explaining why "xenophobic propaganda has always depicted immigrants as bearers of disease" (ibid.: 62). "[T]here is a link between imagining disease and imagining foreignness. . . . Part of the centuries-old conception of Europe as a privileged cultural entity is that it is a place which is colonized by lethal diseases coming from elsewhere" (ibid.: 50; see also Haraway 1989: 4). There is also a link between affirming racial discrimination and gendering the national space as feminine, subject to penetration and rape. Hence, bound up in the urgency to control female sexuality is the imperative to preserve racial differentiation, manifest at the level of "public health" and the management of disease, pollution, and contamination. In short, the gendering of a national space serves racial imperatives as well as the gender imperatives discussed in chapter 2 in connection with the feminizing of the garden landscape and its relationship to colonial and postcolonial gazes.

Jean Baudrillard adds a twist to this perceived threat of external invasion. Baudrillard is primarily concerned with AIDS in his writing about the viral and virulent excesses involved in current society's "endless process of self-reproduction" (Baudrillard 1993). Nonetheless, he offers greater insight into the seemingly irrational terrors evoked by the threat of rabies by highlighting the insidious and imminent forces of "radical otherness" and disorder now emerging from within (Napier 1992: 139–75). In an insightful discussion of the impact of the colonized, Baudrillard writes:

> It lies in their power to destabilize Western rule. . . . It is now becoming clear that *everything* we once thought dead and buried, everything we thought left behind for ever by the ineluctable march of universal progress, is not dead at all, but on the contrary likely to return—not as some archaic or nostalgic vestige (all our indefatigable museumification notwithstanding), but with a vehemence and a virulence that are modern in every sense—and to reach to the very heart of our ultra-sophisticated but ultra-vulnerable systems, which it will easily convulse from within without mounting a frontal attack.
>
> (Baudrillard 1993: 137–38)

Terror of the "enemies within" is heightened at a time when the mythological sense of being British has lost some of its vitality, and the country is culturally and politically fragmenting (Hall 1988: 8). The influx of postcolonial peoples since the 1950s and 1960s has been instrumental in developing two general versions of Britishness, discussed in chapter 3. These two visions of Britishness in a way reflect two different trajectories of modernity; the first is regressive, conservative, and based on the presumption of a stable, unified culture; the second is motivated by the tense, and at times bloody, overlapping of cultural histories and traditions, which in their link to class and ethnicity, challenge the very notion of British homogeneity (see Gilroy 1991; Rustin 1994; Wheeler 1994: 107; Nairn 1988: 246–50). While the repeated successes of the Conservative party throughout the 1980s and 1990s suggest the dominance of the regressive type of British identity, its contestation is highlighted by increasing minority dissidence and the dramatic defeat of the Tories by Tony Blair's Labour party in the 1997 general elections. In the volatile and distrustful political environment of Britain in the past decade, it is hardly surprising that in the fight against rabies, the Conservative British government required three lines of defense and an electrified fence to be built inside the Tunnel, and, moreover, that a large percentage of the English public refused to believe that this was adequate.

RAILWAYS AND COLONIALISM

While fear of rabies can be viewed as representing English people's heightened sensibility of the internal disintegration of their own nation, does the high-speed rail link on which rabies supposedly rides modify this interpretation?

Railways are symbolic of a national heritage and hold a special place in the English imagination (Nock 1947: v). In no other country would you find the same number of hobbyists spending hour after hour "trainspotting," spending fortunes on Hornby model railways, and belonging to clubs that maintain old engines and run steam-train rides (see Whittaker 1997). One only has to walk into almost any bookshop and see the abundance of literature on railway history, or visit the new National Railway Museum in York, in order to realize the extent of this national obsession. If anything, this interest seemed to have escalated throughout 1993 and 1994 with the government's moves toward rail privatization, which is opening up to rail enthusiasts the possibility of owning their own rolling stock and rights to rail lines (see Lowe 1994).

Within Britain, railways played a dramatic historic role by functionally and symbolically altering the relationships between cities.[3] By 1848, one could travel by rail from Edinburgh to London. The reduction of travel times between towns and places led to an "enormous shrinkage in the national space" and instrumentally united the British nation (Thrift 1990: 463; Kellett 1969; Faith 1990: 58–70; Schivelbusch 1986). The first railway line was laid in the industrial north between Manchester and Liverpool. As railways developed and transformed the "whole surface of the land," they visually brought home to the wider population the impact of the Industrial Revolution (Barman 1950: 6). With mobility came the opening up of job opportunities and the rising economic power of the middle class. And in this transition, capitalism's accompanying ideology of individualism took hold, fundamentally disrupting the rural, and in a sense still feudal, social fabric (Faith 1990: 59). "The railway was the embodiment of the new equalitarian civilization of the towns" (Barman 1950: 26). Railways touched all dimensions of the physical and experienced landscape, altering how people moved through it and viewed it. "[T]he metropolitan

---

3. "[A] train is an extraordinary bundle of relations because it is something through which one goes, it is also something by means of which one can go from one point to another, and then it is also something that goes by," observes Foucault (1986: 23–24). Michel de Certeau likens the train to a form of incarceration. As the rail carriage hurtles along, passing through abstract spaces and illegible frontiers, the traveling individual leaves behind his/her proper place and in a sense is suspended in time, separated from reality. The train "not only divides spectators and beings, but also connects them; it is a mobile sym-bol [*sic*] between them, a tireless shifter, producing changes in the relationships between immobile elements" (1984: 113).

corridor objectified the ordered life, the life of the engineered future," John Stilgoe observes apropos of the United States. "Industrial zones, small-town depots, railway gardens, suburbs, even backyard vegetable gardens and lawns all drew characteristics from the railroad and its fabulous trains. For one half-century moment, the nation created a new sort of environment characterized by technically controlled order" (1983: 339).

Particularly in country areas, the coming of the railway was often met with violent and bitter opposition (Faith 1990: 35–57). In arguments that are strongly reminiscent of today's local reactions against the high-speed rail link to London, it was claimed that the new railway lines would carve up the fields like a knife and "brutally amputate every hill on their way" (Barman 1950: 25). Railways altered conventional perceptions of space and time, and in the process redefined the identities of localities: "The regions, joined to each other and to the metropolis by the railways, and the goods that are torn out of their local relation by modern transportation, shared the fate of losing their inherited place, their traditional spatial-temporal presence, or, as Walter Benjamin sums it up in one word, their 'aura'" (Schivelbusch 1986: 41).

Against these objections, the railway engineers and entrepreneurs stood firm. Apart from satisfying private investors, they saw their mission as one of improving the visual landscape. In 1837, the historian Arthur Freeling wrote that these engineering projects were things that "in their moral influence must affect the happiness and comfort of millions yet unborn," and another commentator suggested that the engineer's "will to conquest appears to be dominated by a deep 'sense of moral obligation to put the conquered territory to productive use'" (both quoted in Barman 1950: 35).

This moral overlay helped rationalize the extension of rail across Britain throughout the nineteenth century and introduce it to its wider empire. Perceived as a feat of universal progress, rail represented a revolution in international transport necessary to bring the rest of the world within European reach. The railway was the agent and primary generator of Britain's informal nineteenth-century colonial expansion, helping to stake out Britain's imperial territories, opening up its colonial markets and resources, and promoting investment and immigration (Robinson 1991: 1–6; Headrick 1988). Providing the means for both overseas integration and territorial annexation, it could be reasonably argued, railways were critical in shaping the colony-metropole relationship in almost every colonial context (see Davis and Wilburn 1991). Moreover, the enormous use of railways in the second half of the nineteenth century as a means of opening up new regions of exploitation in South America and southern Africa explicitly marks a shift in imperial vision away from a protectionist policy over dominions toward a free-trade economy of rampant exploitation.

Since they were as much a part of the nation's internal development as they were of empire-building (Robinson 1991: 4), railways integrally affected British politics. Analogous to the way in which Britain's internal railroads altered the distance between town and country, and hence the spatial organization of work, leisure, and domesticity, Britain's overseas railroads affected the spatial relations between the imperial power and its peripheral colonies. For as much as railways were a feature of Britain's nineteenth-century colonial expansion, they were also in a large way responsible for the empire's eventual demise. For instance, in the 1890s, Cecil Rhodes built a railroad north from Kimberley to Bulawayo and Salisbury (Harare) in a bid to take control of the territory that is now the Republic of Zimbabwe. However, once built, the railroad became the focus of a claim to independent power on the part of the settlers, giving first Rhodes's British South Africa Company (which was chartered to exploit the mineral resources of the region) and then, after 1923, the self-governing colony of Southern Rhodesia "more with which to bargain against the metropolis" (Hanes 1991: 65). "The railways proved crucial not only in the creation of the empire and efforts to maintain it, but also in shaping the successor states that replaced it," W. T. Hanes argues (ibid.: 44).

This brief discussion of British colonial railroading may hint at ways in which the rabies metaphor may be embellished by the image of the fast train on which it rides. The somewhat irrational public fear of rabies can be interpreted as embodying the English people's heightened sensibility of the internal disintegration of their own nation in the face of the encroaching New Europe. At the same time, the rabies fascination sustains the need for the island state's legal defense against external intervention. Thus the rabies scare expresses disillusionment in the establishing of ethnic harmony, which is intimately tied to England's future open borders with mainland Europe. What the image of the fast train does is to intensify this cultural anxiety and fear. By alluding to England's rail heritage, it evokes historical images of the railway's capacity to carve up the countryside in the nineteenth century, alter relations of distance between cities, towns, and villages, and ultimately centralize the industrial nation. But today, in the fast train's linking London to Paris and Brussels, these evocations of the national past are fundamentally distorted. New ground networks emphasize a theme of connection that is distinctly different from, yet reminiscent of, Britain's expansionist imperial history. This longer historical perspective provides the background to English anxiety about the Tunnel's potential for promoting transnational territorial integration. In the context of Europe's transport network and the penetration of the island nation, the fast train materially highlights a turning point in the shifting spatial relations between Brussels and an increasingly peripheral England.

EUROPEAN TRANSNATIONALISM

The fast train in Europe brings to the fore the issue of transnationalism, which is often interpreted as heralding the breakdown of the nation-state. Against this, I suggest that, somewhat paradoxically, transnationalism, which marks forces moving beyond and geographically transcending state boundaries, at the same time affirms that ideas of nation-state and national borders exist, and, to the extent that they can be transcended, are fixed. Transnationalism draws its meaning from, and so intrinsically reifies, a modernist theory of nation-building. In short, nationalism and transnationalism, in ways similar to colonialism and postcolonialism, are distinct but aligned processes (see Verdery 1994; Darian-Smith 1996).

This is not to argue, however, that the increasing scale of transnationalism does not pose particular problems and raise issues that challenge conventional institutions of modernity. My concern is in exploring the intersections between law and transnational activities, where the reification of modernist conceptions as they relate to law become overtly problematic. In this way I want to consider a presumption often made in transnational studies, which is that legal systems, while responding and adapting to new pressures, are nonetheless holistic, coherent, and state-bound. Transnational activity raises jurisdictional issues of cross-border legality. But in connecting new legal configurations such as immigration and trademark legislation, I suggest, what also needs to be explored is the very authority of law through which these new connections are made. Since transnationalism involves not only a confrontation of the nation-state with external forces, but also a confrontation of those external forces with the internal diversities within any one nation-state, how may transnational activities pose new questions about the nature of law, its sources of legitimation, its powers of inclusion and exclusion, and its ready conflation with particularized territories?

A brief examination of the creation of the nation-state in the nineteenth century suggests parallels with current transnational formations. The rise of the modern nation-state was essentially an imperialist project, requiring the idea of a distant other to consolidate internal state divisions. As outlined in chapter 3, no country better exemplifies this need than Britain, where the "protective shield of empire" was critical. The otherness of Europe, and even more so the colonial other, came to be popularized and domesticated, forming a central ideological force in smoothing over internal political, cultural, and class divisions and shaping everyday conceptions in the production of an authentic "British" community (Bhabha 1986: 153–56).

Following this argument, today's transnationalism can be interpreted as a neo-imperialist process, requiring as much as any form of nationalism an abstracted other through which to define itself as a coherent force. But in contrast with nationalism's location within the nation, what is interesting is that in the trans-nation, there is a greater willingness to acknowledge the integral presence of the other within (Fitzpatrick 1995b). In an essay entitled "Reluctant Euro-centrism," Hans Magnus Enzensberger discusses this converse position:

> [I]f a cultural other is no longer available, then we can just produce our own savages; technological freaks, political freaks, psychic freaks, cultural freaks, moral freaks, religious freaks. Confusion, unrest, ungovernability are our only chance. Disunity makes us strong. From now on we have to rely on our own resources. No Tahiti is in sight, no Sierra Maestra, no Sioux and no Long March. Should there be such a thing as a saving idea, then we'll have to discover it for ourselves.
> (Enzenberger 1990: 33)

The European Union is a conspicuous example of both trans-state formation and the potential of transnational "ungovernability." Driven by the need to redefine faltering member-state economies, national resources are being united in order that Europe may become a viable world power. In this way the EU embodies an ambitious new phase of global integration and cooperation. According to Charles Tilly, as seen from Eurasia, there have been numerous waves of political and economic globalization since the tenth century. Today's phase of globalization is certainly not the same as its historical predecessors, with technology and speed of communications characterizing its distinct difference. Nonetheless, there are parallels between today's globalization, which destabilizes the concept of nation-state, and that experienced in the nineteenth century, which resulted in the crystallization of the modern nation-state in conjunction with "a rush for empire" (Tilly 1994: 1).

These historical parallels become more concrete in the context of the EU's fast-train network. As already noted, in the second half of the nineteenth century, Britain quickly realized the capacity of railways to extend its colonial empire. Railways were used for the purposes of territorial annexation, primarily by imposing lines of integration on often fragmented and diverse conquered communities. In the context of the Channel Tunnel fast train, there is a clear sense that a transnational rail network is vital to enhance European integration. Mitterrand's comment that the Tunnel means that "the whole of Community Europe will have one nervous system," and that no one country will be able to run independently of the others, is a strong reminder of hopes for an interconnected transport system.

Drawing upon insights from its postcolonial heritage, what England most fears about this transport system linking it to the European mainland, and hence weakening its national borders, is not a sudden influx of rabies. Rather, the greatest anxiety for the English people and the British government is that the train, which Michel de Certeau calls a "tireless shifter" in the production of relational change (1984: 113), will alter spatial relations and the balance of power between the island nation and mainland Europe. And in this transitional reshuffling, the train may facilitate new political discourses and fundamentally affect the capacity of national governments to control their transportation systems and economies. Already the high-speed rail link, institutionalized through British, French, and EU law, contests the presumption of England's legal autonomy within its island-bound jurisdiction.

LEGAL SOVEREIGNTY AGAIN

Fear of the idea of a more integrated Europe reflects English fear for the country itself. And nowhere is this anxiety so well articulated as in the context of law and the issue of national legal sovereignty (Appadurai 1996b). The EU constitutes a new and authoritatively superior legal order binding its member states. Where EU law applies, notes Mary Robinson, a former president of Ireland, it has in effect brought into the national English system "a written constitution through the European back-door" (Robinson 1992: 138). She goes on to say that "in recent years there has been a realization that there must also be a possibility of different groups using the wider European framework, but using it in a way that penetrates right down to the local level. . . . I think there is a very strong movement at European level for more regional and local taking of decisions" (ibid.: 139).

The EU's constitutional challenge dislodges the ideology of England's legal autonomy. Europe creates an increasingly powerful legal forum through which Scottish, Welsh, Irish, and other, less territorially defined nationalisms may reform their relative positioning and significance inside and outside Britain. "Europe is somehow a way of Scotland getting into the world," observes the Scottish journalist and author Neal Ascherson (1992: 20), for example. Thus in shaking up legal relations within the country, the EU also introduces new cultural and political opportunities. Splinter groups in Britain can, in some cases, now appeal directly to Brussels and sidestep the centralized hierarchy of British state power. Admittedly, such appeals are somewhat limited. Nonetheless, the breakup of Britain by its multinational elements envisaged by Tom Nairn in the late 1970s is now being promoted by new forces of fragmentation (Nairn 1977; Anderson 1989: 35–50). Regionalism is increasingly being exploited through the EU's regional and structural fund schemes as a substitute for ethnonationalism, alongside the potential of the principle of subsidiarity and new institutions such as the European Committee of Regions (see chapter 7). It is these localized spatial reconfigurations of transnational activity, which both subdivide and extend the borders of England, that disrupt a modernist reading of law and legal meaning.

But how does this argument correlate with my earlier claim that nationalism and transnationalism should be considered, not as opposed political processes, but rather as interconnected and mutually sustaining? In pointing to how the nation-state is undergoing internal and external transnational challenges, I do not mean to suggest that as an institution it is on the way out. On the contrary, the heady claims for the nation-state's demise are now being revised and countered, particularly in Europe (see Milward 1992). Rather, what I argue is that it is not appropriate to analyze national versus transnational processes as though they were distinct, opposing, and mutually exclusive. Nor is it appropriate to presume that law is coherent, holistic, and state-bound. In the very connectedness of national and transnational processes, what should be recognized are the complex political and cultural shifts that underlie the contradictions of the coexisting endurance and vulnerability of law as an expression of national unity. In other words, that the state may well continue to override all other political structures is not questioned in my argument. But I ask how the state can maintain that position despite coexisting nationalisms and regional ventures both within and outside its borders that increasingly make use of multiple sources of legal legitimation. In short, strategies both endorsing and resisting transnationalism, and through such strategies the reflexive modification of what constitutes a legal system and legal sovereignty, may increasingly have to be recognized as problematizing our understandings of law.

CONCLUDING COMMENTS

In this chapter, I have treated the perceived threat of rabies, and the fast train on which rabies may ride, as a powerful and complex metaphor, the potency of which derives from the continuing significance of England's postcolonial heritage. Particularly important is the understanding that railways promoted both the rise of the British empire and its eventual demise.

Reacting against and through this postcolonial legacy, what many English people fear is that the EU's high-speed rail link will "colonize" the nation, and alter its spatial, legal, and political relations with Europe. This means a national subordination to EU law and, more important, suggests the internal fragmentation and reconstitution of what is defined as England, as against mainland Europe. In Kent, the completion of the Channel Tunnel and early work on the high-speed rail link to London have generated legal challenges and changes. In particular, the Kent County Council's involvement in the control of the Tunnel through the creation of the Euroregion uniting it with Nord–Pas de Calais, Flanders, Wallonia, and Brussels points to the development of more accessible channels for local government control and legal reform through the EU. I take up these issues in the next chapter. What I have stressed here is that infrastructural possibilities do already exist for heightening awareness of Kent as a new form of regional entity not categorized as English or contained by the state. In short, the Tunnel and rail link practically illustrate an instance of the wider jurisdictional limitations of British, and more specifically English, law.

The historical parallels between imperial Britain and a transnational Europe are illuminating and insightful. While the two entities cannot be equated, like Britain, the EU today is primarily an economic and commercial venture, with fluid, vulnerable, and contested borders. Like Britain, the EU seeks to consolidate multiple nationalisms, not so much through internal cohesion as by imposing a single institutional frame, legal system, and citizenry that create exclusivity vis-à-vis the rest of the world. Unfortunately, the EU, like Britain, has not fully reconciled the promise of modernity to transcend cultural differences with its failure to do so. And so the EU may in the future have to cope with painful conflicts that accompany an institutionalization of democracy without either populist consensus or territorial solidity. Perhaps, as has often been argued, there are no easy solutions, and cultural and political struggles at the level of state, region, and city are inevitable in Europe. If this is the case, it is no wonder that the British government and many English people do not view the Channel Tunnel, symbolic of the EU's neo-imperialist integration and territorial annexation, with the same optimism as their European counter-parts. England's postcolonial legacy is forever present and suggests the ominous internal presence of further social fragmentation. Rabies riding the fast train may be useful as an interpretative metaphor, but it represents real fears of impending radical change.

7 Locating a Reinvigorated Kentish Identity

New Connections, New Divisions

A NEW KENTISH IDENTITY?

Today, Kentish identity represents many different things to different people. Some academics at the University of Kent in Canterbury—particularly in the anthropology department—assured me that a Kentish identity did not exist. Steve Dawe, the Green party candidate for East Kent who ran for the European parliamentary elections in May 1994, strongly declared, however, that the academics at the university live "in a village up there on the hill, and have no sense of what really goes on in any way." According to Dawe, there is a sense of Kentish solidarity, which "is a remarkably strong identity and should not be underestimated when something controversial comes up" (interview, 7 Mar. 1994). In his view, actions around the conservation of land highlighted this Kentish sensibility. He spoke of a petition of 10,000 local residents protesting the Shepway Council's plan to destroy the largest remaining single tract of English forest in 1993:

> I went to this fantastic meeting where local people basically turned up—there were hundreds of people—and this chairman of Shepway Council . . . was trying to defend his position of ignoring the petition. There were a number of features to it all. One is that these people were bloody well going to keep their forest and no one was going to stop them. That feeling was very strong. But there was also a feeling that our job as a community was not only to protect our immediate vicinity. The general question of protecting Kent came up again and again. Now I was very active in London for a number of years. But people

there would never talk about protecting London, or even parts of it! It wasn't expressed in those terms. But this business of protecting the long-term interests of people in Kent is a very strong emotion.

(interview, 7 Mar. 1994)

Hazel McCabe, the former mayor of Canterbury, herself a Conservative, confirmed this strong sense of Kentish identity:

I can't speak for a lot of people but I think particularly as Kentish people, at the back of our minds there always is that we've been an island and withstood quite a lot of nasties over the centuries, and I suspect we feel we are losing something—and I know that this may seem very parochial and all the rest of it, but that is at the bottom of it somewhere. We have a strong history of independence, and Kent was a kingdom, and that's why we have the white horse Invicta as the Kent motto because we never surrendered to the Normans.

(interview, 20 Jan. 1994)

Of course it is almost impossible to articulate what the Kentish identity is and how to recognize it. As pointed out to me by Steve Dawe's wife, Hazel, "you have a coast identity and a town identity and a rural identity all criss-crossing here" (interview, 7 Mar. 1994). And compounding the complexities between local communities within Kent are the external contexts through which these local negotiations are played out—namely, an encroaching and omnipresent London to the north, and the increasingly interventionist European Union to the east. And these two sources of pressure are not mutually exclusive nor unrelated to the operation of each other.

What can be said with some confidence is that there is currently a heightened consciousness of Kent as a regional entity, distinct from London, that is not determined by political party lines. In the county paper *Kent Messenger*, this question of Kentish identity was expressly addressed in February 1994, when there were calls for a restructuring of local government. According to the bishop of Maidstone, "Clearly Kent is one of the oldest Kingdoms we know in this country. If it is split into unitary authorities, the historical reality will vanish" (*Kent Messenger*, 11 Feb. 1994, p. 54). Lord Kingsdown backed up this sentiment:

I think there is a Kent character. I think that people have a special sense of the special position we occupy geographically. . . . If you look at Kent's history and geography, you can see it's different from any other county in England in a substantial way. . . . in our county's history, it has either received invasion, like the Romans, or resisted invasions, at the time of Napoleon and the last war. The modern equivalent of that, in my view, is both taking responsibility and reacting to the enormous demands that are made by cross-Channel traffic.

(*Kent Messenger*, 11 Feb. 1994, p. 54)

Such political rhetoric has to be set against the results of a Market & Opinion Research International (MORI) poll of Kent residents, which indicated that Kent commands more loyalty than many other English counties, but also that people's first loyalties are to their town and village rather than to the county. Perhaps as a counter to this, the Kent County Council published a list of reasons why Kent is unique among counties, which include, amongst other things:

It is England's front line. In the second World War the Battle of Britain was fought above the fields of Kent.

Kent is a peninsula. The sea forms much of its border. This has helped make the county feel separate from the rest of the South.

Nowhere else in Britain has such strong links with the Continent. People in Kent travel to France regularly, people living elsewhere do not.

There was a Kingdom of Kent in the Dark Ages when the county was a bastion of the Jutes. The rest of England was run by the Angles and the Saxons.

Christianity arrived in England via Kent. St. Augustine was received by the Kentish King Ethelbert in the year 597.

William the Conqueror did not conquer Kent. He had to reach an agreement with its people: hence the motto Invicta [unconquered].

(*Kent Messenger*, 11 Feb. 1994, p. 54)

Against this list's reiteration of a mythologized historical past, another impulse currently informing Kentish identity speaks to a much more open and flexible future. Particularly among younger generations who have no clear memories of World War II, there is a more open receptivity to and enthusiasm for change. This sentiment was often reaffirmed for me when I went swimming each morning at a private school in Canterbury that made its pool available to the general public. Here I struck up relationships with some of the young people in their late teens who worked at the swimming center. We had lots of conversations about what they wanted to do with their future, how much they wanted to travel, and the new cultural and economic opportunities represented by the EU. In contrast to many older people whom I talked to in the security of their own kitchens and gardens, this younger generation appeared full of excitement and enthusiasm for the new system precisely because it is in the process of developing before their very eyes.

In education, there are escalating opportunities for cultural exchange, and among school programs, links between Kent and Calais are rapidly expanding. Children go across the Channel to learn French, receive French friends into their homes, learn French history, and generally are encouraged to take an active interest in EU developments. Kent County Council has been prominent in promoting change. Given the recognized centrality of geographical education in the creation of a national identity (Foucault 1980: 73–74), it is revealing that the Kent County Council has its own geography curriculum consultant. According to this consultant, Marcia Foley:

> Schools with a strong European dimension and proximity to north east France will want to include it as part of their "home region." If you live in Dover and your mum or dad has been working on a cross-Channel ferry or may be soon employed driving a Channel Tunnel shuttle from Cheriton to the Coquelles terminal, then north east France is much more part of your home's region than Essex.
> (*Kent Messenger*, 12 Nov. 1993, p. 12)

These links between Kent and Nord–Pas de Calais are also occurring through cultural organizations and music exchanges, such as the Education Art Link, the Cross Channel Photographic Mission, and a constant crossing of theater and dance groups from mainland Europe into Kent. And it is also happening at the level of business with networks such as the East Kent Initiative, cross-Channel farmers' cooperatives, English companies opening up offices in Calais, and the vast number of twinning schemes between Kent villages and European villages sponsored by groups such as the Kent Rural Community Council through their European Partners Competition. Indicative of wider changes is the seriousness with which these twinning schemes are approached.[1] Often representatives of local municipalities come together to sign an official treaty, usually somewhere aboard a ferry symbolically moored in mid-Channel, and double receptions are often presided over by a member of the European Parliament. Canterbury's chief executive, Christopher Gay, affirmed the development of these schemes:

1. More than 1.5 million Europeans, in 4,000 towns, have so far been involved in town twinning, which has an EU budget of 10 million ecus for 1998.

Each town has a twin; we are twinned with Rheims, Whitstable and
Herne Bay have separate relationships, and so on, and all these things
tend to be done on a voluntary basis not run by council. One particularly good link has been set up between Herne Bay and a town just
outside Bologne. These are two seaside towns, both with the desire to
do works to beautify their seafronts and provide related facilities, and
it has been a very good relationship, developed effortlessly and people
have got on very well.

(interview, 21 Dec. 1993)

In my conversations with Gay, we talked about the impact of the EU
on England, Kent, and Canterbury, as well as popular Kentish reactions to
Europe. We returned again and again to the origin of the anxiety that
characterized these complex relations. "I think it is because we are next to
France, which is the traditional foe in some way, that makes it more difficult to get over the joining of Europe. Maybe if we were physically next
to Italy or Spain, it wouldn't be so difficult," he said (interview, 21 Dec.
1993). Which begs a question: isn't proximity key to the construction of
France as England's traditional adversary?

This feature of spatial proximity points to another issue. Although England's traditional foe, France has also been its ally in two world wars.
Now with the threat of war between England and France virtually eliminated, in a large part owing to the European Union, the clandestine relations that have always existed between Kent and Calais are no longer of
any marked significance. In fact, with the opening up of borders and the
increasing cross-Channel traffic, Kent is getting more and more squeezed
between London and northern France. No longer able to draw upon its
nineteenth-century identity as an English resort coast (Urry 1990: 16–39),
or upon its historical separateness from England through its independent
relations with France, Kent communities are reinventing their older essentializing image as the Garden of England. Of course, other less prominent images of Kent are also being promoted, such as its advantages for
the relocation of service industries, light manufacturing, and agricultural
enterprises. Yet more important than which particular identity of Kent is
more widely promoted than another is that increasingly the impulse of
change beats strongly across the water from Brussels in the east, and not
from London in the north.

In this chapter, I explore some of the new connections and divisions
emerging in Kent that have in part been brought about by the building of
the Channel Tunnel. As a result of increasing communications across the
Channel and the attenuation of national jurisdictional borders, broad

changes are occurring both in the institutional frame of the European Union and informally through personal networks. In contrast to the feeling of despair expressed by many Kent residents at the signing of the Channel Tunnel Treaty in 1986 (see chapter 5), today, in the late 1990s, there is a new sense of optimism about the opportunities being opened up by the EU. Transnational exchanges between people living in Kent and on the European mainland now characterize local businesses and educational and cultural programs in towns such as Canterbury. For many people in Kent, the presence of the EU is becoming more accepted and acceptable over time.

However, simultaneously with the increasing connections between people and places on either side of the Channel, new boundaries are emerging and old divisions are being redefined. Kent is experiencing a need to reclaim its own identity and to assert its own independence as a region within England and a borderland with France. In chapter 2, I analyzed the apparent retreat to the ideal of a localized community through reaffirmation of Kent's historical claim to be the Garden of England. In the following sections of this chapter, I return to the theme of a reintensification of local identity and localized narratives as a central feature of postmodernity (Harvey 1989; Lyotard 1984; Ley 1989). My focus is on some of the very new methods by which Kent people are claiming independence for themselves, which have only become available under the increasing impact of the EU on Kent. What I suggest is that historical narratives are being revamped and merged with new political and economic strategies into a dynamic, complex mix of local, regional, national, and transnational exchanges.

Having begun this chapter by describing how some Kent residents are expressly trying to define themselves as Kentish, and looking at what it might mean to have a "Kentish identity," I switch gears to examine EU politics and law, which are changing the Kent County Council's local forms of government. Specifically, the EU has been critical in helping Kent create a trans-border administration over the past decade. From this level of transnational policy and law, I move again to local changes and focus upon the revitalization in Kent of the ritual called "beating the bounds." Finally, I discuss the introduction into Kent by the EU of a new crop, rapeseed, which has dramatically altered the aesthetics of Kent's country landscape. Like the Tunnel itself, the growing of rape (*Brassica napus*), a crop of the mustard family, underscores the presence of the European Union on English soil. Throughout these explorations, my aim is to highlight the myriad ways in which Kentish people and their respective localized identities are increasingly being pulled into the EU's orbit, and how this ultimately affects social practices and what we construe as law.

My oscillation between so-called "global" and "local" spheres of action is deliberate, if somewhat confusing. There now exists a great deal of theoretical literature on local and global politics within which an analysis of Kent, England, Britain, and Europe can be situated. Yet much of this work takes for granted that we all recognize and know what "local" and "global" mean and represent. On the one hand, formal institutional change is presumed to operate at the global level, while on the other hand, personal perceptions relating to cultural identity and subjective interpretation of place occur at local levels. The problem with this model is that global (structure) and local (agency) are too often neatly distinguished as separate processes. In fact, these arenas of exchange and transition are interdependent. For despite the appearance of local and global as extreme opposites, they depend upon and mutually define each other.

The following analysis of activities in Kent over the past decade suggests that it is impossible to differentiate spatially where the global ends and the local begins, and what gets bracketed within these categories (see Buchanan 1995, 1996; Santos 1995; Darian-Smith 1996, 1998; Cvetkovich and Kellner 1997; Brenner 1997). Instead, I argue that new connections and new divisions are constantly being forged in push-and-pull relational processes that redefine the meanings people attribute to Kent's place in the New Europe. These meanings, of course, shift across the global/local continuum according to the various perspectives, at any particular moment, of any one individual. But what they underscore are the explicit challenges to the modernist notion that there is one law relevant to any one agent, that this is the nation-state's law, and that it correlates to a unified legal system within a particular state territory that itself has a unified identity.

LOCAL GOVERNMENT IN THE NEW EUROPE

The Channel Tunnel provided the political and economic impetus for Kent County Council to take advantage of the new opportunities for local government bodies introduced by the EU. The history of local government in England is long and complicated, and there is an abundance of literature on the subject. What is important here is that throughout the 1980s, Thatcherism created an increasingly more powerful central government to the detriment of local councils. At the same time, Kent County Council's involvement in Brussels in the 1980s illustrates that local government can increasingly bypass London and to an extent operate with a measure of independence.

Christopher Gay discussed with me the relations between national and local government from his perspective as representative of a small city:

> Those of us working in local government had no strong love for Margaret Thatcher because she was perceived as somebody who very much looked down on local government. . . . there has been a process of centralization going on in this country, and the last major step was in education, where what was one of our major functions in local government was being rapidly eroded away by this business of funding schools directly from Whitehall. . . . I am not sure if people realize the implications of it, but it is [Prime Minister John] Major's latest thing in a long campaign of centralization. Our Parliament seems to be obsessed with sovereignty issues—they are so sort of terrified that their powers are going to Europe that they are grabbing them all back from local governments.
>
> (interview, 21 Dec. 1993)

Earlier, in 1986, the Greater London Council (GLC) was abolished by the Thatcher government and its powers were distributed among thirty-two London boroughs, much to the consternation of Labour supporters (Rhodes 1991: 88; see Welfare 1992).[2] The abolishing of the GLC was symbolic of widespread restructuring of local government by Thatcher. Power was spread thinly among many local authorities, whose financial resources were increasingly controlled by the central government. Expenditure targets and financial penalties were introduced that further reduced the autonomy of local bodies (Preston 1992: 113; Buck et al. 1989). This forced local governments to raise local tax rates, which were eventually replaced by a national poll tax in 1990, further diminishing the freedom of local authorities and creating widespread public outrage (Gibson 1992: 67–76). At the same time that local financial responsibility was curtailed, more and more welfare responsibilities were thrust onto local governments through the privatization of local services (Pickvance 1991: 68–85; Marsh and Rhodes 1992: 37–40). Thatcher's streamlining of local bodies included what has been called a strategy of "placelessness" (Johnston 1991: 245), which sought to eliminate all local and regional variations in policy. Throughout the 1980s and early 1990s, increasing centralization led to a

---

2. Note, however, the discussion in chapter 5 of the introduction of a mayor of London as mandated by referendum on 5 May 1998.

general sense of crisis in the relations between the central and local governments.

One consequence of the changes in central-local government relations in England is that both spheres have become increasingly politicized. These alterations have corroded former ideals of cooperation and coordination and the customary limits on central government. Ten major acts of Parliament were introduced during the 1980s to curb the power of local governments,[3] forcing local authorities to consciously reevaluate their role as employers, regulators, and administrative bodies (Loughlin 1986: 191). According to Martin Loughlin, the legal relationship between the central and local bodies, which had previously been of minor significance, became critical throughout the 1980s and 1990s.

> Local authorities have been required to examine closely the nature of their legal powers and duties because expenditure constraints cause them to re-examine the pattern of their activities and also because the law defines the parameters of their formal autonomy. Central departments are concerned about their legal powers because they outline the limits of their available power to control local authorities. In this sense, the collapse of traditional administrative arrangements results in juridificiation of the central-local relationship.
>
> (ibid.: 193)

EUROPEAN INFLUENCE ON BRITAIN'S LOCAL GOVERNMENT

The rupture in relations between Britain's central and local governments was accompanied by the perception of encroachment by the Europe Union, as reflected in Councilor Gay's remarks. Surprisingly, the impact of the EU is still often unappreciated in commentaries on British local government (e.g., Kingdom 1991). But as much as central government practices cannot be understood without attention being given to their implementation at the local level, so too the intervention of the EU throughout

---

3. Under the Local Government Act of 1972, all local authorities (with the exception of the City of London) are created by statute and so have no independent legal status. Theoretically, this means that local authorities are entirely subject to the central government, which can add to or detract from local powers by passing legislation. Thatcher took full advantage of local authorities' legal vulnerability in enacting the Local Government and Planning Act of 1980, Housing Act of 1980, Local Government (Interim Provisions) Act of 1984, Rates Act of 1984, Local Government Act of 1985, Local Government Finance Act of 1988, Education Reform Act of 1988, Local Government Act of 1988, Housing Act of 1988, and Local Government and Housing Act of 1989.

English and British government has to be taken into account. This is despite the refusal of the British government to sign the European Charter of Local Self-Government (1986),[4] and despite the assertion of Michael Portillo, British minister of local government in 1990, that "[l]ocal government is not a suitable subject for regulation by an international convention" (quoted in Crawford 1992: 69).

By the end of the 1970s, a number of English local authorities, including some in Kent, had close informal relations with bureaucrats in Brussels. This steadily increased, with some local bodies establishing offices there. Kent County Council was one of the first to take advantage of these informal processes and established a department in Brussels in 1987. It became increasingly apparent that British local authorities could both lobby Brussels to apply pressure on Whitehall and seek EU support for projects of explicitly local significance:

> There is no doubt that the link between EC powers and the local government authorities is becoming greater in terms of substantive issues. On the one hand . . . powers will be transferred to the European level, "reinforcing trends towards supranational decision-making and curtailing local and regional autonomy in specific fields." On the other hand, Europe has sometimes found it useful to bypass recalcitrant central governments of member states and deal directly with local governments, such as in the area of regional assistance.
>
> (Crawford 1992: 83; also see Duchacek 1986)

The EU explicitly calls into question its member states' conventional central and local governmental frameworks. In short, it is no longer possible to accept as given a hierarchy in which local governments are exclusively subject to a central national state system. Of course, this raises further questions about what constitutes sovereignty (Appadurai 1996b; Rosas 1993; MacCormick 1993; Wæver et al. 1993: 68–71; Camilleri and Falk 1992: 4, 98; Santos 1992: 134). New forms of politics, new centers of power, new conceptions of social space, and how these spaces relate to multiple layers of legal meaning, simultaneously show that the concept of sovereignty is changing. Today, "it seems obvious that no state in Western Europe any longer is a sovereign state," despite John Major's declaration in the House of Commons as recently as 1993 that "[t]he sovereignty of this House is not up for grabs" (MacCormick 1993: 1, 8).

The shift in legal and political relations between central and local governments is most evident since the Maastricht Treaty of 1992, which in-

4. Ireland is the only other EU member not to have signed.

troduced both the Committee of Regions and the principle of subsidiarity, both aimed at creating a new balance of power more favorable to local authorities. At this stage it is difficult to determine how effective these measures will be in altering conventional center/periphery state relations. Nonetheless, the Committee of Regions and the subsidiarity principle are significant in that they procedurally and theoretically formalize a shifting relationship between national capitals and local authorities in the New Europe. Certainly, these innovations have attracted a great deal of attention in Scotland and Wales, where many people are anxious to reassert their independence of English political institutions. Also encouraging a growing sense of regional independence has been the shift in government policy toward decentralization and devolution of state power initiated by Tony Blair and his Labour party. In 1997, Scottish voters voted overwhelmingly for the return of their own parliament and its right to raise taxes. The referendum subsequently in Wales was not nearly so dramatic a success, with the "yes" vote for devolution just coming out ahead. Nonetheless, despite concerns about the full implications of a transfer of power to regional entities, people in Wales and Scotland are envisioning new opportunities in their future relationships with London and Europe.

THE COMMITTEE OF REGIONS AND THE
PRINCIPLE OF SUBSIDIARITY

Under the authority of the Single European Act (1986), the European Parliament promoted the establishment of the Consultative Council of Regional and Local Authorities in 1988. For the first time, local governments in Europe now meet with the European Commission to discuss policy initiatives and general issues of regional concern. This Consultative Council also works with the two main European organs involved in local affairs, the Council of European Municipalities and Regions (which has existed in some form since 1952 and creates a vertical dialogue between regions and EU institutions), and the Assembly of European Regions (established in 1985 to create a horizontal network among regions). The Assembly of European Regions operates as the first tier of government below the national level and treats English and Scottish counties as de facto regions on a par with large-scale authorities on the European mainland (Barber and Millns 1993: 3).

Regions, as social and spatial constructs and political paradigms, have a complicated history in Europe. What is clear is that despite Britain's denigration of the region as an important administrative and political entity (Harvie 1991, 1994: 63, 724), a strengthening regionalism in Europe potentially undermines the central dominance of national governments (Thrift 1995; Salem 1991; Amin and Thrift 1994; Murphy 1993; Kearney 1993; Albrechts et al. 1989; Marquand 1991; Mellors and Copperthwaite 1990). In recent years, regions have emerged in even greater focus with discussion of the function and possible impact of the Committee of Regions. Created as a consultative body under the Maastricht Treaty in 1992, the committee has 222 elected members, who are in principle officials most immediately accountable to EU citizens, and whose main goal is to involve the regions and localities as much as possible in the design and implementation of EU policies. It is still too early to anticipate the long-term influence of the Committee of Regions. Regional politicians, especially representatives of the German Länder and the Spanish Comunidades Autónomas, hope to transform it into an organ with direct decision-making powers alongside the Council of Ministers and the European Parliament. However, the Committee of Regions' position is juridically weak since it can only give advisory opinions to the commission or council when the competencies of regions are affected or in the case of trans-European networks that involve economic, social and cultural regional interrelations (Maastricht Treaty, arts. 126[4], 128[5], 129c, and 130b, d, and e).

One of the most significant contributions of the Committee of Regions is that it embodies the principle of subsidiarity in a move to make the EU more accountable and so more legitimate in the eyes of ordinary people (Armstrong 1993; Norton 1992; Schaefer 1991). Very simply, the purpose of the subsidiarity principle is to bring the processes of decision-making closer to citizens by allowing local governments to make decisions in appropriate instances. Article 3b of the Maastricht Treaty (1992) says:

> In areas which do not fall within its exclusive competence [i.e., security, monetary, and trade matters, etc.], the Community shall take action, in accordance with the principle of subsidiarity, only if and in so far as the objectives of the proposed action cannot be sufficiently achieved by the Member States and can therefore, by reason of the scale or the effects of the proposed action, be better achieved by the Community.

Since subsidiarity implies a vertical division of political power, it has been referred to as the basic characteristic of federalism. However, its conceptual ambiguity, such that it could be used by the EU to increase its sovereign powers as much as to redistribute them to subnational entities, makes it questionable whether it can ever become justiciable and so constitute a ground for reviewing the legality of actions taken by the council or the commission. Still, some analysts do see subsidiarity as a principle of noncentralization, and so a way of institutionalizing direct contacts between the EU and substate governments, including interest groups and citizens, without too much concern for the opinions of member states (Emilliou 1994: 67). How subsidiarity will play out in the future is a question of much debate. Certainly at the level of local and regional governments, it has raised many hopes, and perhaps nowhere more so than in England, where local governments experienced a steady decline of their relative autonomy under the Conservative party, which governed Britain for eighteen years between 1979 and 1997.

KENT COUNTY COUNCIL IN BRUSSELS: CREATING THE EUROREGION

The principle of subsidiarity in a sense formalizes an evolving and deepening relationship between some English local authorities and the EU's administrative offices in Brussels. In the mid 1980s, as fears mounted in England about the effects of the Tunnel, and as Britain's central authority refused all economic responsibility for needed infrastructural improvements, the Kent County Council decided it had to act for itself. Accordingly, in 1987, it established a European Operations Unit. "There are no regions in the UK, and there was no chance under a Conservative government that regions would be created. Yet within Europe there is no doubt that we are heading towards a Europe of Regions. So what KCC did was to go and create our own region," Stephen Barber, head of the KCC's European Operations Unit, told me (interview, 19 Nov. 1993).

KCC agents in Brussels thereupon negotiated with the Conseil Régional du Nord–Pas de Calais and signed a cooperation agreement with it in April 1987 that resolved "to promote as far as possible across the border the development and strengthening of the friendship and ties which already unite the populations of their two regions . . . [and to] contribute thus to the economic and social progress of the two border regions and to the solidarity which unites the people of Europe." This agreement was formalized to create the Transmanche Region, joining Kent and Nord–Pas de Calais (map 3), which received a grant of £6 million from the EU's Interreg Agency in 1989 for cross-border projects.[5]

5. Getting this grant was quite a coup, given that prior to this, Interreg had almost exclusively targeted land borders. To date, Kent has been the only area in Britain to attract benefits under the Interreg cross-border scheme, although there

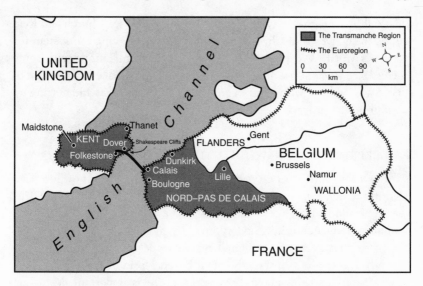

Map 3. The Transmanche Region and the Euroregion, incorporating Kent, Nord–Pas de Calais, Flanders, Wallonia, and Brussels Capital. Courtesy of Dirk Brandts.

In 1991, the Transmanche Region was reconstituted to form a new Euroregion with the addition of the three Belgian regions of Flanders, Wallonia, and Brussels Capital. The Euroregion is more extensive in its networks and powers than the Transmanche Region, and its larger institutional and administrative framework qualifies it as an Economic Interest Group. This in turn provides it with a legal status sanctioned by the EU, easing "the problems which would otherwise stem from collaboration within a multitude of different legal systems and regulations" (Sinclair and Page 1993: 482; see also Martin and Pearce 1993). With 15.5 million inhabitants, the Euroregion is one of the most densely populated areas in Europe, and it is often called the "heartland" of Europe. Although it also handles tourism, employment, transport, and spatial planning, the Euroregion authority is particularly concerned with the environment. On the basis of Interreg funding and the securing of other European regional development funds, Kent County Council and its cooperative partners on the European mainland had secured well over £35 million pounds from the EU for trans-border programs by the mid 1990s. The Euroregion initiative has also brought to the attention of other local British authorities the

now are strong bids being made by other areas, including Sussex, Portsmouth, Wales, and Merseyside.

financial benefits that may be gleaned from the EU (see Church and Reid 1994). In the words of Christopher Gay: "We are playing the system for what it's worth. We have been getting grants from Europe with some success recently, and we are regrouping ourselves to make what we can of that, forming links with cities in Nord–Pas de Calais areas and putting up joint projects" (interview, 21 Dec. 1993).

FINGERPRINTING A NEW IDENTITY?

All this cross-border activity may perhaps increase a sense of European identity among Kent residents. Some critics have argued that the Euroregion "could look, in a few years time, like a Channel Tunnel state, with innumerable bilateral links underpinned by multilateral trade flows, and the possibility, even, of a bilingual culture, at least in the younger generation" (Robinson 1990: 71). Stephen Barber, head of the KCC's European Operations Unit, noted, however, that "it is important not to get carried away, because despite what [European Commission President Jacques] Delors says, our lives are not going to be dramatically changed, and in ten years' time, it is still going to be a British way of life" (interview, 19 Nov. 1993).

Nevertheless, there certainly exists a new awareness of Kent as a regional entity neither categorized as English nor contained entirely by the present British state. Kent and Nord–Pas de Calais market themselves to foreign investors as a single region, and international travel agents are beginning to promote the region "as a single overseas holiday destination." As part of a frontier region with France and Belgium, and as a co-recipient of EU funds with the other territories of the Euroregion, Kent is in many small ways somewhat independent of the rest of Britain. In effectively extending Britain's border across the Channel with the sanction of EU law, Kent County Council has reconfigured both the country's spatial territory and its political, economic, and social positions. At the same time, it has challenged the concept of the bounded territory of the state, which Max Weber, among others, has argued to be a critical characteristic of modern statehood (Weber 1946: 78).

The Euroregion's logo, designed by a team from Nord–Pas de Calais, is a thumbprint, and when I asked Stephen Barber the reason for using such an image, he suggested that it symbolized the uniqueness of the Euroregion, and that its shape matched the region's geographical area. However, the common French idiom *donner un coup de pouce*—literally, "to give a hit of the thumb"—means "to give a boost to" or "to nudge in the right direction," and this is most likely what the Francophone designers of the logo intended it to convey. The thumbprint brings to mind the use of passports as a mechanism of classification and social control by modern nation-states to govern the borders of exclusive and inclusive territories (Foucault 1977; Torpey 1995). In any event, in marking out a new political and legal space, Kent and the local authorities in France and Belgium have represented themselves as a distinctly new area, encompassing particular challenges and needs, largely generated by the building of the Channel Tunnel. In these ways, Kent County Council has consciously acted against the strategy of "placelessness" imposed by Britain's former Conservative government, making it safe to say that in this instance, "Central government consistently failed to anticipate the responses of local authorities and pressed ahead with policies which often produced the opposite of what was intended" (Marsh and Rhodes 1992: 47).

BEATING THE BOUNDS

While many of the economic and political links being forged by Kent County Council with the wider Euroregion may pass unnoticed by the majority of Kent residents, indirectly these connections do have significant local repercussions. With the EU's penetration, which has greatly enhanced the power of British local governments, there is a concurrent move by some people in Kent to retreat to reassuring rituals of localism and community. One of these is the current revival of a peculiar ceremony called "beating the bounds." What is significant about this ritual to do with land is that it is one way of "laying down" the law locally that does not necessarily bear a clear relationship with either the British nation-state's legal system or that of the New Europe.

According to the historian John Brand, in his *Observations on the Popular Antiquities of Great Britain*, written in 1795, beating the bounds has its origins in the Roman festival of the god Terminus, who was considered the guardian of fields and landmarks and the keeper of peace among men (Brand 1795; Reed 1984). It occurred on the third day before Ascension Day, when the minister, churchwardens, choir boys, and local community would processionally walk around the limits of the parish, and stop to beat the white boundary stones with willow wands and chant litanies beside them.[6] The procession blessed nature's bounty. More important, it rein-

6. There are numerous variations on this theme. For instance, the opening scene in Thomas Hardy's *Tess of the d'Urbervilles* depicts a women's club that, for hundreds of years, has walked in an annual "processional march of two and two

forced a sense of justice and local authority by marking property rights and the property owner's responsibilities to the parish poor. According to Brand:

> These religious processions mark out the limits of certain portions of land, under which the whole kingdom is contained; and in all these the principle of God's fee is recognized by the law and the people. The . . . church-rate is admitted as due throughout the bounds, and the tithes, also as a charge on the parish; but, together with these admissions, there is formed in the mind a mental boundary, and a sacred restraint is placed upon the consciences of men, that co-mingles religious awe with the institution of the landed right and landed inheritance, and family succession to it. . . . The walking of the parish bounds on the *gang-days*, in religious procession, very materially contributed to form and keep fresh in the mind of each passing generation the terms on which property was held, and some of the duties belonging to the holding.
>
> (Brand 1795: 197–98)

In reinforcing local knowledge about land and clarifying community responsibilities, beating the bounds helped sustain a "mental boundary" around the parish and confirm people's places in society as laborers or manor lords.[7] In times when parish boundaries were rarely created by statute or evidenced in writing, unless the bounds were occasionally patrolled, this knowledge might be lost. Those who lived beyond the village were "savage," while insiders were "civilized." Critical to the endurance of these identity distinctions was the capacity of the village to define its

---

round the parish. . . . In addition to the distinction of a white frock, every woman and girl carried in her right hand a peeled willow wand, and in her left a bunch of white flowers" (Hardy 1891: 6–7).

7. In England, beating the bounds affirmed a lord's duties to his poor tenants, as well as the peasants' right to bring their lord to trial through an established system of manorial courts. The terms of this reciprocal relationship and the balance of hierarchical power shifted significantly throughout the seventeenth and eighteenth centuries (Holmes 1962; Williamson and Bellamy 1987). But there are enough cases on record to suggest that the threat of legal redress by the poor against their superiors had some force (Daniels 1988: 45; Drescher 1964: 91). Thus continuities of custom allowed poorer people to stand their ground, assert their inherited rights, and to take "combative, socially-critical and threatening roles" (Bushaway 1992: 130; and see also King 1989). In this way, throughout premodern England and into the eighteenth century, beating the bounds exemplified a set of mutual social relations and a powerful legal ideology that went beyond the realm of property rights in legitimating peasant and emerging working-class activities. This in turn informed popular notions of justice in social contexts that transcended parish limits (Bushaway 1992: 114; and see Thompson 1991, pl. ix).

local constituency. Beating the bounds was a public spectacle designed to demarcate who had rights (or not) to charity, access to common lands, and historically to a lord's knights for military protection. "Those within the boundary were a part of a particular moral world and those without were outsiders" (Bushaway 1992: 126). This moral dimension of insider/outsider is disclosed in written records of beating the bounds, where a slippage of word use between "processioning" and "possessioning" is often found. This slippage suggests that in a particular way, the local community belonged to, or was in the possession of, the parish. In many ways, the performative ritual stressed that a relational sense of locality was inextricably bound up with a moral and legal code of rights identifying community members. Beating the bounds helped solidify social relations within the local community.[8] This consolidation was important, given that England's medieval system of feudal tenure was based on a hierarchy of reciprocity and exchange. Thus beating the bounds was one of numerous rituals that helped establish people's place in society and their mutual responsibilities.[9]

BEATING THE BOUNDS IN 1994

Mr. Humphreys, a retired lawyer living in Barham, Kent, is something of a local expert on beating the bounds, having written an article on it in the *Kent News*, published by the Kent branch of the Council for the Protection of Rural England (CPRE). He explained that the article was written because the custom was "of topical interest" to a Kent audience, since "there were quite a lot of parishes doing it last year" (interview, 25 Feb. 1994).[10] Ac-

8. Parishes by definition had a church and were the basic units of ecclesiastical jurisdiction. On average, they contained 300 to 400 people. Thus town parishes were cramped compared to those in agricultural communities. Whether in towns or villages, the importance of beating the bounds was that it ensured that property owners provided for the parish poor and, as a corollary to this, that small communities retained a measure of local authority and autonomy (Holmes 1962: 42, 59–67).

9. In many ways, it calls to mind Evans-Pritchard's description of the Shilluk marching around the northern bounds of the kingdom in the ritual investiture of the new king (Evans-Pritchard 1948: 22–29).

10. With respect to the ritual's history, Mr. Humphreys stressed that establishing the parish or manor limits was necessary to exclude incorrigible rogues, vagabonds, and itinerants. While each parish had its own share of burdensome individuals, whose care and welfare reinforced the idea of the righteous insider as "civilized," the local elite were nonetheless anxious not to have to feed and clothe another parish's "roguish" poor. Moreover, Mr. Humphreys thought this need to exclude outsiders stemmed from fourteenth-century outbreaks of the Black Death,

cording to the Open Spaces Society,[11] there has been an unprecedented resurgence of interest in beating the bounds since 1989. Over fifty villages beat the bounds in 1993, and even more villages participated in 1994. The society has been the main stimulus to current interest in beating the bounds. From the society's perspective, the ritual's importance lies in its public declaration of concern for the local common, which in turn helps to reinstate an informal property regime that puts value in "public" land (and so runs contrary to the utilitarian legal and economic position endorsed by Thatcherism). According to one of its pamphlets about Rogation Sunday (the Sunday before Ascension Day):

> There are all too many interests keen to encroach on the margins of our commons and greens. If no one objects in time, it can mean common land is permanently lost. So beating the bounds is just as important *today*. It reminds your local community that they *have* a common or green with a boundary to be guarded, and in the process also shows them how much enjoyment and interest the area has to offer. It's a practical and enjoyable way to protect a valuable part of our heritage.
>
> (Open Spaces Society n.d.: 2)

Most of the villages that beat the bounds are in southeast and southwest England (Open Spaces Society 1993, 1994). One of these is Fordwich, a small, well-preserved village about four miles outside Canterbury, where issues of local heritage are taken very seriously.[12] Here beating the bounds is performed every year. In muddy Wellington

---

which periodically swept across the Continent and spread into England (Brand 1795: 201; Jessup 1974: 63; Mingay 1990: 59–63). People traveling from distant lands generally disembarked on the shores of East Kent, the closest coast to France. These foreigners were more likely to be carriers of disease, and not surprisingly— foreshadowing contemporary panics about outbreaks of the plague in India—"were not looked upon kindly." On the perceived relationship between foreignness and disease, see chapter 6.

11. The Open Spaces Society was established in 1865 by public-spirited reformers (including John Stuart Mill) in response to the enclosure acts and the widespread appropriation by the modernizing state of premodern common lands (Walsh 1992: 71).

12. Here the community is keen to preserve its local traditions and heritage as a reminder of the days when Fordwich was a thriving inland port in the twelfth and thirteenth centuries. Indeed, in 1994, under the direction of a local historian, the community of some fifty households created a film about the village's rise and decline, stressing its still functioning "ducking stool," which once lowered witches into the Great Stour River (now only a few feet deep), and parochial legal jurisdiction, administered in what is England's smallest town hall (see McIntosh 1975).

boots, anoraks, woolen sweaters, and limp cloth caps, people arrive in the main square around 10 A.M. on the morning of Rogation Sunday, accompanied by their dogs, and in anticipation of a hearty pub lunch. It is a family event, friendly and congratulatory, as people slowly walk the outskirts of the village pointing out and tapping with walking sticks the few remaining boundary stones designating the parish limits. In some villages, a child is "bounced" or "bumped" at these boundary stones in imitation of the old custom of bouncing the choirboy in order to "knock sense into the child" and help him (it is usually a boy) remember the parish limits. This involves hoisting the child upside-down and symbolically knocking his head against the stone. The custom evokes the days when village records and statistics were contained in the memories of parishioners rather than written down.

Of course, Fordwich is not representative of Kent. Many villages, even the smaller ones, are now populated by people who do not know each other, such as the touristy village of Chilham, which is occupied by a disproportionate number of London weekend commuters prepared to pay handsomely for their rustic retreats. As discussed in chapter 5, tranquil rural life is, for the most part, an illusory ideal. Nonetheless, it is important to reflect upon this nostalgia for a disappearing countryside. For purposes of this brief discussion, the aesthetic deterioration of the countryside is of secondary importance to the forms through which this loss is being perceived, vitalized, and politicized. In Kent, the revival of beating the bounds is one of many expressions of a popular anxiety to preserve the landscape, and specifically the communal right to public property. Beneath this anxiety, however, runs the related but deeper English identification with the land. This is linked historically to the loss of empire and more currently to the diminishing of Britain as a political and economic world leader. In recent years, this fear has become even more intense, as illustrated by the commodification and commercialization of heritage, which has become a huge English industry (Walsh 1992; Ashworth 1994).

Against the background of popular obsession with all things to do with English heritage, the resurgence of interest in beating the bounds becomes both more complicated and more interesting. This is particularly so when its main advocates tend to be, not natives of Kent, but recent arrivals from London and other urban areas, escaping the city in search of a sense of morality, community, and locality in which to play out their rural fantasies. Village life is changing dramatically, a full feature article in the *Kentish Gazette* concluded (11 Feb. 1994, p. 11). In Barham, according to Mr. Humphreys:

a lot of the people living here are ex-urban people really and funnily enough, the chairman of the parish council who organized the previous beating of the bounds was a Londoner, who became a farmer. . . . He came here and took an enormous interest. It's rather like a convert, I suppose, whereas local people took it all rather for granted. It's often like that, when an outsider picks things up. . . . It came I think with broader education, which happened with the war, and which took longer to get down to East Kent, mind you. I'm not sure that ought to have gone on record. . . . Another thing is that all that happened through the women's institutes in those days [i.e., interest in local history], and you hear more about it now because it's the projection business; there's a Barham Society, a Petham Society, an Ash Society, and all of these are independent of the parish council, and they all started thinking about it. I think partly it's because other people come from other areas and want to find out where they've come to, search around, and get to know the people who live here.

(interview, 25 Feb. 1994)

The resurgence of interest in village customs and local practices cannot simply be dismissed as sentimental yearnings for a past golden age. In consciously linking the past with the future, the force of custom rests on its symbolic capacity to historically ground and in a sense legitimate shifting cultural aspirations. Custom today, as throughout history, exemplifies particular social ideologies and community relations. Of course, it is important not to interpret too much. There is an attractive element of security in the continuities of ritual, and most people would agree with Mr. Humphreys that they participate in beating the bounds "for fun, really." Yet I argue that the current impetus, especially by "city" people,[13] to revive a practice so central to the production of locality in premodern life is more telling of deep social and political undercurrents than is immediately apparent. Maintaining ritual is about more than merely the asserting of continuities. Customary ritual is also a way of remaking the world, of changing the present, of redirecting a sense of history.

OTHER LOCAL COMMUNITY ACTIVITIES

Beating the bounds is only one of many local events in Kent that seek to lay down and reinstate a sense of local community imagined through

13. Other anthropologists have pointed to the irony of incomers to small villages and towns taking over local committees and groups in an effort to "keep alive" local customs that natives are not particularly concerned about (see Forsythe 1982: 94–95; Rapport 1993).

a rural landscape and aesthetic sense of order. The Open Spaces Society, Common Ground, and other charities fear that the privatization schemes promoted by recent Conservative governments threaten the remaining common lands accessible to the general public. And as anyone who has traveled in southern and other parts of England can attest, common land in the form of the village green is the focus around which village life circulates. It is the site of festivals, fairs, and markets, and on summer weekends it may function as a cricket pitch, providing a centralized space for the local community's sport and leisure activities. Other forms of common land are parks and gardens, nature reserves, and beaches. All of these sites are theoretically collectively owned by the crown in the name of the people. And they help substantiate a sense of community justice, in a similar vein to the commons of medieval England, which provided a plot of land for individual tenant farmers and affirmed a community right to graze one's cow on common pasture.

Groups such as the Open Spaces Society and Common Ground inevitably came into conflict throughout the 1980s and 1990s with the capitalist ideology and the so-called "enterprise culture" fostered under Thatcherism (Heelas and Morris 1992). Under Thatcher, substantial tracts of common land were sold off to private owners. Against such action, in 1993, the Open Spaces Society launched an "Open Spaces—Special Places" campaign and established a charter proposing legislation to guarantee the protection of open land for collective recreational purposes. The Open Spaces Society advocates that local authorities be vested with the control of common land, which contests the efforts over the past decade of the Tory government to divest local bodies of power, as discussed above. With the Labour party voted into office in 1997, the extent to which these centralizing trends will continue remains an open question. For my purposes here, what is important is that the Open Spaces Society and other organizations like it, in seeking to legally reinstate the value of localism by generating interest in common lands and village greens, promote an alternative sense of justice that in theory rejects exclusive property rights and selfish individualism.

It is hardly surprising that the Open Spaces Society's aims resonate somewhat ironically with other, more explicitly insurgent local practices in Kent.[14] At one extreme are the few but conspicuous gypsies and itinerants who claim rights to squat on common land. More significant in

14. On the paradoxical convergence of Green and Conservative perspectives in England, see Gray 1993.

terms of their political strength are the many supporters of the environment who are involved in a variety of projects concerned with noise, pollution, road construction, bicycle paths, and train lines, as well as with the stabilizing of micro-environments exclusive for the survival of rare species of birds and wildlife. In Kent, the Council for the Protection of Rural England (CPRE) has heightened anxiety about losing the island nation, and specifically the "Garden of England," as a national landscape. On the front cover of its 1993 Annual Report, it depicts a prehistoric image of a horse inscribed with the words "This Island, our Home, the Lost Land." To counter this perceived loss, CPRE advocates using European law, while striving for "better decision-making and greater public participation in the decision making process," which it claims "can result in tangible, practical improvements in procedures and legislation" (Sheate 1992: 90). CPRE's *Campaigner's Guide to Using EC Environmental Law* outlines step by step how local lobbying groups can petition Brussels and draw attention to the British government's numerous environmental transgressions. This strategy was put into action when CPRE joined up with four Kent groups, including the Kent Association of Parish Councils, as the local watchdog body on the implementation of the Channel Tunnel Rail Link (Kent Action Group 1993).

Now that the Channel Tunnel has been in operation for some years, the forms and strategies of local Kent politics have shifted. The focus of contention has moved away from the Tunnel itself toward the implementation of the fast-rail link between London and the coast. Energies have been dispersed. What remains, however, is an invigorated sense that Kent's environment is of value and must be protected. Local leaders operating out of the Canterbury Environment Center told me about the heightened enthusiasm on the part of residents to get involved in environmental projects over recent years. When I asked why they thought this was, there were vague assertions that it was the spirit of the times, and that everyone now has to be more environmentally aware. In Canterbury, this has resulted in independent umbrella bodies such as the Canterbury District Environmental Network, which seeks to link up small volunteer groups, bicycle clubs, and local green interests. In early 1995, the network involved fifty-one organizations, ranging from regional branches of Friends of the Earth, Greenpeace, and the Body Shop to the Kent Bat Group, Kent Farming and Wildlife Advisory Group, and Action on Canterbury Traffic group. As an indication of the extent of their activities, during the unusually cold and miserable winter of 1995, these groups, which are composed almost equally of men and women, young and old, organized fifty-three events, workshops, conservation tasks, and evening information nights. One member from the Chartham Conservation and Recycling Enterprise (CARE), which, like many of these groups, was launched sometime during the past decade, informed me: "[W]e were not directly influenced by the Channel Tunnel, but like many of our parishioners, we are concerned about the effect on Kent countryside that the works have caused. Our conservation activities are mainly concerned with the parish of Chartham, e.g. maintenance of Public Rights of Way, Tree preservation and preservation of ancient features such as Parish boundary banks and stones" (letter to the author, 23 Nov. 1993). This sentiment was endorsed by the leader of Canterbury Conservation Volunteers, another local environmental group, who wrote: "In the past few years, there has certainly been an explosion of public interest in conservation issues, and I'm sure the Channel Tunnel has played its part in convincing local people that they have to do something before the Kent countryside gets swallowed up. . . . The development generated by the Tunnel will certainly be a major catalyst to this trend" (letter to the author, 19 Jan. 1994).

A sense of locality is further supported by emerging groups such as the Canterbury group of LETS (Local Exchange Trading System), which replaces money with a supposedly medieval system of bartering goods and services. This group was set up in early 1994 and appears to have been relatively successful. I went along to some of its planning meetings, which seemed to always take place in a local pub over numerous pints of beer, as did most of the Greenpeace and other environmental meetings I attended. It was very interesting to hear the founding members present their arguments and outline how they proposed to publicize their message to the general public. Noteworthy about this system, which is also in operation in Manchester, South Devon, and elsewhere, are both its objections to government authority and its use of alternative units of currency, which means that it can only operate within a limited local territory (Worpole 1994: 171). In Canterbury, the unit of currency is called "Tales" (as in Canterbury Tales) in order to immediately identify the local vicinity in which the system operates. According to Andy Ryrie, a former businessman and now co-ordinator of Canterbury LETS, "By using an interest free unit of currency, which only has value locally, people are given the chance to regenerate community facilities and spirit rather than see the fruits of their labour taken for investment in more lucrative markets elsewhere" (*Kent Adscene*, 14 Jan. 1994; *Guardian*, 25 April 1995, p. 13). To my mind, one of the biggest drawbacks to the scheme is that it only encourages participation by those who can commit themselves to being certain of a long-term residence in the area. If one wants to move, there is no mechanism whereby you can take your accrued points and transfer them to a new location. In short, one's horizons are limited to the physical space of Canterbury, marking the participants as "real insiders."

This brings the discussion back to the wider symbolism embodied in customary rituals such as beating the bounds. Just as beating the bounds rearticulates the village space, these other activities, be it a hedgerow restoration project or the setting up of a recycling scheme, are also consciously committed to building up a locality and carving out a sense of place. Revealingly, for the first time, many people from various political perspectives are becoming involved in local politics and have helped push green issues to the forefront. It seems that many individuals are clearly feeling a need to participate in the "laying down" of law and order in localities and for reasserting a "law of the countryside" in the old footpaths and rights-of-way that criss-cross the local landscape. For instance, the Kentish Stour Countryside Project has put out a pamphlet calling on landowners, farmers, community groups, Parish councils, and schools to become involved in the conservation and preservation of hedgerows. The pamphlet states that "[w]ith the disappearance of hedges, Rights of Way can be threatened as many follow original hedge boundaries. Footpaths may be ploughed up, making public access more difficult. Traditional field systems are lost, and the sense of place altered" (Kentish Stour Countryside Project, Wye, Kent).

The theme that runs through all these activities—"What Kind of Kent?"—was the subject of a regional meeting held in Maidstone in February 1994, which attracted about a hundred people from a wide range of interest groups and community projects anxious to debate the future of their place in the county. People representing different bodies were given slots to speak, and many questions were asked of the official local government representatives. It seemed to me that there was not a great deal of new information exchanged and that the debates circled around a few questions to which there were no simple solutions, such as public health, transportation, and pollution. However, what was interesting was that this rather diffuse range of people explicitly asked what sort of people lived in Kent and what their future identity would be. Here, alongside serious challenges to the mythology of Kent as the "Garden of England" and a unique historical county, was a level of consciousness about issues of identity construction and self-labeling for which I was unprepared.

YELLOW HORIZONS

Fields of rape, a prolific crop, grown for the production of rapeseed oil (called canola oil in America), are one feature that Kent shares with many other counties in Britain and much of mainland Europe. In a good year, three harvests can be reaped between early spring and late summer, and the rape crop is a constant vibrant yellow splash across the skyline. Rape is the visible emblem of a new set of economic and political interests, and as the basis of a new visual aesthetics, expanding the limits of the horizon, it also bespeaks shifting strategies of power. Horizons of yellow extend out and beyond British boundaries, linking up to similar yellow vistas throughout France, extending across the flank of western Europe and down into northern Tuscany. As one journalist put it: "As a result [of such monoculture], many natural features have disappeared. Woodlands, marshes and invaluable 'wildlife corridors' such as hedgerows, riverbanks and even roadside verges have been ploughed over. In their place, from Scotland to southern Spain, have emerged vast expanses of fields, swathed in single crops, which offer neither variety to the eye nor cover for wildlife, with few corners for wildlife" (*European: élan*, 27 May–2 June 1994, p. 2).

Since 1960, the Common Agricultural Policy has encouraged uniform European agricultural practices and policies directed toward maximum food productivity. In the past decade, this has meant that for English farmers to compete economically against their mainland neighbors, they had to pull out an estimated 42,000 kilometers of hedgerows in order to plant wheat, rape, and other crops producing oil and grain. As a result, smaller specialized crops like blackcurrants, hops, grapes, and English apples such as Cox's Orange Pippin have suffered dramatic setbacks. In Kent, rape has a substantial presence, standing out against the soft white and pink blossoms of the steadily diminishing apple orchards and vertical poles of Kent's hop gardens. According to one Kent native: "Perhaps if they would grow the old types of cattle food instead of the foreign rape, the glaring colour of which blots out a lot of the lovely green slopes of the Downs in Spring and spreads into the roadside hedges, it would be better for cattle, and for us. Will someone please soon declare that margarine made from rape seed is poisonous" (Laker 1992: 72).

Such monoculture runs directly counter to the aims of environmentalists and groups such as the Countryside Commission and the Council for the Protection of Rural England, which in recent years have sought new environmental legislation to introduce, among other things, regulations to protect hedgerows. British legal authority is being evoked against the wide-spread changes in the agricultural landscape that illustrate the EU's at-tempts to create sustainable local economies. In Kent, the building of the Channel Tunnel, while dramatically polarizing public opinion, has had less visible impact on the countryside than the widespread, pervasive changes in farming. In certain areas, "[European] Community legislation may pro-foundly affect the use of the British landscape," observes J. D. C. Harte (1985: 52; and see also *Guardian*, 11 May 1998, pp. 8–9).

Now, as a result of Common Agricultural Policy's promotion of the rape crop, there is an embarrassing backlog of surplus oil seed. This has resulted in the Common Agricultural Policy and the National Farmer's Union having to reverse their laws and regulations. Under the EU's new set-aside scheme, 1.4 million acres across Britain are lying fallow. Farmers are paid £253 per hectare per year to set aside land from cultivation, and further subsidies are offered for wheat and oilseeds. The total cost of all these schemes is calculated at £759 million for the whole of Europe, with Britain alone forking out over £200 million in compensation costs to farm-ers for land now sitting idle. In the southeast of England, where farmers are receiving over £30 million, set-aside payments have been the highest in the country (*Guardian*, 23 May 1994, p. 8).

Apart from robbing "a generation of aspiring youngsters of the chance to get started in farming," the set-aside schemes have caused much anxiety and bitterness both amongst farmers and environmentalists (*Guardian*, 8 Feb. 1994, p. 18). Having seen old landscapes cleared and subjected to intensive farming, involving harsh pesticides, many now fear that fields will be abandoned and that the environment will suffer further. In Kent and across England, the set-aside schemes, as much as the building of the Channel Tunnel, have altered people's perceived relations to the idealized rural countryside and angered local residents, fueling antagonisms toward the idea of a legally dominant Europe. The apple "invasion" from France led to the grubbing out of many Kent orchards, only a few having been left for the sake of the tourist industry, according to Roger Arnold, a Kentish farmer. Other agricultural products typical of Kent are likewise now being imported—cherries from Turkey, blackcurrants from Poland, and eggs from Germany. Calling the situation "absolutely horrendous," Arnold said: "I'm fighting like hell to save our farming industry from total destruction. It looks as though the European Commission and the whole of Europe is out to destroy our agriculture and make us totally dependent" (*Kent Gazette*, 2 June 1994, p. 12).

Changes in the landscape provide a constant reminder that European law can have a material and startling impact. Whereas in the past, landscape may have been taken for granted, legal intervention has forced a new consciousness of its presence and significance, altering people's "forms of subjectivity and sociability and their aesthetic appreciation of nature, landscapes, townscapes, and other societies," observes John Urry, who calls this a "growth of an aesthetic reflexivity" (Urry 1992: 127–28). Alongside continuing open resistance by the British government and many English citizens to the idea of a united Europe, there is thus increasing public awareness of an alternative and more authoritative local legal power.

Trains, roads, crops, pollution, beaches, noise, car exhaust, seat belts, bicycle helmets—in England all of these are increasingly regulated by the EU, affecting how one moves through, gazes upon, and perceives the environment and one's place and identity within it. Horizons of relations of power are shifting, expanding, and contracting, as well as accommodating new political centers and new modes of spatial operation. "The modern absence of actual physical horizons or boundaries poses its own set of problems, including possible loss of identity," remarks Dale Segrest (1994: 224). The national myth of a cohesive community looking out over a landscape delimited by Britain's coasts has thus received an "interruption," to use the terminology of Jean-Luc Nancy (1991: 43–70).[15] In other words, the need to forget the artificiality of Britain's fictitious national identity, sustained by an ideology of sovereign law and natural island borders, is now competing with the need to maintain equally fictitious resurrected local identities and new forms of transnational European identity.

CONCLUDING COMMENTS

In seeking to establish a united territory—a European legal, political, and social community—the European Union is employing all sorts of tactics and strategies. Whether or not the EU technically qualifies as a state is immaterial to the realities of it emerging as the most regulatory and the most powerful of all modern institutions in contemporary Europe. In Michel Foucault's terms, it embodies new techniques in the art of governmentality, both over states and in the managing of individuals. And control over the landscape is, I have argued throughout this book, a critical

---

15. But as Jean-Luc Nancy points out, this does not necessarily mean that the myth of nation-state is "demythologized" or abandoned. In the very act of acknowledging its absence, "myth says what is and says that we agree to say that this is" (Nancy 1991: 50). The recognition that Britain is no longer a unified nation-state affirms the possibility of such a state existing, albeit in another form.

dimension in the construction of what the New Europe will look like. Hence the legal presence of the EU, in the form of fast trains, yellow rape fields, clean beaches, and exhaust-free cars, may be subtly affecting a range of people and their perceptions of the landscape as an aesthetic symbol of their identity and a possible icon of national allegiance. One consequence is that the nature of English law, its intimate connection to the land, and its relationship to the conceptualization of Britain as an autonomous island nation are being seriously challenged.

Foucault's concern with the "workings of power" and the "techniques for 'governing' individuals" cannot be separated from the constructions of territory through which people are managed as a population (Foucault 1984: 337–38). Territory, according to Foucault, is merely a variable in the practices of modern government, because governmentality extends beyond the limits of the state—a conceptualization of territory that presumes its conflation with nation-state borders (Foucault 1980: 122; 1991: 93–94). I have tried to show that focusing on landscape as the cultural practice of territory shows the link between territory and state to be problematic. Landscape is not bound to territory any more than governmentality is to the state. Landscape should be conceived of as an instrumental strategy of power among various actors and agencies—as a contested domain through which individuals seek to manage their own destinies, "not as an object to be seen or a text to be read, but as a process by which social and subjective identities are formed" (Mitchell 1994a: 1).

In the context of England in the New Europe, issues of law, territory, and identity are coming to the fore in unprecedented ways. Certainly, with the building of the Channel Tunnel and the impact of EU agricultural and environmental law in Kent, it is now more difficult to imagine the nation's mythologized green landscapes and link them to an identity that is exclusively and quintessentially English. At the same time, at least for some people, this symbolic destabilizing makes even more pertinent the sustaining of an English nationalist, or more specifically Kentish, landscape imagery. Evident too throughout Kent are the variety of ways in which different people, with different interests and needs, are trying to manage a membership of Kent in Europe. Across these push-and-pull processes, landscapes, always political, contested, and dynamic, spill out across borders and seas, linking and confronting peoples and nations, shaping and being shaped by new forms of governmentality and spatial aesthetics.

Conclusion
A Shifting Perspective on Europe

> Thresholds, especially very old, heavily passed thresholds, require some attention now and then.
>
> John Stilgoe, *Alongshore* (1994)

LOOKING EAST, LOOKING RIGHT

In many modern maps of the world, Europe is still placed at the center. Following this logic, England is to the left of France, and the English visualize their relationship to Europe by turning eastwards. This mapped positioning between nations solidified in the eighteenth century with the rise of modern nation-states and the consolidation of national borders. Today, modern cartography remains remarkably formulaic in presenting this image of projected "reality" (Wood 1992: 4). It is when the world is visually rearranged, with, for instance, some maps placing Africa in the pictorial center, that the presumption of this ethnocentric "worldview" perspective from which the west spatially conceptualizes itself and the rest is dramatically exposed.

This conclusion locates my overall arguments about the Tunnel within this theme of conventional spatial relations between people, nations, and supposedly natural geopolitical borders. In focusing on the implications of perspective as a way to locate and analyze the impact of legal authority, I am not arguing that one point of view represents the "truth" more than another. Rather, I stress that there exist multiple centers and horizons in which people are located and from which perspectives are produced, often simultaneously (Bryson 1983: 133–62). These various positions operate as "symbolic forms," containing qualities of both objective rationality and subjective distortion, according to Erwin Panofsky:

> [T]he perspectival view, whether it is evaluated and interpreted more in the sense of rationality and the objective, or more in the sense of contingency and the subjective, rests on the will to construct pictorial space, in principle, out of the elements of, and according to the plan of, empirical visual space. . . . Perspective mathematizes this visual

space, but it is very much *visual* space that it mathematizes; it is an ordering, but an ordering of the visual phenomenon.

(Panofsky 1991: 71)

It is when such perspectives are "naturalized" in rhetoric, or taken for granted as actually existing, that they become powerful in the organizing of social worlds. What happens, I ask, when changes occur in the perspective that English people adopt in their relations with the European mainland?

LAW AND THE ORDERING OF LAND

The Channel Tunnel is both monument and spectacle. But its construction also allows an exploration of the role of law in reordering spatial and social relations. How does law, as a source of power, relate to visual and cultural phenomena embedded in the landscape, and how does this in turn affect people's understanding of law, and ultimately of themselves? Radiating outwards from London across the nation's peripheral territories, legal jurisdiction operates as a spatial rationalization and a logical ordering of the landscape. As discussed in chapter 1, this creates what I call a technology or strategy of governmentality. From the eighteenth century on, the embodiment within law of a particular spatial aesthetics became explicit with the territorial consolidation of nation-states. Law solidified the new nation of Britain, delimiting its territorial reaches, concealing its political artificiality, constructing a citizenry, and extending a nationality across the island through the joining of England, Scotland, Wales, and Northern Ireland (chapter 3). In this sense, modern western law encapsulates the liberal presumption inherited from absolutism that power necessarily emanates from the state's center.

But to what extent does this presumption still hold in the context of the New Europe? Law has the capacity to generate subjective affiliations and national identities. This ability is intrinsically related to how law orders the landscapes in which people live. Of course, political, economic, and social factors are implicated in these processes. The European Union, a dramatically new legal entity, provides the central force through which challenges are made to member states' sovereign autonomy. This new potential in turn affects a state's institutional rights to manage its finances and foreign affairs. Furthermore, since legal control marks jurisdictional boundaries, law directly relates to the exclusion of foreigners and the affirmation of citizens. Thus because Brussels has challenged the nation-state, cultural identities across national, regional, and local contexts are

Figure 19. Untitled cartoon by Nicholas Garland. *Independent,* 6 November 1991. Prime Minister John Major and Foreign Secretary Douglas Hurd are shown on the cliffs of Dover affirming their commitment to the European Union by repainting Britannia's shield with the EU's stars. By kind permission of Nicholas Garland.

also in flux. A wonderful political cartoon that sums up the interrelations between law, state, geography, and cultural identity shows Prime Minister John Major and Foreign Secretary Douglas Hurd on the cliffs of Dover, facing east toward the European mainland, painting over the Union Jack on Britannia's shield with the yellow stars of the EU (fig. 19).

In many EU member countries, there is a perceived need, although variable in its intensity and pervasiveness, to legally consolidate national borders in the face of an increasingly interventionist Brussels. England fears being colonized by the New Europe, for example, provoking new formulations of the relations between law, identity, and territory. This nexus frames the research and shapes the primary question with which I began the book: What is the significance of the EU's legal blurring of the material and symbolic borders around what is imagined as England?

In chapter 3, for instance, to illustrate my argument about the relationship between law and landscape, I refer to the 1994 stamp issue of country views of Scotland, Wales, and England painted by Prince Charles. These empty rural scenes draw together the separate regions of Britain and position the viewer "inside" looking out onto a delimited island horizon. What I suggest is that this is an explicit—although not necessarily conscious—instance of a particular construction of territoriality being used in the imposing of order and reinforcing of state legal authority.

Similarly, I explore the interconnections between country and city as another significant dimension in the institutionalizing of central power and its extended reach over a rural periphery. The country/city dualism underscores my examination in chapter 2 of the importance of Kent as London's idealized "garden" landscape, and it helps to explain reactions to the Channel Tunnel's perceived destruction of this rural idyll. By cutting across Kentish properties, orchards, hedgerows, and a dense network of public footpaths and bridle paths deemed to have existed for centuries, both the Tunnel and the fast rail that links it to London, literally and metaphorically undermine an established aesthetics of order. Such order is the indispensable basis for imagining the natural authority of English law and notions of Englishness (chapter 1). Thus the much-used military rhetoric of "penetration," "invasion," and "rape" emphasizes the Tunnel's violent destabilizing of the "naturalized" perspective and perceived stable history of an implicitly gendered landscape.

COMPETING LEGAL SYSTEMS

Law is critical to this realignment of spatial and political relations in the New Europe. After Margaret Thatcher was compelled to support the Channel Tunnel in 1984 as a public demonstration of Britain's commitment to the EU and reconciliation with France (chapter 4), the national boundary between England and France was legislatively redrawn halfway across the Channel, replacing the coast as the limit and threshold of the nation. Although the British government was able to push through the Channel Tunnel Hybrid Bill (1986), this alienated many people. In some instances, it generated open resistance in Kent against the central government. Because of the capacity of law to fabricate a new legal entity, Kent County Council was able in part to reconstitute itself through its participation in the Euroregion linking it to Nord–Pas de Calais, Flanders, Wallonia, and Brussels Capital in 1991 (chapter 7).

The legal dominance of the European Union has ruptured the apparent predictability, confidence, logic, and objectivity promulgated by English law. And this rupture suggests deep ramifications for the construction of legal and cultural identities. The EU is an alternative legal authority (and perspective) that transcends, intersects, and competes with the legal authority of member nation-states. As an artifact of this new legal structure, the Channel Tunnel represents the undermining of Britain's island status and the encroachment of France and Europe. The Tunnel calls into question concepts of sovereignty, territorially based democracy, and the exclusivity of nationalism that have historically been critical in the legitimization of modern principles of law. In this way, it precipitates political and economic transformation, generating discussions about the EU's principle of subsidiarity, Committee of Regions, and regionalism, as well as the devolution of power to local governments (chapter 7). The Tunnel materially represents a reordering of power relations between local, regional, national, and transnational entities through its disruption of an idealized national landscape.

This study, though, is about much more than the Tunnel. I set out to bridge the gap between image and text that normally hampers legal analysis. By exploring historical narratives, tunnel stories, and the legal myths that surrounded the building of the Channel Tunnel, I have shown the interconnections between people's memories of the past and current history, subjective interpretations and legal viability, and strategies of power and aesthetic transformation. In my concern with both textual and textural dimensions of law, explicit legal change has been only one facet of my research. By this I mean that there is more to an understanding of law than can be accounted for through a narrow focus on the obvious legal arenas of courtrooms, Parliament, legislation, and the legal profession. As Peter Goodrich has noted: "A reading of the legal text which ignores the power of its imagery or the aesthetic of its reception is a reading which is in many senses beside the point in that it ignores precisely that dimension of the text and its context which performs the labour of signification and so gives the text its effect" (Goodrich 1991: 236–38).

To return to Panofsky's definition of perspective, quoted above, the objective and subjective interpretations of any particular view are "really the double face of the same issue" (Panofsky 1991: 71). A particular perspective, legal or otherwise, consists of both seemingly rationalized objective rules and regulations and apparently contingent individualistic interpretations. In stressing how law is intimately connected to visual phenomena, what I have explored is how an aesthetic redefinition of people's view of their material, symbolic, and metaphoric landscapes influences how people experience the powers that order those landscapes. So while EU law constitutes a new legal rationality, this alternative legal authority is subjectively interpreted by individuals although seemingly an objective legal code.

OVERLAPPING LEGAL SUBJECTIVITIES

Subjective interpretations of legal change underscore and center my substantive analysis. Discussions about Channel Tunnel legislation, the limitations of England's parliamentary process, the creation of the Euroregion, and the implications of law in guarding against terrorism must, I argue, be supplemented by the less tangible implications of competing legal perspectives. For it is in these moments of formal and informal legal interaction that the mythology of modern law is most challenged. Such challenges proceed both with respect to the universalistic claim made through law to provide an overarching juridical framework and in the particularistic functioning of law as a "potent figure of national identity" (Fitzpatrick 1992: 117).

For instance, the European Union has changed the relationship between country and city, and London is now characterized as a global city, associating it with such places as Paris, Sydney, Hong Kong, Mexico City, and São Paulo. People living on the periphery of London, such as in Kent, are seeking to distance themselves from the nation's center in a variety of ways, the most radical method being through direct connections to the EU's legal and financial institutions. Revitalization of local customs like "beating the bounds" can be interpreted as expressions of local anxiety about London and an encroaching Europe.

The deliberate interrelation between "transnationalism" and "postcolonialism" that I describe in chapter 6 highlights another way in which apparent historical continuities can affect analyses of current legal change. Railways historically symbolized England's imperial power, and the EU's role in promoting the fast train thus suggests England's potential colonization by the New Europe, echoing the nation's past. Heightening apprehension about the Tunnel among the wider English population is an irrational fear of disease and its linking to ideas of "foreignness." These fears are made more acute by images of a high-speed penetration of English territory by people formerly colonized.

The city/country dichotomy, the historical role of the railroad, and the illusion of local land boundaries all come together in chapters 5, 6, and 7, which draw their premise from and build upon my discussion of Kent as the Garden of England in chapter 2. For it is here that I establish the significance of Kent as a particularly symbolic landscape in the English imaginary. Kent, the closest point in England to the European mainland, has historically enjoyed much trans-Channel traffic. It has always been the most cosmopolitan of English counties. At the same time, much of its identity as a region derives from its historic role as defender of the nation, most recently in World War II's Battle of Britain. Cosmopolitanism and parochialism, I argue, have shaped Kent's idealized landscape imagery and its intimate relationship to the authority of English law in complementary ways. In Kent, law is still perceived as being bound to the land by the oak trees, hedgerows, hop fields, and boundary walls that carve up the landscape according to customary property laws mythically existing from time immemorial.

Local, regional, and national concern for protecting the Kent landscape has to be understood against an environment of cultural anxiety in which the British government is often the laughing stock of Europe, and where the very notion of Englishness is being re-created. The widespread obsession with heritage in Kent shows that for some people, the past is being used in the planning of the future in reaction against, rather than subservience to, the idea of an all-powerful Mother England. This shift in people's reactions to their nation cannot be separated from an emerging sense of the legal potential of Brussels. These new links to Europe are concretely promoted through such activities as the building of the Tunnel and the introduction of new commodity crops, for example, rape seed. These physical manifestations symbolize a new spatial ordering and the new landscapes that accompany legal realignments.

A SHIFTING PERSPECTIVE ON EUROPE?

The European ethnocentrism often inscribed on conventional maps of the world may not be challenged by the European Union. In fact, with the increasing power of the EU, this particular worldview is arguably stronger. But even modest local activities like beating the bounds underscore emerging points of conflict at once below and beyond the level of the nation-state. In the New Europe, the contained centrality of the nation-state, and how various member countries interrelate, is precarious. Internal legal tensions within countries can be significant in their influence on wider EU relations, as well as on the EU's interaction with other power blocks, including the United States, Russia, and the other countries that formerly constituted the Soviet Union. The conventional map of Europe, in which England is spatially represented as lying to the left or west of France, is no longer entirely self-evident. Rotating the map, one could reimagine England as a sublot of the New Europe and now lying below or south of the mainland.

We need to pay attention to changing visual phenomena in the landscapes that represent a constant negotiation of legal perspectives in the European Union. Acknowledging the aesthetic dimensions, spatial relations, and experiential realities of law underscores the role of people's participation in legal practice through such things as myth and custom as critical facets of governance in western legal discourse. This shatters the supposition within the history of legal anthropology that modern law is superior to "primitive" law on the basis of its written, objective, and rational reproduction. In the face of the collapse of a naturalized English/British legal order, the residents of Kent, the bedrock of "civilized" Tory England, are fighting to preserve the rituals associated with premodern forms of performative and customary law. Thus it is not enough to approach law as an abstract text or metaphor. Rather, law should be understood as meaningful social practices that become visible and tangible in everyday life. In their visual and spatial reordering of the places we experience, through which we all try to find perspectives on ourselves, the symbols of law—the oak tree, the cliff face, the common land, the fast train—are crucial to how we live.

APPENDIX 1

Key Dates in the History
of the Channel Tunnel Project

1785   Jean-Pierre Blanchard and John Jeffries make the first crossing of the Channel by air, traveling by balloon from Dover Castle to France.

1802   At the Peace of Amiens, England formally renounces its claim to Calais and recognizes French sovereignty over it.

           Albert Mathieu, a French engineer, proposes a tunnel to link Cap Gris-Nez with East Wear Bay, near Folkestone, running via the submerged Varne Bank in mid-Channel and then parallel to the English coast. On the Varne Bank, where the water is as shallow as fifteen feet at low tide, Mathieu envisages an artificial island with a relay station for changing horses, and he proposes to ventilate the eighteen and a half miles of tunnel by chimneys reaching above the waves, with drainage by means of a smaller tunnel at a lower level. Mathieu has almost no knowledge of the complicated geology of the Channel seabed, however, and suggests no means of construction. Napoleon Bonaparte expresses some interest, and during the short period of peace between the warring countries, the tunnel plan is seen as a symbol of friendship between France and England.

1803   An Englishman called Mottray suggests that a submerged steel tube could be laid across the seabed, as opposed to a

---

This brief summary is based on the following sources: Hunt 1994: 272–75; Eurotunnel information papers, October 1992 (B1 and B3); and the private notes of Alex Brown, Honorable Librarian of the Channel Tunnel Association, 22 Feb. 1982 (Channel Tunnel Archives, Churchill Archives Center, Cambridge).

tunnel through the chalk bottom. Like Mathieu's, this plan is short-lived, for in 1803, war resumes between the two nations.

1830   Interest in a permanent link across the Channel is revived in the 1830s by another remarkable Frenchman, Thomé de Gamond, a civil engineer, who during the next twenty-five years comes up with various tunnel and bridge schemes. In 1856, he submits his plans to Napoleon III, and they are published the following year to some acclaim in both France and England.

1868   An international committee reports that a tunnel could be completed in ten years, but the inquiry is interrupted by the breaking out of the Franco-Prussian War in 1870.

1875   A new proposal for an undersea tunnel captures the imaginations of many of the great financiers of the day, including the Rothschilds, and eventually results in the formation of the English and French Channel Tunnel companies. A British engineer, Colonel Frederick Beaumont, is asked to come up with a machine to bore through the chalk, and his design proves surprisingly successful. The British Parliament authorizes the Channel Tunnel Company to begin preliminary work.

1878–79   In the late 1870s, tunneling commences on both sides of the Channel, at Sangatte on the French side, and at Shakespeare Cliff, near Dover, on the English side. Two shafts are sunk from Abbots and Shakespeare cliffs, and about 2,000 yards of tunnel is bored out under the seabed. The Board of Trade requests that the War Office investigate the military implications of the tunnel, however, and as a result, in 1882, work is halted for reasons of defense. English generals imagine a French army marching through the tunnel unimpeded.

1884   A joint select committee of Parliament is appointed to investigate and concludes that it is not expedient for England to have submarine communication with France. All work stops. At this stage, the estimated cost of twin rail tunnels is in the region of £16 million.

1903   Wilbur and Orville Wright fly the first motorized airplane at Kitty Hawk, North Carolina.

1909   Louis Blériot becomes the first man to cross the Channel by plane.

1900s   New plans for a tunnel in the early years of the twentieth century are frustrated by World War I.

1923   A trial tunnel 420 feet long is dug at Folkestone.

1930   Interest in the tunnel project is once again revived in 1930, when a royal commission comes out in favor of the scheme by a majority vote, but the House of Commons turns the project down by seven votes. If the Commons had not done this, the Committee of Imperial Defence would have prevented the tunnel from being built on the grounds that its likely success would cause some of the south coast ports to become redundant.

1931   A regular car-ferry service opens between Dover and Calais.

1939–45   Sir Winston Churchill was all in favor of the tunnel project and wished it had been available during World War I, although Field Marshal Bernard Montgomery is quoted as having said that a tunnel would have endangered British security during World War II. He was not alone in this attitude. It is reported that there were sentries on duty all through World War I guarding the original tunnel opening at Dover, as though the Germans might pop up there like moles.

1947   From 1947 on, there is more or less continuous interest in the project on the part of various groups. Three possible forms of mixed link are investigated—a bridge, a tube on the seabed, and a tunnel.

1954   As minister of defence, Harold Macmillan finally disposes of the old fears of military invasion, admitting that strategic considerations no longer apply.

1957   The Channel Tunnel Study Group is formed and commissioned to begin a geological study and full-scale inquiry into possible forms of fixed link.

1959   The hovercraft makes its first Channel crossing.

1960–61   New proposals for fixed crossings of the Channel are put forward by the Channel Tunnel Study Group. A working group of British and French officials examines these proposals and concludes that the tunnel project is technically feasible, and that twin railway tunnels would be economically viable. In 1961, the British government announces its decision to apply for membership in the European Common Market.

1963   The working group's report, *Proposals for a Fixed Channel Link*, is published in September.

1964   British Minister of Transport Ernest Marples announces on 6 February that as a result of studies undertaken jointly, the British and the French governments have agreed that the construction of a Channel rail tunnel is technically possible and that it would be a sound investment for the two countries. Subject to further discussion of the legal and financial problems involved, the two governments thereupon decide to proceed with the project. A geological and geophysical investigation is undertaken into the conditions on and under the seabed in the Straits of Dover. The results confirm that a bored tunnel is feasible.

1966   In July, the British and French prime ministers, Harold Wilson and Georges Pompidou, issue a joint statement approving construction of a Channel tunnel. Tenders are sought from interested private groups for the financing and construction of a tunnel, and three proposals are submitted, although none is deemed acceptable as it stands.

1968   Civil unrest in Paris delays proceedings but does not dampen French enthusiasm for the tunnel.

1970   A new consortium of companies is formed and joins the British and French members of the Channel Tunnel Study Group.

1971   In March, the British and French ministers of transport, John Peyton and Jean Chamant, accept new proposals. The Channel Tunnel Study Group is now organized into the British Channel Tunnel Company and the Société française du Tunnel sous la Manche. The two governments and the group agree on a program of financial, economic, and technical studies to decide whether or not to proceed with the project.

1972   On 20 October, parallel agreements are concluded between the British and French governments and the members of the group, providing for studies to be completed by the middle of 1973 and setting out a framework for subsequent action if the tunnel goes ahead. The studies are expected to cost £5 million, about half of which is to be provided by the companies, with the balance raised under government guarantees.

1973   A green paper reviewing all the progress made on the tunnel project during the previous twelve years is presented to Parliament by the secretary of state for the environment in March. The Channel Tunnel (Initial Finance) Bill is passed, and an Anglo–French treaty is signed. Preparatory work begins at Shakespeare Cliff and Sangatte. The total cost is estimated at £846 million, of which the British are to contribute half. In October, war breaks out between Israel and Egypt and Syria.

1974   War in the Middle East escalates into a major oil crisis. Prime Minister Edward Heath declares a state of emergency and imposes a three-day work week to conserve energy.

1975   The British government unilaterally abandons the tunnel project on grounds of economic uncertainty. The companies are compensated for preliminary diggings.

1977   All the machinery used in the abandoned project is put up for sale, but there are no takers.

1979   The Conservative party is returned to power under the leadership of Margaret Thatcher.

1981   On 10 May, François Mitterrand is elected president of France. In September, Thatcher and Mitterrand revive the tunnel project officially by concluding in a joint statement that a further feasibility study should be done. A joint study group is formed by the French and British departments of transport.

1982   The joint study group reports that it favors twin rail tunnels to take conventional trains and a vehicle shuttle service. The House of Commons standing select committee begins consideration of the Channel Tunnel Bill.

1984   At the end of a Franco-British economic summit in Avignon, Thatcher and Mitterrand issue a joint statement that a fixed link is in the mutual interests of both countries. An Anglo–French working party is formed to draw up the specifications for prospective tenders.

1985   France-Manche and the Channel Tunnel Group merge to form Transmanche-Link (TML). Ten companies submit tenders.

1986   Thatcher and Mitterrand sign the Channel Tunnel Treaty in Canterbury Cathedral's chapter house, and grant a 55-year concession to Transmanche-Link, selected as the most promising bidder. Transmanche-Link then signs a contract with Eurotunnel as its administrative company, commencing a complicated and turbulent financial relationship. The Channel Tunnel Hybrid Bill, on second reading, is passed in the House of Commons by 309 votes to 44.

1987   On 22 April, the French National Assembly unanimously approves legislation for the Channel tunnel. On 23 July, the Channel Tunnel Act receives royal assent, marking the end of a long legislative process in the United Kingdom. On 29 July, the Channel Tunnel Treaty is ratified by Thatcher and Mitterrand. By December 1, tunneling has begun on the English side at Shakespeare Cliff. Throughout 1986 and 1987, complicated financial arrangements are made to raise sufficient equity for the project to go ahead through a series of stock market flotations and extensive bank and other financial loans.

1990   Eurotunnel announces financial difficulties, saying that a further £300 million loan is to be made by the European Investment Bank (without a letter of credit support). Transmanche-Link completes one half of the tunnel, and on 30 October, the first contact is made between British and French undersea working crews in the middle service tunnel.

1991   Breakthrough is made on 22 May in the north rail tunnel, and on 28 June in the south rail tunnel.

1992   Britain joins the European Economic Monetary Union. Eurotunnel announces that the opening of the tunnel will have to be delayed from 15 June 1993 until the end of that summer.

1993   The European Single Market Agreement comes into force. Eurotunnel reconfigures itself to become an international rail company, and Transmanche-Link hands over all control of the tunnel to it.

1994   Official inauguration of the Channel Tunnel occurs on 6 May. Queen Elizabeth II and President François Mitterrand attend official receptions in Calais and Folkestone, and to-gether ride in the queen's Rolls-Royce through the Tunnel. Service is not open to the public until the end of the year, when passengers can finally board at Waterloo International Terminal in London or take themselves and their cars across on the shuttle service from Folkestone. A national poll shows, however, that 70 percent of English people refuse to travel to the European mainland by undersea transport.

1994–98   The financial chaos and woes of Eurotunnel continue. The new Labour government elected in 1997 is pushed to take over all Eurostar services and the building of the fast-train link between London and Dover from the private sector. TGV service between Paris and Calais and Brussels and Calais is up and operating, but there are still no solid plans to build the fast-rail link in England, much to everyone's increasing embarrassment.

An Analysis of European Union Survey Statistics on Attitudes toward the Channel Tunnel

POPULAR OPINION

It is easy to dismiss sentiments for or against the Channel Tunnel as of relevance only to those immediately affected by it. Within England, this presumption suggests that the Tunnel has been and is of public interest only in London, where commuters to the European mainland benefit from it, and in east Kent, where the Tunnel emerges and the fast-rail link is being built. The rest of the country, divided along the infamous industrial north/capitalist south line, is held to be not really concerned about the plight of what is commonly perceived as the rich southeast (see Balchin 1990; Lovering 1991: 13).

There may be some truth in this. As argued by Lord Sefton of Garston at the second reading of the Channel Tunnel Bill in the House of Lords in 1986, "this nation does not consider itself as one nation. The North-South divide . . . is real, and it will get worse because of the way this tunnel has been planned." But at the same time, as Baroness Carnegy of Lour responded as representative of a Scottish constituency, "It is time that we in Scotland woke up to the fact that the tunnel could present us with the most enormous and much-needed opportunities if only we had the sense to exploit them. . . . I believe that far from this project increasing the so-called North-South divide, in very many respects Scotland is going to gain an enormous advantage from it." Lord Ezra added in support, "the opportunities this is going to provide for all regions are very considerable. I cannot see this resulting simply in a further development of the South-East" (Channel Tunnel Bill, *Parliamentary Debates*, vol. 484, nos. 40 and 41 [1987], cols. 926, 957, 958, and 972).

Here I briefly examine British and European attitudes toward plans to build a Channel tunnel in 1986, when Thatcher and Mitterrand signed the Channel Tunnel Treaty in Canterbury, receiving media attention in the national papers. The information is derived from a 1986 Eurobarometer survey, *Public Opinion in the European Community, Spring 1986*, in which respondents were asked whether they were "for," "against," or "neither for nor against" plans to build a tunnel. Unfortunately, this question was not asked in subsequent Eurobarometer surveys, which thus does not enable me to measure any shift in opinion since the Tunnel's construction and completion in 1994. That said, what I am interested in is the extent to which the Tunnel had an impact on those not necessarily directly affected by it in a material sense. Although in 1986 there were only plans to build a tunnel, the Eurobarometer survey results go some way toward indicating British attitudes toward France and mainland Europe more generally. For this reason I also compare attitudes toward plans to build a tunnel with findings on attitudes toward European unification.

"NOT IN MY BACK YARD": KENTISH AND BRITISH ATTITUDES TOWARD THE CHANNEL TUNNEL

Throughout the second half of the 1980s, the slogan "Not in my backyard!"—NIMBY—was often used in the debates surrounding the building of the tunnel and the fast-rail link in Kent. It was hurled as a form of abuse against anyone seen to be in support of a scheme that did not in a physical sense affect that person directly, forcing one to sell up one's house and move. Not surprisingly, bureaucrats and politicians who descended upon Kent in a flurry of activity attempting to calm locals and persuade people that everything would be all right were often met with this response.

While humor was an effective means of charting the ironies, confusions, and blatant ineffectiveness of political activity, it did not veil the real hardships that were to be faced by many east Kent residents. In 1986, fears about what a tunnel would bring were high among those immediately living near the terminal site and along the coast in Dover and Folkestone, the home of many ferrymen and their families. Not surprisingly, the highest percentage of people against a tunnel was recorded among residents of east Kent (region South-East 2), 63 percent, with only 21 percent for a tunnel (table 1). In west Kent (region South-East 1), 44 percent were against and 33 percent for the building of a tunnel. This slight regional variation can be explained by west Kent's greater distance from the coast, making the likely impact of a tunnel less immediate there. In west Kent, greater concern was focused upon the route of the fast-rail line and how this would affect the local community, rather than upon the tunnel terminal. David Wilson, who was Field Marshal Viscount Montgomery's military assistant in 1957 and involved in drawing up a report on the building of a Channel tunnel and its defense, and a borough councilor in Tunbridge Wells in west Kent between 1984 and 1992, confirmed this difference in local concerns: "As [a councilor] I attended various meetings at which the questions of the effect of the Tunnel were discussed, but in our case it mostly concerned the proposed high speed rail link, which barely touched the Borough. In our particular case the main problems were those of disgruntled property owners" (letter to the author, 12 May 1994).

The differences in attitudes across Kent indicate that not all residents feared tunnel plans for the same reasons and to the same degree. It would be misguided to talk about the inhabitants of Kent, or in any other British region, as a cohesive group. Still, the Eurobarometer survey presents interesting findings on regional variation in British attitudes toward construction of the tunnel (see table 1). In London, Wales, and the North, people are least against the tunnel, although London and the North have about a third of the population not committed either way, while the Welsh are much more for the tunnel. Citizens in Wales have been, like the Scots, relatively consistently in support of the EU, although support in Scotland did not really emerge until the late 1980s, when regional protest again blossomed under a strengthening Scottish Nationalist Party. But unlike Scotland, Wales is geographically closer to the southeast coast, and so presumably people thought in 1986 that a Channel tunnel might materially improve their connections with both London and Europe, as they evidently continue to do today.

Strikingly, apart from a more pronounced antagonism to the tunnel in east Kent, there is not much regional variation in opinions on the subject across Britain. This runs counter to the House of Lords tunnel debates, conducted at roughly the same time as the Eurobarometer survey, where some lords, speaking on behalf of their western and northern constituents, suggested that the proposed tunnel was not even an issue of public note. No one had heard of it or cared. Contrary to this presumption, the survey information suggests that this was not the case. For instance, people in the West and North Midlands felt strongly about the issue and were almost as opposed to the Tunnel as people in east Kent itself. Kent's backyard was perceived as the backyard of all British citizens.

Table 1. British Attitudes to the Channel Tunnel, 1986
(percentages)

Region	against	neither	for
North	37.5	28.6	33.9
Wales	38.3	11.7	50.0
London	38.5	25.6	35.9
Northwest	43.8	15.2	41.0
Southeast 1	44.2	22.1	33.7
West Midlands	48.9	21.3	29.8
Yorkshire–Humberside	50.0	25.0	25.0
Scotland	51.5	18.4	30.1
North Midlands	57.6	13.6	28.8
East Anglia	58.2	16.4	25.5
Southwest	59.3	16.3	24.4
Southeast 2	63.0	15.7	21.3

SOURCE: Directorate General of the European Commission, Eurobarometer No. 25, *Public Opinion in the European Community, Spring 1986.*

$N = 1{,}017.$

A TUNNEL OF EUROPE?: EUROPEAN ATTITUDES TOWARD THE TUNNEL

Table 2 shows that in 1986, Europeans generally supported plans to build a Channel tunnel, with 66 percent for and only 12 percent against. However, there are some notable differences between countries. Respondents from Spain, Italy, Ireland, and particularly Greece and Portugal (at this stage these countries were not yet members of the EU) were most strongly in favor. Opinions in Luxembourg, the Netherlands, France, and the former West Germany were very similar, with about two-thirds of the population in support, while in Denmark, Northern Ireland, and Belgium, people were slightly less enthusiastic.

British attitudes toward the tunnel project become truly remarkable in comparison to those of other Europeans. Only 30 percent of British citizens were for the proposed tunnel in 1986, considerably less than the 66 percent for all of Europe. Belgium ranks second in terms of absence of support for the tunnel (56 percent), but it also has a low level of opposition (11 percent). Considering that Britain incorporates Wales, whose people were rel-

Table 2. European Attitudes to the Channel Tunnel, 1986 (percentages)

Country	against	neither	for
Great Britain	50.0	19.2	30.9
Belgium	11.4	32.4	56.2
Northern Ireland	16.7	22.7	60.5
Denmark	20.7	18.5	60.7
West Germany	7.8	27.1	65.0
France	6.8	27.5	65.7
Netherlands	9.0	23.6	67.3
Luxembourg	5.0	26.2	68.8
Ireland	11.0	14.4	74.6
Spain	5.0	18.7	76.3
Italy	5.1	17.4	77.5
Portugal	2.7	15.8	81.5
Greece	3.1	11.3	85.7
All Europe	12.6	21.2	66.2

SOURCE: Directorate General of the European Commission, Eurobarometer No. 25, *Public Opinion in the European Community, Spring 1986.*
$N = 10,225.$

atively more in favor of the tunnel, the percentage of Britons supporting the tunnel is exceptionally low. Moreover, with 50 percent against, Britain was also the country with the most opposition to the tunnel. Denmark's relatively high percentage of citizens opposing the tunnel (20 percent) is counterbalanced by its high level of support (60 percent).

It is instructive to compare these findings with attitudes toward European unification in order to examine whether the tunnel can be considered a symbolic indicator of the new Europe and of shifting relations between Britain and the European mainland. In a revealing analysis entitled "The Myth of Post-National Identity: Popular Support for European Unification" (1996), Mathieu Deflem and Fred Pampel examine attitudes toward unified Europe. On the basis of Eurobarometer surveys conducted in 1982, 1986, 1989, and 1992, they find that Europeans on average were consistently much in favor of European unification. However, they also found important variations in levels of support between countries, which could not be attributed to variables such as age, sex, education, profession, and ideological cleavages in terms of left and right political identification. This may raise further questions about sweeping statements such as that made by Lord Pennock, chairman of Eurotunnel, who said that with respect to the Tunnel "from many of the surveys we have carried out we have noticed that almost universally our young people under the age of 25 welcome the project with open arms. However, regrettably some of our older and, from today's debate, less intelligent members of our community over the age of 55 feel equally strongly the other way" (Channel Tunnel Bill, *Parliamentary Debates*, vol. 484, no. 40 [1987], col. 920).

In 1986, nearly 85 percent of all respondents were for or very much for efforts to unify Europe (see Deflem and Pampel 1996). With respect to national differences in attitudes, Luxembourg was most in favor, followed by the Netherlands, Spain, the former West Germany, Italy, France, Portugal, and Belgium. Less supportive of European unification were Ireland, Greece, Northern Ireland, and particularly Britain and Denmark. These findings indicate that country differences in attitudes toward the tunnel generally correspond to country differences in attitudes toward European unification. However, there are some notable exceptions. Specifically, Germany was less supportive of the tunnel than it was of European unification. Relative to Europe as a whole, Greece was more against unification of Europe but most in support of the Tunnel. And, compared with Britain, Denmark was more in favor of the tunnel but even more opposed to a unified Europe.

What these findings suggest, then, is that at least in some countries, the tunnel was perceived as a matter pertaining to France and Britain, rather than as a symbol of a transnational Europe. However, in sharp and clear contrast, British attitudes were as negative toward the tunnel as toward European unification. In Britain, in other words, the tunnel was a highly charged icon of European intervention, additionally tainted by its association with France. In some British regions, this involved less opposition to the Tunnel, such as in Wales, which favored the idea of a united Europe and its weakening of British power over the region. In other areas, such as in the southeast and southwest of England, the tunnel was strongly opposed, perhaps because perception of it as a potential invasion route, breaching the country's island isolation, made it seem threatening. Thus, reactions toward the building of the tunnel are revealing of the wider cultural responses to the idea of united Europe and of perceptions of the role the tunnel might play in this process. But it was only on the English side of the Channel that this association between the tunnel and European unity lead to forceful opposition.

The English are known for their antagonism to the notion of membership in a European community (Worcester 1990; Stephenson 1993; Pinder 1991; Friend 1994). It is against this background, related to the country's geographical isolation, peculiar legal and political institutions, mixture of Welsh, Scottish, Irish, and English nationalisms, and decline as an industrial and imperial power that the Channel Tunnel has to be considered. British attitudes toward European unity remained negative between 1986 and 1992, and in 1994, in one of many phone surveys conducted by national newspapers, respondents voted 13 to 1 for the British government to "grab back its sovereignty from Brussels and have trade only links with Europe" (*Sun*, 29 Apr. 1994). Only 32 percent of English people considered their country powerful in the eyes of other nations in 1994, in contrast to 73 percent in Japan, 73 percent in Germany, and 87 percent in the United States (*Guardian*, 2 Apr. 1994). These figures and surveys are not conclusive by any means and only help to round out the wider picture. But they do provide some insight into why the Channel Tunnel has become such a highly charged emblem of European intervention: it "represents in a symbolic sense what '1992' [the year of the signing of the Maastricht Treaty] does in terms of political reality" (Ratcliffe 1992: 110).

A Summary of European Union Treaties, Legislation, and Agreements Relevant to the Channel Tunnel

The idea of a united Europe has a long historical genealogy and is not simply a modern phenomenon that has emerged in the second half of the twentieth century. It has existed since at least the fourteenth century and endures in the political and economic aspirations of the Roman Catholic Church, which through its missionizing activities has sought to "civilize" and unite the old and new worlds (see Hay 1957; Delanty 1995). However, it is through the Treaty of Rome (1957) that the idea of a united Europe has taken on a modern and concrete form.

The original six signatory member states to the Treaty of Rome have expanded by 1998 to include fifteen countries, with 368 million citizens, and there are constantly new (and often bitter) petitions by outside states to join. Some theorists of the European Union predict that opening it up or "widening" it to incorporate central and eastern European countries will increase its economic and political presence in international politics and its overall capacity to affect power relations between trading blocs. Other theorists, however, argue that with its current fifteen members, the EU is already too large and unwieldy to effectively govern and maintain itself as a functioning, popularly supported supranational political, economic, and legal entity. As a consequence, it is argued that there should first be a "deepening" of its internal policies before membership can be opened up to other less economically stable nations, which might become financially dependent upon EU funding. Whether one advocates widening or better integrating the EU, all the member countries face looming major obstacles associated with the European Monetary System and the institutionalizing of the EU's new common monetary unit, the euro. In May 1998, Britain, along with Denmark and Sweden, opted not to participate in the initial establishment of a common monetary system, which came into effect in 1999, with the new currency to be in use by 2002. Britain's reluctance to fully commit to a common currency does not come as a surprise, and follows a long and very turbulent relationship with the other EU member states over recent decades.

The following discussion is a very brief summary of a few of the major treaties and agreements that have punctuated Britain and the EU's common history, which may help to contextualize both the significance of the EU and the wider historical, legal, political, and cultural background to the building of the Channel Tunnel. For an excellent and detailed history of Britain's relations with the European Union, see Stephen George's *An Awkward Partner: Britain in the European Community* (Oxford: Oxford University Press, 1990).

THE TREATY OF ROME (1957)

The Treaty of Rome was signed by Belgium, France, (West) Germany, Italy, Luxembourg, and the Netherlands on 27 March 1957 to take advantage of market growth and economic recovery after World War II. The European Economic Community (ECC), as it was then known, was originally conceived of largely as a common free market for capital and trade through a customs union between the Benelux countries and two of the three largest economic powers in Europe, France, and Germany. However, the Treaty of Rome also embodied a more profound ideological and political rationale, which was to avert future European wars by institutionalizing intrastate integration and interdependence. The treaty was very much a document reflecting the anxieties of the Cold War. It sought to amend inter-European tensions and in the process consolidate Europe's resources to better cope with its rather ambiguous and vulnerable position between an increasingly polarized and antagonistic United States and USSR. These various sentiments are reflected in article 2 of the treaty, which states a desire to "promote throughout the Community a harmonious development of economic activities, a continuous and balanced expansion, an increased stability, an accelerated raising of the standard of living and closer relations between its Member States."

At the turn of the nineteenth century, and particularly after World War I ended in 1918, British federalists were very strong advocates of the idea of a modern united Europe. This support intensified throughout the 1930s with the rise of Hitler and in the 1940s with the revelation of war horrors. Clement Attlee, Britain's first postwar prime minister (1945–51), went so far as to say: "Europe must federate or perish" (quoted in Ward 1996: 3).

However, by the time of the signing of the Treaty of Rome in March 1957, the British government had adopted a very different attitude. There was open hostility to and xenophobic anxiety expressed against any idea of a federal Europe. The fact that federalism was not canvassed or promoted by the six signatory countries to the Treaty of Rome apparently did not matter to the British public and administration. Sir Anthony Eden, prime minister in the period immediately preceding the signing of the treaty, declared that joining a European community was "something which we know in our bones we cannot do," and Prime Minister Harold Macmillan is asserted to have said a few years later that European integration was an idea put about by "the Jews, the planners, and the old cosmopolitan element" (Ward 1996: 15).

The British government quickly realized its mistake in failing to join the EEC in 1957 and made numerous applications in the late 1950s. With colonial independence and the dismantling of Commonwealth monopolies in the 1960s, Britain began exporting more goods to the European Community than to its former colonies, a shift in trade that made membership in the EEC even more desirable. However, France's President Charles de Gaulle was not impressed by Britain's sudden about-face. After public skirmishes with Macmillan, de Gaulle determinedly blocked all British requests for membership, arguing that Britain was not sufficiently stable economically to join.

Finally, in the early 1970s, amid world oil crises and a very depressed world economy, the six member states decided that their own financial security required the EEC to open its doors in an attempt to share the burden of worldwide economic recession. Britain, Denmark, and Ireland joined the EEC in 1973; Greece joined in 1981; Portugal and Spain in 1986; and Austria, Finland, and Norway in 1995.

THE SCHENGEN AGREEMENT (1985)

The Schengen Agreement was signed in 1985 at Schengen in Luxembourg, at the intersection of Luxembourg, France, and Germany. Its purpose is to remove all internal controls at land, sea, and air frontiers between the signatory countries and maintain common visa policy and security controls at the external borders of "Schengenland," the area of free circulation within the European Union created by its signatories, Belgium, the Netherlands, Luxembourg, France, Germany, Portugal, and Spain (Italy signed in 1990, Greece in 1992, and Austria in 1995, but each of these countries has yet to prove the capacity to effectively monitor its external borders). It is an intergovernmental agreement that was established outside the EC framework in an environment of frustration at the slow pace of the developing European Community and especially the emerging state differences over the exchange rate mechanism and the long-term future of integrated political and economic union.

Part I of the Schengen Agreement came into force in 1986 and deals with short-term conditions for the transfer of goods and services across borders, while Part II, which deals with the free movement of peoples, came into force in 1990. This second section was largely delayed because of the fall of the Berlin Wall in 1989 and the many uncertainties surrounding the potential movement of East Germans into the former West Germany and the rest of the EU. However, the Schengen Agreement was not fully implemented until 1995, with the dismantling of internal border controls, creating genuine freedom of movement for individuals within six of the seven signatory states. Drug trafficking, common asylum and visa policies, and capacities to effectively police the movement of peoples, especially third world nationals, are the mutual concerns of the Schengen signatories.

Britain has refused to sign the Schengen Agreement, since it neither entirely trusts the effectiveness of external border controls across Schengenland nor is yet willing to give up its own sovereign jurisdiction in that respect. With respect to the policing of the Channel Tunnel, the British government continues to treat the Channel waters as a border zone and so subject to full surveillance and maintenance, as if an external frontier. However, in practice, the Kent police operate as if the Channel is, for all intents and purposes, an "Internal Frontier" according to the definition set out in article 1 of Schengen Agreement II (1990) (Fijnaut 1993). As discussed in chapter 4, this has led to increased communication and cooperation between police forces in England, France, Belgium, and the Netherlands, institutionalized in technologies such as Policespeak and the Schengen Information System, among other interesting developments. It appears that localized, on-the-ground trans-European policing practices are to some extent developing independently of international treaties and official state and EU policies. Of course, issues of trust and confidence still inhibit full police cooperation between Britain and the Schengenland state members, as well as across the EU's Europol police force and TREVI's (Terrorism, Radicalism, Extremism and Political Violence) four working groups on terrorism, public order, international crime, and cross-border police and security.

THE SINGLE EUROPEAN ACT (1986)

After significant political and economic stagnation throughout the 1970s and 1980s, concerted efforts were made to revitalize the European Community through constitutional reform. Apart from the need to streamline internal market control and regulation, real concerns over the lack of democratic process (commonly referred to as the "democratic deficit") in the Community urgently required attention.

In the spirit of reform and cooperation, a draft treaty was drawn up in 1984, and various intergovernmental conferences were held in the years preceding the implementation of the Single European Act signed in 1986, which became effective in July 1987, after the Irish approved the document in a referendum. However, despite all these efforts, for many people the end result was extremely disappointing. The Single European Act did provide some institutional structure for the EEC's economic recovery in the very important article 8A. Yet on the more emotionally charged and ideological issue of democratic reform, it made very little change. The European Parliament was officially recognized in article 3.1, and legislative "co-operation" between the European Council and Parliament was indicated in articles 6 and 7. Perhaps most promisingly, article 149 granted Parliament the right to reject or amend propositions suggested to it by the council. Notwithstanding these concessions, the practical technicalities involved prevented Parliament from assuming any real power or ultimate right to modify decisions made in the council. According to Pierre Pescatore, the act was a deceptive piece of legislation designed in appearance only to read as reform:

> The Single Act does not contain any tangible commitment by the Member States, no obligation which could be defined in precise terms. It opens or seems to open some new avenues, though most of them had already existed under the original EEC Treaty [Treaty of Rome], but each new possibility is outweighed by corresponding loopholes, reservations and new unanimity requirements. . . . Thus, the lip service paid in paragraph 4 of the Preamble to the "European idea" is no substitute for real progress towards democracy and political cooperation.
>
> (Pescatore quoted in Ward 1996: 33)

THE CHANNEL TUNNEL TREATY (1986)
AND CHANNEL TUNNEL ACT (1987)

Under article 10 of the Channel Tunnel Treaty, the British and French governments set up an intergovernmental commission to supervise the Tunnel, but its status caused some anxiety, since it was, on the one hand, a neutral international authority, and, on the other, possessed powers sufficient to produce changes in the internal legal system of each state. Moreover, disputes among the sixteen members of the commission were to be arbitrated by a tribunal sitting in Brussels, indicating that ultimate control did not lie with state governments. Under article 19(2) of the treaty, this tribunal was to consist of one representative each chosen by Britain and France, with scope to appoint a representative of another state as a third arbitrator, subject to mutual consent. Article 19(2)(c) provided for the president of the European Court of Justice to make the necessary appointment if mutual consent could not be obtained.

Although the treaty gives Eurotunnel a great deal of leeway to apply its own procedures and negotiate its own terms with British and French governments, it also specifically states that the EU, both with respect to arbitration and legality, is the ultimate authority. So ostensibly while the treaty is between a construction company located in two states, the overriding jurisdiction of the EU lurks in the background. For example, under article 19(6), resolution of any dispute requires that the "rules of English law or the rules of French law may, as appropriate, be applied when recourse to these rules is necessary for the implementation of particular obligations under English law or French law," but article 9(3) decrees that national law is applicable only if subject to and consistent with EU law.

Similar to the ambiguous status of the intergovernmental commission is the status of Eurotunnel itself. At times, it has been represented as independent of national interests, but at other times the company has been split along national lines. With respect to the frontier between England and France, for example, which amounts to an imaginary line out at sea midway along the line of the Tunnel, article 3(3) states that if any works from any "one of the two States [not Eurotunnel] extend beyond the line of the frontier, the law that applies in that part which so extends shall, in relation to matters occurring before that part is effectively connected with works which project from the Other State, be the law of the first mentioned State." This language was clarified the following year under the Channel Tunnel Act (1987), however, which clearly differentiates between Eurotunnel crews working from the direction of England and France and separate state entities. Under article 10 of the act:

1. The land comprising the tunnel system as far as the frontier, so far as not forming part of the United Kingdom before the passing of this Act, shall, as it becomes occupied by or on behalf of the Concessionaires working from England, together with so much of the surrounding subsoil as is necessary for the security of the part of the system so occupied, be incorporated into England and form part of the district of Dover in the county of Kent, and the law of England shall apply accordingly.

3. Until the English section effectively joins the French section, any crossfrontier extension of the English section shall be treated as being in England and, except for rating purposes, as forming part of the county of Kent and the law of England shall apply there.

Specific issues for England raised by the Tunnel, such as race relations and immigration, passport controls, and customs and taxation, are referred to in supplementary protocols and agreements between England, France, and Eurotunnel. On the Tunnel itself, the Channel Tunnel Act (1987) gives legal guidelines for the status of the Tunnel system and surrounding lands, construction and building regulations, safety precautions, labor and workers' compensation, maintenance of the Tunnel system, supervision of the intergovernmental commission, compulsory land acquisition, and so on. Besides the comprehensive legal details, the central difference between the Channel Tunnel Treaty and the Channel Tunnel Act is that the latter also deals with the road and rail networks connected to the fast-rail link in Kent. Debated at length in the House of Commons and subjected to public objections, like the Channel Tunnel Hybrid Bill, the act attempts to go beyond the more immediate problems of constructing the Tunnel and deal with the Tunnel's infrastructure and wider impact on Kent's landscape.

THE TREATY OF EUROPEAN UNION (MAASTRICHT TREATY) (1992)

The Treaty of European Union, signed in the town of Maastricht in the Netherlands in 1992, and commonly referred to as the Maastricht Treaty, was viewed as a necessity in the wake of the disappointment and frustration of the Single European Act. Implemented some five years after the Single European Act, the Maastricht Treaty represented real efforts on behalf of the EEC state leaders to achieve economic, political, and social integration. Up to this point, many had held on to the belief that the European Community was solely an entity providing structural institutions for economic integration, and that the political and social arenas would still be solidly contained within and controlled by sovereign nation-states. With the increasing realization that these three arenas are not mutually exclusive emerged a more widespread appreciation that the alienation of the general public owing to the "democratic deficit" was detrimental to the progress and success of the European Community. In short, Brussels bureaucrats, led by Jacques Delors, the European Commission's enthusiastic and visionary president, came to see that without the support of ordinary citizens, and the introduction of a social charter that dealt with issues such as employment, immigration, and political representation for people moving across internal borders, the European Community would remain a sterile and ultimately limited mechanism.

Throughout the 1980s and into the early 1990s, Britain stood firmly against these proposals for higher levels of integration between member states. Prime Minister Margaret Thatcher took a strong stand against any moves to institutionalize and standardize wages, working conditions, and public health policy across state jurisdictions or to make political representation more accessible and more accountable to ordinary people. According to one onlooker, her strategy for European diplomacy was to rampage "from summit to summit as a sort of fishwife Britannia demanding her money back" (quoted in Ward 1996: 37). It was at precisely this time that Thatcher rather cynically agreed to sign the Channel Tunnel Treaty (1986) as a public demonstration of the country's commitment to the European Union. In this context, it is hardly surprising that many in Kent felt that their country had sold them out, sacrificing their heritage, homes, and livelihood to a European ideal that Thatcher in her famous Bruges speech openly denounced as threatening to the spirit of Magna Carta.

A great deal has been written about the implementation and significance of the Maastricht Treaty, and I can in no way do justice to its complexity here. For many commentators, it was felt that it did not go far enough in effecting social reform through the Social Charter and equalizing the balance of power within the European Union's central institutions. One of the most strident criticisms has been directed against the treaty's vague introduction of the principle of subsidiarity, making it almost impossible to implement in any meaningful way its ideology of bringing processes of decision-making closer to citizens, as spelled out in its article 3b.

Since subsidiarity implies a vertical division of political power, it has been referred to as the basic characteristic of federalism. Some analysts see subsidiarity as a principle of noncentralization and so a way of institutionalizing direct contacts between the European Union and substate governments, including interest groups and citizens, without too much concern for the opinions of member states. How subsidiarity will play out in the future is a question of much debate. Certainly, at the level of local and regional governments, it has raised many hopes, and perhaps nowhere more so than in England, where local governments experienced a steady decline of their relative autonomy under the Conservative party that governed Britain for eighteen years between 1979 and 1997. As discussed above in chapter 7, Kent County Council is taking advantage of this opening up of avenues of authority and financial support that exist beyond the reach of London.

Bibliography

Abèles, Marc. 1991. *Quiet Days in Burgundy: A Study of Local Politics.* Translated by Annella McDermott. Cambridge: Cambridge University Press. Originally published as *Jours tranquilles en 89: Ethnologie politique d'un département français* (Paris: O. Jacob, 1988).

Abrams, Philip. 1988 [1977]. "Notes on the Difficulty of Studying the State." *Journal of Historical Sociology* 1: 57–89.

Adams, James. 1993. *Taking the Tunnel.* London: Michael Joseph.

Agnew, John A. 1987. *Place and Politics: The Geographical Mediation of State and Society.* Boston: Allen & Unwin.

Albrechts, L., F. Moulaert, P. Roberts, and E. Swyngedouw, eds. 1989. *Regional Policy at the Crossroads: European Perspectives.* London: Jessica Kingsley.

Aldridge, Trevor M. 1967. *Boundaries, Walls and Fences.* London: Oyez.

Alfrey, Nicholas, et al. 1993. *Towards a New Landscape.* London: Bernard Jacobson.

Alison, J., and B. Lardinois, eds. 1994. *Soundings.* Maidstone, Kent: Cross Channel Photographic Mission in cooperation with South East Arts.

Amin, Ash, and Nigel Thrift. 1994. "Living in the Global." In id., eds., *Globalization, Institutions, and Regional Development in Europe*, pp. 1–22. Oxford: Oxford University Press.

Anderson, Benedict. 1991. *Imagined Communities: Reflections on the Origin and Spread of Nationalism.* Rev. ed. New York: Verso.

Anderson, J. 1989. Nationalisms in a Disunited Kingdom. In J. Mohan, ed., *The Political Geography of Contemporary Britain*, pp. 35–50. London: Macmillan.

———. 1992. *The Territorial Imperative: Pluralism, Corporatism, and Economic Crisis.* Cambridge: Cambridge University Press.

Anderson, M. 1987. "Planning and Environmental Concern in Britain." In C. Church, ed., *Approaching the Channel Tunnel*, pp. 34–45. University Association for Contemporary European Studies Occasional Paper 3. Canterbury: University of Kent.

Andrews, M. 1992. "Englishness and English Landscape." Open Lecture, University of Kent, Canterbury.

Appadurai, Arjun. 1991. "Global Ethnoscapes: Notes and Queries for a Transnational Anthropology." In R. G. Fox, ed., *Recapturing Anthropology: Working in the Present*. Santa Fe, N.M.: School of American Research Press, distributed by University of Washington Press.

————. 1996a. *Modernity at Large: Cultural Dimensions of Globalization*. Minneapolis: University of Minnesota Press.

————. 1996b. "Sovereignty without Territoriality: Notes for a Postnational Geography." In P. Yager, ed., *The Geography of Identity*, pp. 40–58. Ann Arbor: University of Michigan Press.

Armstrong, H. W. 1993. "Subsidiarity and the Operation of European Community Regional Policy in Britain." *Regional Studies* 27, 6: 575–606.

Arnason, Johann P. 1990. "Nationalism, Globalization and Modernity." *Theory, Culture and Society* 7: 207–36.

Ascherson, Neal. 1992. "Nations and Regions." In R. Kearney, ed., *Visions of Europe*, pp. 13–22. Dublin: Wolfhound Press.

Ashworth, G. J. 1994. "From History to Heritage: From Heritage to Identity: In Search of Concepts and Models." In G. J. Ashworth and P. J. Larkham, eds., *Building a New Heritage: Tourism, Culture and Identity in the New Europe*, pp. 13–30. London: Routledge.

Balchin, Paul N. 1990. *Regional Policy in Britain: The North-South Divide*. London: Paul Chapman.

Baldwin, T. 1992. "Territoriality." In H. Gross and R. Harrison, eds., *Jurisprudence: Cambridge Essays*, pp. 207–30. Cambridge: Cambridge University Press.

Bale, John. 1994. *Landscapes of Modern Sport*. London: Leicester University Press.

Barber, Stephen, and T. Millns. 1993. *Building the New Europe: The Role of Local Authorities in the UK*. London: Association of County Councils.

Barman, C. 1950. *Early British Railways*. Harmondsworth, Eng.: Penguin Books.

Barnes, Julian. 1995. *Letters from London, 1990–1995*. London: Picador.

Barry, A. 1993. "The European Community and European Government: Harmonization, Mobility and Space." *Economy and Society Review* 22: 314–26.

Barth, Frederick. 1969. *Ethnic Groups and Boundaries*. Boston: Little, Brown.

Baudrillard, Jean. 1993. *The Transparency of Evil: Essays on Extreme Phenomena*. Translated by James Benedict. London: Verso. Originally published as *La Transparence du mal: Essai sur les phenomenes extremes* (Paris: Galilee, 1990).

Bauman, Zygmunt. 1987. *Legislators and Interpreters: On Modernity, Post-Modernity and Intellectuals*. Ithaca, N.Y.: Cornell University Press.

Behrman, Cynthia F. 1977. *Victorian Myths of the Sea*. Athens: Ohio University Press.

Bender, Barbara. 1993. "Introduction: Landscape—Meaning and Action." In id., ed., *Landscape: Politics and Perspectives*, pp. 1–18. Providence, R.I.: Berg.

Bently, Lionel. 1996. Introduction. In id. and Leo Flynn, eds., *Law and Senses: Sensational Jurisprudence*, pp. 1–20. London: Pluto Press.

Bently, Lionel, and Leo Flynn, eds. 1996. *Law and Senses: Sensational Jurisprudence*. London: Pluto Press.

Berdahl, Daphne. 1999. *"Where the World Ended": Transition and Identity in the German Borderland*. Berkeley and Los Angeles: University of California Press.

Bergeron, John H. 1998. *An Ever Whiter Myth: The Colonization of Modernity in European Community Law*. In P. Fitzpatrick and J. H. Bergeron, eds., *Europe's Other: European Law Between Modernity and Postmodernity*, pp. 3–26. Aldershot, Hants.: Ashgate.

Bermingham, Ann. 1994. "Redesigning Nature: John Constable and the Landscape of Enclosure." In Roger Friedland and Deirdre Bodin, eds., *Now Here: Space, Time and Modernity*, pp. 236–56. Berkeley and Los Angeles: University of California Press.

Beynon, H., and R. Hudson. 1993. "Place and Space in Contemporary Europe: Some Lessons and Reflections." *Antipode* 25: 171–90.

Bhabha, Homi. 1986. "The Other Question: Difference, Discrimination and the Discourse of Colonialism." In F. Barker, P. Hulme, M. Iverson, and D. Loxley, eds., *Literature, Politics and Theory*, pp. 148–72. London: Methuen.

———, ed. 1990. *Nation and Narration*. London: Routledge.

———. 1994. *The Location of Culture*. London: Routledge.

Bianchini, Franco. 1993. "Remaking European Cities: The Role of Cultural Policies." In id. and Michael Parkinson, eds., *Cultural Policy and Urban Regeneration*. Manchester: Manchester University Press.

Bignell, Alan. 1983. *Kent Lore: A Heritage of Fact and Fable*. London: Robert Hale.

Birch, R. 1989. "Policing Europe in 1992." *Police Journal* 62, 3: 203–10.

———. 1991. "International Cooperation of the Police." *Police Journal* 64, 4: 289–98.

Bird, J. B. Curtis, T. Putnam, G. Robertson, and L. Tickner, eds. 1993. *Mapping the Futures: Local Cultures, Global Change*. London: Routledge.

Black, Jeremy. 1986. *Natural and Necessary Enemies: Anglo-French Relations in the Eighteenth Century*. Athens: University of Georgia Press.

Blacksell, M., A. Clarke, K. Economides, and C. Watkins. 1988. "Legal Services in Rural Areas: Problems of Access and Local Need." *Progress in Human Geography* 12: 47–65.

Blackstone, William. 1765. *Commentaries on the Laws of England*. 2d rev. ed. Vol. 1. Chicago: Callaghan, 1879.

Blomley, Nicolas K. 1989a. "Text and Context: Rethinking the Law-Space Nexus." *Progress in Human Geography* 13: 512–34.

———. 1989b. "Interpretative Practices, the State, and the Locale." In J. Wolch and M. Dear, eds., *The Power of Geography: How Territory Shapes Social Life,* pp. 175–96. Boston: Unwin Hyman.

———. 1994. *Law, Space and the Geographies of Power.* New York: Guilford Press.

Blomley, Nicolas K., and Gordon L. Clark. 1990. "Law, Theory, and Geography." *Urban Geography* 11, 5: 4333–46.

Bloomfield, P. 1987. *Kent and the Napoleonic Wars.* Vol. 10 of *Kentish Sources.* Gloucester: Allan Sutton for Kent Archives Office.

Bohm, K. 1994. "Urban Innovations in Nordic Countries." In European Foundation for the Improvement of Living and Working Conditions, *European Conference on Urban Innovations, Seville, 6–8 October 1993,* pp. 99–112. Lanham, Md.: UNIPUB (distributor).

Bonyhady, Tim. 1987. *The Law of the Countryside: The Rights of the Public.* Milton Park Estate, Abingdon: Professional Books.

Borneman, John. 1992. *Belonging in the Two Berlins: Kin, State, Nation.* Cambridge: Cambridge University Press.

Boyes, Georgina. 1993. *The Imagined Village: Culture, Ideology and the English Folk Revival.* Manchester: Manchester University Press.

Brand, John. 1795. "Rogation Week and Ascension Day." In id., *Observations on the Popular Antiquities of Great Britain,* rev. H. Ellis, pp. 197–212. London: Henry G. Bohn, 1853.

Brandon, P. F. 1979. "The Diffusion of Designed Landscapes in South-East England." In H. S. A. Fox and R. A. Butlin, eds., *Change in the Countryside: Essays on Rural England 1500–1900,* pp. 165–87. London: Institute of British Geographers.

Brandon, P. F., and B. Short. 1990. *The South East from AD 1000.* London: Longman.

Brennan, Teresa. 1993. *History after Lacan.* London: Routledge.

Brenner, N. 1997. "Global, Fragmented, Hierarchical: Henri Lefebvre's Geographies of Globalization." *Public Culture* 10, 1: 135–68.

Briggs, Asa. 1994. *A Social History of England: From the Ice Age to the Channel Tunnel.* New ed. London: Weidenfeld & Nicolson.

British Museum. 1992. *Europeans in Caricature, 1770–1830.* Exhibition Guide. London: British Museum Press.

Brockway, Lucile H. 1979. *Science and Colonial Expansion: The Role of the British Royal Botanic Gardens.* London: Academic Press.

Brownwell, M. R. 1978. *Alexander Pope and the Arts of Georgian England.* Oxford: Clarendon Press.

Bryant, Sir Arthur. 1967. *Protestant Island.* London: Collins.

Bryson, Norman. 1983. *Vision and Painting: The Logic of the Gaze.* New Haven, Conn.: Yale University Press.

———. 1988. "The Gaze in the Expanded Field." In H. Foster, ed., *Vision and Visuality*, pp. 87–114. Seattle: Bay Press.

Buchanan, Ruth. 1995. "Border Crossings: NAFTA, Regulatory Restructuring, and the Politics of Place." *Indiana Journal of Global Legal Studies* 2, 2: 371–94.

———. 1996. "Re-Viewing *Local Hero*: Problems of Perspective and Scale in Research on Globalization." Paper presented at the Law and Society Annual Meeting, Glasgow, July.

Buck, N., I. Gordon, C. Pickvance, and P. Taylor-Gooby. 1989. "The Isle of Thanet: Restructuring and Municipal Conservatism." In P. Cooke, ed., *Localities: The Changing Face of Britain*, pp. 166–97. London: Unwin Hyman.

Bulpitt, Jim. 1983. *Territory and Power in the United Kingdom*. Manchester: Manchester University Press.

Bunn, David. 1994. "'Our Wattled Cot': Mercantile and Domestic Space in Thomas Pringle's African Landscapes." In W. J. T. Mitchell, ed., *Landscape and Power*, pp. 127–74. Chicago: University of Chicago Press.

Bunyan, Tony. 1991. "Towards an Authoritarian European State." *Race and Class* 32, 3: 19–30.

———. 1993. "Trevi, Europol and the New European State." In id., ed., *State-watching the New Europe: A Handbook on the European State*, pp. 15–36. London: Statewatch.

Burchell, G., C. Gordon, and P. Miller. 1986. *The Foucault Effect: Essays on Governmental Rationality*. Brighton: Harvester.

Burke, Edmund. 1955 [1790]. *Reflections on the Revolution in France*. Intro. by T. H. D. Mahoney. New York: Liberal Arts Press.

Burt, R., and J. M. Archer, eds. 1994. *Enclosure Acts: Sexuality, Property, and Culture in Early Modern England*. Ithaca, N.Y.: Cornell University Press.

Bushaway, R. W. 1992. "Rite, Legitimation and Community in Southern England, 1700–1850: The Ideology of Custom." In B. Stapleton, ed., *Conflict and Community in Southern England*, pp. 110–34. New York: St. Martin's Press.

Caenegem, R. C. van. 1973. *The Birth of the English Common Law*. Cambridge: Cambridge University Press.

Camilleri, Joseph A., and Jim Falk. 1992. *The End of Sovereignty?: The Politics of a Shrinking and Fragmenting World*. Aldershot, Hants.: Edward Elgar.

Campbell, I. 1993. "From the 'Personal Union' between England and Scotland in 1603 to the European Communities Act 1972 and Beyond—Enduring Legal Problems from an Historical Viewpoint." In B. S. Jackson and D. McGoldrick, eds., *Legal Visions of the New Europe: Essays Celebrating the Centenary of the Faculty of Law, University of Liverpool*, pp. 37–106. London: Graham & Trotman / Martinus Nijhoff.

Carlyle, Thomas. 1891 [1837]. *The French Revolution*. London: Chapman & Hall.

Carter, E., J. Donald, and J. Squires, eds. 1993. *Space and Place: Theories of Identity and Location*. London: Lawrence & Wishart.

Carty, Anthony. 1991. "English Constitutional Law from a Postmodernist Perspective." In P. Fitzpatrick, ed., *Dangerous Supplements*, pp. 182–206. London: Pluto Press.

Casey, Edward S. 1993. *Getting Back Into Place: Toward a Renewed Understanding of the Place-World*. Bloomington: Indiana University Press.

Castells, Manuel. 1994. "European Cities, the Informational Society, and the Global Economy." *New Left Review* 204: 18–32.

Certeau, Michel de. 1984. *The Practice of Everyday Life*. Berkeley and Los Angeles: University of California Press.

———. 1998. *Culture in the Plural*. Introduction by L. Giard. Minneapolis: University of Minnesota Press.

Chambers, Iain. 1990. *Border Dialogues: Journeys in Postmodernity*. London: Routledge.

———. 1994. *Migrancy, Culture, Identity*. London: Routledge.

Channel Tunnel Archives. Churchill Archives Centre.

Channel Tunnel Bill. 1987. Second reading before the House of Lords. *Hansard*. 16 February.

Channel Tunnel Group. 1985. *Channel Tunnel Project Protection against Rabies*. London: Channel Tunnel Group.

———. 1990. *Rabies and the Channel Tunnel*. Eurotunnel Publications, E253. London: Channel Tunnel Group.

———. 1991. *From Ice Age to Tunnel: A Story of Life in South East Kent*. From the works of Canterbury Archaeological Trust. Eurotunnel Publication. Folkestone, Kent: Channel Tunnel Group.

———. 1992. *Eurotunnel Information Paper: Rabies and the Channel Tunnel*. Eurotunnel Publications, M3. London: Channel Tunnel Group.

Chatterjee, Partha. 1993. *The Nation and Its Fragments: Colonial and Postcolonial Histories*. Princeton, N.J.: Princeton University Press.

Cheshire, P. C., and I. R. Gordon, eds. 1995. *Territorial Competition in an Integrating Europe*. Aldershot, Hants.: Avebury.

Church, A., and P. Reid. 1994. "Anglo-French Co-operation." In R. Gibb, ed., *The Channel Tunnel: A Geographical Perspective*, pp. 199–216. Chichester, Sussex: John Wiley & Sons.

Clamp, Hugh. 1988. *Landscape Professional Practice*. Aldershot, Hants.: Gower Technical Press.

Clark, Gordon L. 1989. "The Geography of Law." In R. Peet and N. Thrift, eds., *New Models in Geography*, pp. 310–37. London: Unwin Hyman.

Classen, Constance. 1993. *Worlds of Sense: Exploring the Senses in History and across Cultures*. London: Routledge.

Claval, Paul. 1992. "The Museification of Landscape." In S. T. Wong, ed., *Person, Place and Thing: Interpretative and Empirical Essays in Cultural Geography*, pp. 335–51. Vol. 31 of *Geoscience and Man*. Baton Rouge: Louisiana State University Press.

Clifford, James. 1986. "Introduction: Partial Truths." In id. and G. E. Marcus, eds., *Writing Culture: The Poetics and Politics of Ethnography*, pp. 1–26. Berkeley and Los Angeles: California University Press.

Clifford, James, and George E. Marcus, eds. 1986. *Writing Culture: The Poetics and Politics of Ethnography*. Berkeley and Los Angeles: University of California Press.

Clutterbuck, Richard. 1990. *Terrorism, Drugs and Crime in Europe after 1992*. London: Routledge.

Coastlines. 1992. London: British Council.

Cobbett, William. 1821. *Political Register*. Vol. 39. London: John M. Cobbett.

———. 1830. *Rural Rides*. Edited by G. Woodcock. London: Penguin Books, 1967.

Cohen, Anthony P. 1987. *Whalsay: Symbol, Segment and Boundary in a Shetland Island Community*. Manchester: Manchester University Press.

Cohn, Bernard S. 1987. "The Census, Social Structure, and Objectification in South Asia." In *An Anthropologist amongst the Historians and Other Essays*. Oxford: Oxford University Press.

Cohn, Bernard S., and Nicholas B. Dirks. 1988. "Beyond the Fringe: The Nation-State, Colonialism, and the Technologies of Power." *Journal of Historical Sociology* 1, 2: 224–29.

Colley, Linda. 1992. *Britons: Forging the Nation, 1707–1837*. New Haven, Conn.: Yale University Press.

Collier, Jane, Bill Maurer, and Laura Suárez Navaz. 1995. "Sanctioned Identities: Legal Constructions of Modern Personhood." *Identities* 2, 1–2: 1–28.

Colls, Robert. 1986. "Englishness and the Political Culture." In id. and Philip Dodd, eds., *Englishness: Politics and Culture, 1880–1920*, pp. 29–61. London: Croom Helm.

Comaroff, John L., and Jean Comaroff. 1992. *Ethnography and the Historical Imagination*. Boulder, Colo.: Westview Press.

Comaroff, John L., and Simon Roberts. 1981. *Rules and Processes: The Cultural Logic of Dispute in an African Context*. Chicago: University of Chicago Press.

Connolly, William E., ed. 1984. *Legitimacy and the State*. Oxford: Blackwell.

———. 1991. *Identity/Difference: Democratic Negotiations of Political Paradox*. Ithaca, N.Y.: Cornell University Press.

Cooke, Philip. 1988. "Modernity, Postmodernity and the City." *Theory, Culture and Society* 5, 2–3: 475–92.

Coombe, Rosemary. 1989. "Toward a Theory of Practice in Critical Legal Studies." *Law and Social Inquiry* 14: 69–121.

Corbusier, Le [Charles-Édouard Jeanneret]. 1929. *The City of Tomorrow*. London: Architectural Press.

Corrigan, Philip, and Derek Sayer. 1985. *The Great Arch: English State Formation as Cultural Revolution*. Oxford: Blackwell.

Cosgrove, Denis. 1989. "Geography Is Everywhere: Culture and Symbolism in Human Landscapes." In D. Gregory and R. Walfrid, eds., *Horizons in Human Geography*, pp. 118–53. London: Macmillan.

———. 1993. "Landscapes and Myths, Gods and Humans." In B. Bender, ed., *Landscape: Politics and Perspectives*, pp. 281–306. Providence, R.I.: Berg.

Cosgrove, Richard A. 1987. *Our Lady the Common Law: An Anglo-American Legal Community, 1870–1930*. New York: New York University Press.

Costonis, John J. 1989. *Icons and Aliens: Law, Aesthetics, and Environmental Change*. Urbana: University of Illinois Press.

Council for the Protection of Rural England. 1992. *Campaigner's Guide to Using EC Environmental Law*. London: Warwick House.

Coutine, Susan. N.d. "The 'Real' Americans: Personhood and Belonging in Mass Naturalization Ceremonies in Los Angeles." MS.

Cox, Andrew. 1984. *Adversary Politics and Land: The Conflict over Land and Property Policy in Post-War Britain*. Cambridge: Cambridge University Press.

Crary, Jonathan. 1990. *Techniques of the Observer: On Vision and Modernity in the Nineteenth Century*. An October Book. Cambridge, Mass.: MIT Press.

Crawford, C. 1992. "European Influence on Local Self-Government." *Local Government Studies* 18, 1: 69–85.

Crisp, Frank. 1966. *Medieval Gardens*. Vol. 1. New York: Hacker Art Books.

Cronon, William. 1983. *Changes in the Land: Indians, Colonists, and the Ecology of New England*. New York: Hill & Wang.

Cross, Rupert. 1977. *Precedent in English Law*. 3d ed. Oxford: Clarendon Press.

Crowley, A. J. 1981. "The Passage of Wildlife through Road and Rail Tunnels." Minister of Agriculture, Fisheries and Wildlife, lecture delivered at the World Health Organization Consultation on Natural Barriers of Wildlife Rabies in Europe, Vienna, 28 April–1 May 1981.

Cvetkovich, A., and D. Kellner. 1997. "Introduction: Thinking Global and Local." In id., eds., *Articulating the Local and the Global*, pp. 1–32. Boulder, Colo.: Westview Press.

Dahrendorf, Ralph. 1982. *On Britain*. London: British Broadcasting Corporation.

Daniels, Stephen. 1988. "The Political Iconography of Woodland in Later Georgian England." In D. Cosgrove and id., eds., *The Iconography of Landscape*, pp. 43–82. Cambridge: Cambridge University Press.

Daniels, Stephen, and Denis Cosgrove. 1988. "Iconography and Landscape." In id., eds., *The Iconography of Landscape: Essays on Symbolic Representation, Design and Use of Past Environments*, pp. 1–10. Cambridge: Cambridge University Press.

———. 1993. "Spectacle and Text: Landscape Metaphors in Cultural Geography." In J. Duncan and D. Ley, eds., *Place/Culture/Representation*, pp. 57–77. London: Routledge.

Daniels, Stephen, and S. Seymour. 1990. "Landscape and the Idea of Improvement." In R. Dodgson and R. A. Butlin, eds., *A New Historical Geography of England and Wales*, pp. 487–519. 2d ed. London: Academic Press.

Darian-Smith, Eve. 1993. "Neighborhood Watch—Who Watches Whom? Re-interpreting the Concept of Neighborhood." *Human Organization* 52, 1: 83–88.

———. 1996. "Postcolonialism: A Brief Introduction." In id. and Peter Fitz-patrick, eds., *Social and Legal Studies*, special issue, *Law and Postcoloni-alism* 5, 3: 291–99.

———, ed. 1998a. With Peter Fitzpatrick. *Laws of the Postcolonial*. Ann Ar-bor: University of Michigan Press. In press.

———. 1998b. Review of *Toward a New Common Sense: Law, Science, and Politics in the Paradigmatic Transition*, by Boaventura de Sousa Santos (New York: Routledge, 1995). *Law & Social Inquiry* 23, 1: 81–120.

Darras, Jacques. 1990. *Beyond the Tunnel of History*. Edited by Daniel Snow-man. Ann Arbor: University of Michigan Press. A revised and expanded version of a 1989 BBC Keith lecture.

Davis, Clarence B., and Kenneth E. Wilburn, eds. 1991. *Railway Imperialism*. New York: Greenwood Press.

Davis, M. 1995. "Fortress Los Angeles: The Militarization of Urban Space." In P. Kasinitz, ed., *Metropolis: Center and Symbol of Our Times*, pp. 355–68. London: Macmillan.

Deflem, Mathieu, and Fred C. Pampel. 1996. "The Myth of Post-National Identity: Popular Support for European Unification." *Social Forces* 75, 1: 119–43.

Defoe, Daniel. 1971 [1724–27]. *A Tour through the Whole Island of Great Britain*. London: Penguin Books.

Delanty, Gerard. 1995. *Inventing Europe: Idea, Identity, Reality*. New York: St. Martin's Press.

Derrida, Jacques. 1990. *Force de loi: Le "Fondement mystique de l'authorité."* Paris: Galilée, 1994. Translated by Mary Quaintance under the title "Force of Law: The 'Mystical Foundations of Authority.'" *Cardozo Law Review* 11, nos. 5–6 (July–August): 920–1045.

———. 1992. *The Other Heading: Reflections on Today's Europe*. Blooming-ton: Indiana University Press. Translated by Pascale-Anne Brault and Mi-chael B. Naas. Originally published as *L'Autre Cap: Suivi de la démocratie ajournée* (Paris: Éditions de Minuit, 1991; reprint, 1997).

Dicey, Albert V. 1915. *Introduction to the Study of the Law of the Consti-tution*. 8th ed. London: Macmillan.

Dodd, Philip. 1986. "Englishness and the National Culture." In Robert Colls and id., eds., *Englishness: Politics and Culture, 1880–1920*, pp. 1–28. Lon-don: Croom Helm.

———. 1995. *The Battle over Britain*. London: Demos.

Donnan, Hastings, and Thomas M. Wilson, eds. 1994. *Border Approaches: Anthropological Perspectives on Frontiers*. Lanham, Md.: University Press of America.

Douglas, Roy. 1976. *Land, People and Politics: A History of the Land Question in the United Kingdom, 1878–1952*. New York: St. Martin's Press.

Drabble, Margaret. 1979. *A Writer's Britain*. London: Book Club Associates.

Drescher, Seymour. 1964. *Tocqueville and England*. Cambridge, Mass.: Harvard University Press.

Duchacek, I. D. 1986. "International Competence of Subnational Governments: Borderlands and Regions." In O. J. Martinez, ed., *Across Boundaries: Transborder Interaction in Comparative Perspective*, pp. 11–30. El Paso: Texas Western Press / Center for Inter-American and Border Studies, University of Texas at El Paso.

Duden, Barbara. 1991. *The Woman beneath the Skin: A Doctor's Patients in Eighteenth-Century Germany*. Cambridge, Mass.: Harvard University Press.

Dumm, T. L. 1990. "Fear of Law." *Studies in Law, Politics, and Society* 10: 29–57.

Economides, K., M. Blacksell, and C. Watkins. 1986. "The Spatial Analysis of Legal Systems: Towards a Geography of Law." *Journal of Law and Society* 13, 2: 161–81.

Edgerton, Samuel Y. 1975. *The Renaissance Rediscovery of Linear Perspective*. New York: Basic Books.

Elias, Norbert. 1982. *Power and Civility: The Civilizing Process*. Vol. 2. Translated by E. Jephcott. New York: Pantheon Books.

Elton, C. I. 1867. *The Tenures of Kent*. London: James Parker.

Emilliou, Nicholas. 1994. "Subsidiarity: Panacea or Fig Leaf?" In T. O'Keeffe, ed., *Legal Issues of the Maastricht Treaty*, pp. 65–83. London: Chancery.

Engel, David M. 1993. "Law in the Domains of Everyday Life: The Construction of Community and Difference." In A. Sarat and T. M. Kearns, eds., *Law in Everyday Life*, pp. 123–70. Ann Arbor: University of Michigan Press.

Enzensberger, Hans Magnus. 1990. *Political Crumbs*. Translated by Martin Chalmers. London: Verso. Originally published as *Politische Brosamen*.

Erp-Houtepan, Anne van. 1986. "The Etymological Origin of the Garden." *Journal of Garden History* 6, 3: 227–31.

Evans-Pritchard, Edward E. 1940. *The Nuer*. New York: Oxford University Press.

———. 1948. *The Divine Kingship of the Shilluk of the Nilotic Sudan*. Cambridge: Cambridge University Press.

Everitt, Alan. 1986. *Continuity and Colonization: The Evolution of Kentish Settlement*. Leicester: Leicester University Press.

Faith, Nicholas. 1990. *The World the Railways Made*. New York: Carroll & Graf.

Fardon, Richard, ed. 1990. *Localizing Strategies: The Regionalization of Ethnographic Accounts*. Washington, D.C.: Smithsonian Institution Press.

Febvre, Lucien P. V. 1982. *The Problem of Unbelief in the Sixteenth Century:*

The Religion of Rabelais. Translated by B. Gottlieb. Cambridge, Mass.: Harvard University Press.

Fernandez, James W. 1985. "Folklorists as Agents of Nationalism." *New York Folklore Quarterly* 11, 1–4: 135–47.

———, ed. 1991. *Beyond Metaphor: The Theory of Tropes in Anthropology.* Stanford: Stanford University Press.

Fiennes, Celia. 1982. *The Illustrated Journeys of Celia Fiennes, c. 1682–1712.* London: MacDonald / Webb & Bower.

Finjnaut, C. 1993. "The Schengen Treaties and European Police Co-operation." *European Journal of Crime, Criminal Law and Criminal Justice* 1, 1: 37–56.

Fitzpatrick, Peter. 1990. "'The Desperate Vacuum': Imperialism and Law in the Experience of the Enlightenment." In Anthony Carty, ed., *Post-Modern Law: Enlightenment, Revolution, and the Death of Man,* pp. 90–106. Edinburgh: Edinburgh University Press.

———. 1992. *The Mythology of Modern Law.* London: Routledge.

———. 1995a. "'We know what it is when you do not ask us': Nationalism as Racism." In id., ed., *Nationalism, Racism and the Rule of Law,* pp. 3–26. Aldershot, Hants.: Dartmouth.

———, ed. 1995b. *Nationalism, Racism and the Rule of Law.* Aldershot, Hants.: Dartmouth.

———. 1998. New Europe and Old Stories: Mythology and Legality in the European Union. In id. and John H. Bergeron, eds., *Europe's Other: European Law between Modernity and Postmodernity,* pp. 27–46. Aldershot, Hants.: Ashgate.

Ford, Richard T. 1994. "The Boundaries of Race: Political Geography in Legal Analysis." *Harvard Law Review:* 1841–1921.

Forsythe, Diana. 1982. *Urban-Rural Migration, Change and Conflict in an Orkney Island Community.* London: Social Science Research Council.

Foucault, Michel. 1977. *Discipline and Punish.* New York: Pantheon Books.

———. 1980. *Power/Knowledge: Selected Interviews and Other Writings 1972–1977.* Edited by C. Gordon. New York: Pantheon Books.

———. 1984. *The Foucault Reader.* Edited by P. Rabinow. New York: Pantheon Books.

———. 1986. "Of Other Spaces." *Diacritics* 16, 1: 22–27.

———. 1988. "Technologies of the Self." In L. H. Martin, H. Gutman, and P. H. Hutton, eds., *Technologies of the Self,* pp. 16–49. Amherst: University of Massachusetts Press.

———. 1991. "Governmentality." In G. Burchell, C. Gordon, and P. Miller, eds., *The Foucault Effect: Studies in Governmentality,* pp. 87–104. Chicago: University of Chicago Press.

Francis, Mark, and Randolph T. Hester Jr. 1990. *The Meaning of Gardens: Idea, Place and Action.* Cambridge, Mass.: MIT Press.

Frazer, Sir James G. 1981 [1890–1915]. *The Golden Bough: The Roots of Religion and Folklore*. 2 vols. in one. New York: Avenel Books.

Friedland, Roger, and Deirdre Bodin, eds. 1994. *Now Here: Space, Time and Modernity*. Berkeley and Los Angeles: University of California Press.

Friend, J. W. 1994. "Nationalism and National Consciousness in France, Germany and Britain: The Year of Maastricht." *History of European Ideas* 18, 2: 187–98.

Fuller, C. 1994. "Legal Anthropology, Legal Pluralism and Legal Thought." *Anthropology Today* 10, 3: 9–12.

Gadacz, R. R. 1982. *Towards an Anthropology of Law in Complex Society: An Analysis of Critical Concepts*. Calgary, Alberta: Western Publishers.

Geertz, Clifford. 1983. "Local Knowledge: Fact and Law in Comparative Perspective." In id., *Local Knowledge*, pp. 167–234. New York: Basic Books.

George, M. D. 1959. *English Political Caricature to 1792: A Study of Opinion and Propaganda*. Oxford: Clarendon Press.

George, Stephen. 1990. *An Awkward Partner: Britain in the European Community*. Oxford: Oxford University Press.

Gibson, J. 1992. "British Local Government Finance under the Conservatives." *Local Government Studies* 18, 4: 55–78.

Gibson, R. 1995. *Best of Enemies: Anglo-French Relations since the Conquest*. London: Sinclair-Stevenson.

Gifford, Don. 1990. *The Farther Shore: A Natural History of Perception, 1798–1984*. New York: Atlantic Monthly Press.

Gilroy, Paul. 1991 [1987]. *"There Ain't No Black in the Union Jack": The Cultural Politics of Race and Nation*. Chicago: University of Chicago Press.

Gluckman, Max. 1958. *Analysis of a Social Situation in Modern Zululand*. Rhodes-Livingstone Paper No. 28. Manchester: Rhodes-Livingstone Institute / Manchester University Press. Reprinted from *Bantu Studies* 14 (March–June 1940).

Goddard, Victoria A., Joseph R. Llobera, and Cris Shore, eds. 1994. *The Anthropology of Europe: Identity and Boundaries in Conflict*. Providence, R.I.: Berg.

Godlewska, Ann, and Neil Smith, eds. 1994. *Geography and Empire*. Oxford: Blackwell.

Goldsmith, Oliver. 1759. *The Bee: A Select Collection of Essays on the Most Interesting and Entertaining Subjects*. London: W. Lane.

Goodrich, Peter. 1991. "Specula Laws: Image, Aesthetic and Common Law." *Law and Critique* 2, 2: 233–54.

———. 1992. "Poor Illiterate Reason: History, Nationalism and Common Law." *Social & Legal Studies* 1: 7–28.

Goodrich, Peter, and Yifat Hachamovitch. 1991. "Time Out of Mind: An Introduction to the Semiotics of Common Law." In P. Fitzpatrick, ed., *Dangerous Supplements*, pp. 159–81. London: Pluto Press.

Goody, Jack. 1993. *The Culture of Flowers*. Cambridge: Cambridge University Press.

Gordon, Colin. 1987. "The Soul of the Citizen: Max Weber and Michel Foucault on Rationality and Government." In S. Lash and S. Whimster, eds., *Max Weber, Rationality and Modernity*, pp. 293–389. London: Allen & Unwin.

Gottmann, Jean. 1973. *The Significance of Territory*. Charlottesville: University Press of Virginia.

———. 1990. "Capital Cities." In J. Gottmann and R. A. Harper, eds., *Since Megalopolis: The Urban Writings of Jean Gottmann*, pp. 63–82. Baltimore: Johns Hopkins University Press.

Goulty, S. Mackellar. 1993. *Heritage Gardens: Care, Conservation and Management*. London: Routledge.

Gowan, Peter, and Perry Anderson, eds. 1997. *The Question of Europe*. London: Verso.

Gray, John. 1993. *Beyond the New Right: Markets, Government and the Common Environment*. London: Routledge.

Greenhouse, Carol J. Forthcoming. "Introduction: The Promise of Ethnography in an Uncertain World." In id., K. Warren, and E. Merz, eds., *Ethnography in Unstable Places*.

Greenhouse, Carol J., Barbara Yngvesson, and David M. Engel. 1994. *Law and Community in Three American Towns*. Ithaca, N.Y.: Cornell University Press.

Greenwood, Christopher. 1838. *An Epitome of County History*. Vol. 1: *The County of Kent*. London: 5 Hart Street, Bloomsbury.

Griffiths, J. 1986. "What Is Legal Pluralism?" *Journal of Legal Pluralism* 24: 1–55.

Grillo, R. D., ed. 1980. *"Nation" and "State" in Europe: Anthropological Perspectives*. London: Academic Press.

———. 1989. *Dominant Languages: Language and Hierarchy in Britain and France*. Cambridge: Cambridge University Press.

Grip. 1852. *How John Bull Lost London or the Capture of the Channel Tunnel*. London: Sampson Low, Marston, Searle & Rivington.

Gupta, Akil. 1992. "The Song of the Non-Aligned World: Transnational Identities and the Reinscription of Space in Late Capitalism." *Cultural Anthropology* 7: 63–79.

Gupta, Akil, and James Ferguson. 1992. "Beyond 'Culture': Space, Identity, and the Politics of Difference." *Cultural Anthropology* 7: 6–23.

———, eds. 1997. *Anthropological Locations: Boundaries and Grounds of a Field Science*. Berkeley and Los Angeles: University of California Press.

Gurr, T. R., and D. S. King. 1987. *The State and the City*. Chicago: University of Chicago Press.

Habermas, Jürgen. 1992. "Citizenship and National Identity: Some Reflections on the Future of Europe." *Praxis International* 12: 1–19.

Haining, Peter. 1989. *Eurotunnel: An Illustrated History of the Channel Tunnel Scheme*. Folkestone, Kent: Channel Tunnel Group.

Hall, Stuart. 1988. *The Hard Road to Renewal: Thatcherism and the Crisis of the Left.* London: Verso.

———. 1990. "Cultural Identity and Diaspora." In J. Rutherford, ed., *Identity: Community, Culture, Difference,* pp. 222–37. London: Lawrence & Wishart.

———. 1991. "The Local and the Global: Globalization and Ethnicity." In A. D. King, ed., *Culture, Globalization and the World-System,* pp. 19–40. Binghamton, N.Y.: Macmillan / State University of New York at Binghamton.

Hanes, W. T. 1991. "Railway Politics and Imperialism in Central Africa, 1889–1953." In Clarence B. Davis and Kenneth E. Wilburn, eds., *Railway Imperialism,* pp. 41–70. New York: Greenwood Press.

Haraway, Donna. 1989. "The Biopolitics of Postmodern Bodies: Determinations of Self in Immune System Discourse." *Differences* 1, 1: 3–43.

Harden, Ian, and Norman Lewis. 1986. *The Noble Lie: The British Constitution and the Rule of Law.* London: Hutchinson.

Harding, A., J. Dawson, R. Evans, and M. Parkinson, eds. 1994. *European Cities towards 2000: Profiles, Politics and Prospects.* Manchester: Manchester University Press.

Hardy, Thomas. 1891. *Tess of the d'Urbervilles.* Edited by W. E. Buckler. Boston: Houghton Mifflin, 1960.

Harris, J. 1719. *The History of Kent.* London: The Three Crowns in St. Paul's Church-Yard.

Harrison, S. 1986. *The Channel: Dividing Link between Britain and France.* London: Collins.

Harte, J. D. C. 1985. *Landscape, Land Use and the Law.* London and New York: E. & F. N. Spon.

Harvey, David. 1989. *The Condition of Postmodernity.* Cambridge, Mass.: Blackwell.

———. 1990. "Between Space and Time: Reflections on the Geographical Imagination." *Annals of the Association of American Geographers* 80: 418–34.

Harvie, Christopher. 1991. "English Regionalism: The Dog that Never Barked." In B. Crick, ed., *National Identities: The Constitution of the United Kingdom,* pp. 105–18. Oxford: Blackwell.

———. 1994. *The Rise of Regional Europe.* London: Routledge.

Harwood, E. S. 1993. "Personal Identity and the Eighteenth-Century English Landscape Garden." *Journal of Garden History* 13, 1–2: 36–48.

Hasted, Edward. 1778. *The History and Topographical Survey of the County of Kent.* Reprint, 1972, with introduction by Alan Everitt. Wakefield, Yorks.: EP Publishing / Kent County Library.

Hay, Denis. 1957. *Europe: The Emergence of an Idea.* Edinburgh: Edinburgh University Press.

Headrick, Daniel R. 1988. *The Tentacles of Progress: Technology Transfer in the Age of Imperialism, 1850–1940.* New York: Oxford University Press.

Hechter, Michael. 1975. *Internal Colonialism: The Celtic Fringe in British National Development, 1536–1966*. Berkeley and Los Angeles: University of California Press.

Heelas, Paul, and Paul Morris, eds. 1992. *The Values of the Enterprise Culture: The Moral Debate*. London: Routledge.

Heidegger, Martin. 1977a. "Building Dwelling Thinking." In id., *Basic Writings*, ed. D. F. Krell, pp. 319–40. New York: Harper & Row.

———. 1977b. "The Age of the World View." In id., *The Question Concerning Technology and Other Essays*. Translated by W. Lovitt. New York: Harper & Row.

Helgerson, Richard. 1992. *Forms of Nationhood: The Elizabethan Writing of England*. Chicago: University of Chicago Press.

Helsinger, Elizabeth. 1994. "Turner and the Representation of England." In W. J. T. Mitchell, ed., *Landscape and Power*, pp. 103–26. Chicago: Chicago University Press.

Henderson, Nicholas. 1987. *Channels and Tunnels: Reflections on Britain and Abroad*. London: Weidenfeld & Nicholson.

Herzfeld, Michael. 1987. *Anthropology through the Looking-Glass: Critical Ethnography in the Margins of Europe*. Cambridge: Cambridge University Press.

———. 1992. *The Social Production of Indifference: Exploring the Symbolic Roots of Western Democracy*. New York: Berg.

Hibbitts, Bernard J. 1992. "'Coming to Our Senses': Communication and Legal Expression in Performance Cultures." *Emory Law Journal* 41, 4: 874–960.

———. 1994. "Making Sense of Metaphors: Visuality, Aurality and the Reconfiguration of American Legal Discourse." *Cardozo Law Review* 16, 2: 229–36.

Hobbes, Thomas. 1985 [1651]. *Leviathan*. London: Penguin Books.

Hobsbawm, Eric J. 1990. *Nations and Nationalism since 1780*. 2d ed. Cambridge: Cambridge University Press.

———. 1992. "Ethnicity and Nationalism in Europe Today." *Anthropology Today* 8, 1: 3–8.

Holliday, I., G. Marcou, and R. Vickerman. 1991. *The Channel Tunnel: Public Policy, Regional Development and European Integration*. London: Belhaven Press.

Holmes, George. 1962. *The Later Middle Ages, 1272–1485*. New York: W. W. Norton.

Horn, Pamela. 1984. *The Changing Countryside in Victorian and Edwardian England and Wales*. London: Athlone Press.

Howkins, A. 1986. "The Discovery of Rural England." In R. Colls and P. Dodd, eds., *Englishness: Politics and Culture, 1880–1920*, pp. 62–88. London: Croom Helm.

Hoyles, Martin. 1991. *The Story of Gardening*. Concord, Mass.: Journeyman Press.

———. 1994. *Bread and Roses: Gardening Books from 1560 to 1960*. Boulder, Colo.: Pluto Press.

Hunnings, M. N., ed. 1991. *Commercial Laws of Europe*. London: Sweet & Maxwell.

Hunt, Alan. 1992. "Foucault's Expulsion of Law: Toward a Retrieval." *Law and Social Inquiry* 17, 1: 1–38.

Hunt, Alan, and Gary Wickham. 1994. *Foucault and Law: Towards a Sociology of Law as Governance*. London: Pluto Press.

Hunt, Donald. 1994. *The Tunnel: The Story of the Channel Tunnel, 1802–1994*. Upton-upon-Severn, Worcs.: Images.

Hunt, J. Dixon. 1992. *Gardens and the Picturesque: Studies in the History of Landscape Architecture*. Cambridge, Mass.: MIT Press.

Inglehart, Ronald. 1990. *Culture Shift in Advanced Industrial Society*. Princeton, N.J.: Princeton University Press.

Inglis, F. 1990. "Landscape as Popular Culture." In Simon Pugh, ed., *Reading Landscape: Country, City, Capital*, pp. 197–213. Manchester: Manchester University Press.

Jay, Martin. 1988. "Scopic Regimes of Modernity." In H. Foster, ed., *Vision and Visuality*, pp. 3–28. Seattle: Bay Press.

———. 1993. *Downcast Eyes: The Denigration of Vision in Twentieth-Century French Thought*. Berkeley and Los Angeles: University of California Press.

Jencks, Charles. 1988. *The Prince, the Architects and New Wave Monarchy*. London: Academy Editions.

Jessup, Frank W. 1974. *A History of Kent*. London: Phillimore.

Johnston, R. J. 1990. "The Territoriality of Law: An Exploration." *Urban Geography* 11: 548–65.

———. 1991. *A Question of Place: Exploring the Practice of Human Geography*. Oxford: Blackwell.

Jones, Emrys. 1990. *Metropolis: The World's Great Cities*. Oxford: Oxford University Press.

Just, Peter. 1992. "History, Power, Ideology, and Culture: Current Directions in the Anthropology of Law." *Law and Society Review* 26: 373–412.

Kahler, Miles. 1987. "The Survival of the State in European International Relations." In C. Maier, ed., *Changing Boundaries of the Political*, pp. 287–322. Cambridge: Cambridge University Press.

Karp, J. P. 1990. "The Evolving Meaning of Aesthetics in Land-Use Regulation." *Colombia Journal of Environmental Law* 15: 307–28.

Kasinitz, Philip. 1995. Introduction to pt. 5, "The Future of the City: Space, Race, Class and Politics." In id., ed., *Metropolis: Center and Symbol of Our Times*, pp. 387–94. London: Macmillan.

Kearney, Hugh F. 1989. *The British Isles: A History of Four Nations*. Cambridge: Cambridge University Press.

Keating, Michael. 1988. *State and Regional Nationalism: Territorial Politics and the European State*. New York: Harvester Wheatsheaf.

Keith, Michael, and Steve Pile, eds. 1993. *Place and the Politics of Identity*. London: Routledge.

Kellett, John R. 1969. *The Impact of Railways on Victorian Cities*. London: Routledge & Kegan Paul.

Kent Action Group. 1993. *Response of the Kent Action Group to the Union Railway Proposed Route for the Channel Tunnel Rail Link*. Ashford, Kent: CPRE.

Kent County Constabulary. 1993. *The PoliceSpeak and Intercom Research Projects*. Cambridge: PoliceSpeak Publication.

Kent County Council. 1991. *Kent Impact Study Review*. A report commissioned by the Channel Tunnel Joint Consultative Committee.

King, P. 1989. "Gleaners, Farmers and the Failure of Legal Sanctions in England, 1750–1850." *Past and Present* 125: 116–50.

Kingdom, J. E. 1991. *Local Government and Politics in Britain*. London: Philip Allan.

Kirby, Andrew. 1990. "Law and Disorder; Morton Grove and the Community Control of Handguns." *Urban Geography* 11, 5: 474–87.

————. 1993. *Power/Resistance: Local Politics and the Chaotic State*. Bloomington: Indiana University Press.

Klinck, D. R. 1994. "'This Other Eden': Lord Denning's Pastoral Vision." *Oxford Journal of Legal Studies* 14, 1: 25–55.

Konvitz, J. W. 1990. "The Nation-State, Paris and Cartography in Eighteenth- and Nineteenth-Century France." *Journal of Historical Geography* 16, 1: 3–16.

Kubovy, Michael. 1986. *The Psychology of Perspective and Renaissance Art*. Cambridge: Cambridge University Press.

Kyle, K. 1994. "London: The Unlooked for Conflict." In Seamus Dunn, ed., *Managing Divided Cities*, pp. 53–63. London: Ryburn Publishing / Keele University Press.

Laker, Mary. 1992. *Kent and England*. London: Brookside Press.

Latour, Bruno. 1993. *We Have Never Been Modern*. London: Harvester Wheatsheaf.

Lazarus-Black, Mindie, and Susan F. Hirsch, eds. 1994. *Contested States: Law, Hegemony and Resistance*. New York: Routledge.

Leach, Edmund R. 1954. *Political Systems of Highland Burma*. Boston: Beacon Press.

Leslie, M. 1993. "An English Landscape Garden before 'The English Landscape Garden'?" *Journal of Garden History* 13, 1–2: 3–16.

Lévi-Strauss, Claude. 1966. *The Savage Mind*. Chicago: University of Chicago Press.

Lewis, Pierce F. 1979. "Axioms for Reading the Landscape." In D. W. Meinig, ed., *The Interpretation of Ordinary Landscapes*, pp. 11–32. New York: Oxford University Press.

Ley, D. 1989. "Modernism, Post-Modernism and the Struggle for Place." In J. Agnew and J. Duncan, eds., *The Power of Place: Bringing Together Ge-*

ographical and Sociological Imaginations, pp. 44–65. Boston: Unwin Hyman.

Lincoln, E. F. 1966. *The Heritage of Kent*. London: Oldbourne.

LinguaNet. 1996. *Communicating through the Language Barrier*. Cambridge: Prolingua.

———. 1998. *Communicating through the Language Barrier with Language Controls, Graphics, Standards, Multi Modality and User-Centered Engineering*. Cambridge: Prolingua.

Lock, F. P. 1985. *Burke's Reflections on the Revolution in France*. London: George Allen & Unwin.

Longmate, Norman. 1993 [1991]. *Island Fortress: The Defence of Great Britain, 1603–1945*. London: HarperCollins.

Loughlin, Martin. 1986. *Local Government in the Modern State*. London: Sweet & Maxwell.

Lovering, J. 1991. "Southbound Again: The Peripheralization of Britain." In G. Day and G. Rees, eds., *Regions, Nations and European Integration: Remaking the Celtic Periphery*, pp. 235–64. Cardiff: University of Wales Press.

Lowe, Donald M. 1982. *History of Bourgeois Perception*. Chicago: University of Chicago Press.

Lowe, M. 1994. "The Global Rail Revival." *Society* 31, 5: 51–56.

Lowenthal, David. 1991. "British National Identity and the English Landscape." *Rural History* 2, 2: 205–30.

———. 1994. "European and English Landscapes as National Symbols." In D. Hooson, ed., *Geography and National Identity*, pp. 15–38. Oxford: Blackwell.

Lyotard, Jean-François. 1984. *The Postmodern Condition: A Report on Knowledge*. Translated by Geoff Bennington and Brian Massumi. Foreword by Fredric Jameson. Minneapolis: University of Minnesota Press. Originally published as *La Condition postmoderne: Rapport sur le savoir* (Paris: Éditions de Minuit, 1979).

McCann, M. W., and T. March. 1994. *Legal Tactics and Everyday Forms of Resistance: A Socio-Political Assessment*. Conference on Critical Epistemologies in Law, International Institute for the Sociology of Law, Onati, Spain, October 1994.

MacCormick, Neil. 1993. "Beyond the Sovereign State." *Modern Law Review* 56: 1–18.

McCrone, D. 1993. "Regionalism and Constitutional Change in Scotland." *Regional Studies* 27, 6: 507–72.

MacDonagh, O. 1980. "'Pre-Transformations': Victorian Britain." In E. Kamenka and A. E. Tay, eds., *Law and Social Control*, pp. 117–32. New York: St. Martin's Press.

Macdonald, Sharon, ed. 1993a. *Inside European Identities: Ethnography in Western Europe*. Providence, R.I.: Berg.

———. 1993b. "Identity Complexes in Western Europe: Social Anthropological Perspectives." In id., ed., *Inside European Identities: Ethnography in Western Europe*, pp. 1–26. Providence, R.I.: Berg.

McDonogh, Gary W. 1993. "The Face Behind the Door: European Integration, Immigration, and Identity." In Thomas M. Wilson and M. Estellie Smith, eds., *Cultural Change and the New Europe: Perspectives on the European Community*, pp. 143–66. Boulder, Colo.: Westview Press.

MacDougall, Hugh A. 1982. *Racial Myth in English History: Trojans, Teutons, and Anglo-Saxons*. Montreal: Harvest House / Hanover, N.H.: University Press of New England.

Macfarlane, Alan. 1978. *The Origins of English Individualism*. Oxford: Blackwell.

MacGregor, S. 1994. "Reconstructing the Divided City: Problems of Pluralism and Governance." In Seamus Dunn, ed., *Managing Divided Cities*, pp. 228–43. London: Ryburn Publishing / Keele University Press.

McGrew, A. G. 1992. "Conceptualizing Global Politics." In id., P. G. Lewis et al., eds., *Global Politics: Globalization and the Nation-State*, pp. 1–30. Cambridge: Polity Press.

McIntosh, K. 1975. *Fordwich, the Lost Port*. Ramsgate, Kent: McIntosh.

McLeod, J. 1994. "Postmodernism and Postcolonialism." In Steven Earnshaw, ed., *Postmodern Surroundings*, pp. 167–78. Atlanta, Ga.: Rodopi.

McMichael, P. 1995. "The New Colonialism: Global Regulation and the Restructuring of the Interstate System." In D. A. Smith and J. Borocz, eds., *A New World Order?: Global Transformations in the Late Twentieth Century*, pp. 37–56. Westport, Conn.: Praeger.

Major, Alan P. 1981. *A New Dictionary of Kent Dialect*. Rainham, Kent: Meresborough Books.

Malcolm-Davies, J. 1991. "Heritage Honey-Pot." *Museums Journal*, Feb. 16–17.

Malinowski, Bronislaw. 1985 [1926]. *Crime and Custom in Savage Society*. Patterson, N.J.: Littlefield, Adams.

Manchester, A. H. 1973. "Simplifying the Sources of the Law: An Essay in Law Reform." *Anglo-American Law Review*: 395–413.

Mander, John. 1963. *Great Britain or Little England?* Harmondsworth, Eng.: Penguin Books.

Mann, Michael. 1988. *States, War and Capitalism: Studies in Political Sociology*. Oxford: Blackwell.

Marcus, George E. 1986. "Contemporary Problems of Ethnography in the Modern World System." In James Clifford and id., eds., *Writing Culture: The Poetics and Politics of Ethnography*, pp. 165–93. Berkeley and Los Angeles: University of California Press.

———. 1995. "Ethnography in/of the World System: The Emergence of the Multi-sited Ethnography." *Annual Reviews in Anthropology* 13: 1–23.

Marcus, George E., and M. M. J. Fischer, eds. 1986. *Anthropology as Cultural Critique: An Experimental Moment in the Human Sciences*. Chicago: University of Chicago Press.

Marquand, David. 1991. "Nations, Regions and Europe." In B. Crick, ed., *National Identities: The Constitution of the United Kingdom*, pp. 25–37. Oxford: Blackwell.

Marsh, D., and R. A. W. Rhodes. 1992. "Implementing Thatcherism: Policy Change in the 1980s." *Parliamentary Affairs* 45, 1: 33–50.

Marsh, Jan. 1982. *Back to the Land: The Pastoral Impulse in England from 1880 to 1914*. London: Quartet Books.

Martin, Emily. 1990. "Toward an Anthropology of Immunology: The Body as Nation-State." *Medial Anthropology Quarterly* 4, 4: 410–26.

———. 1992. "The End of the Body?" *American Ethnologist* 19, 1: 121–40.

Martin, Peter. 1984. *Pursuing Innocent Pleasures: The Gardening World of Alexander Pope*. Hamden, Conn.: Archon Books.

Martin, S., and G. Pearce. 1993. "European Regional Development Strategies: Strengthening Meso-Government in the UK?" *Regional Studies* 27, 7: 681–96.

Marx, Karl. 1976 [1867]. *Capital: A Critique of Political Economy*. Vol. 1. Harmondsworth, Eng.: New Left Books.

Marx, Leo. 1964. *The Machine in the Garden*. New York: Oxford University Press.

Massey, Doreen. 1984. *Spatial Divisions of Labour: Social Structures and the Geography of Production*. London: Macmillan.

———. 1991. "A Global Sense of Place." *Marxism Today*, June, pp. 24–29.

———. 1993. "Questions of Locality." *Geography* 78: 142–49.

Maurer, Bill. 1997. *Recharting the Caribbean: Land, Law, and Citizenship in the British Virgin Islands*. Ann Arbor: University of Michigan Press.

Mazzoleni, Donatella. 1993. "The City and the Imaginary." In E. Carter, J. Donald and J. Squires, eds., *Space and Place: Theories of Identity and Location*, pp. 285–302. London: Lawrence & Wishart.

Meinig, Donald W. 1979. "The Beholding Eye." In id., ed., *The Interpretation of Ordinary Landscapes*, pp. 11–32. New York: Oxford University Press.

Mellor, Roy E. H. 1989. *Nation, State and Territory: A Political Geography*. London: Routledge.

Mellors, Collin, and Nigel Copperthwaite. 1990. *Regional Policy*. London: Routledge.

Merry, Sally Engle. 1990. *Getting Justice and Getting Even: Legal Consciousness among Working Class Americans*. Chicago: University of Chicago Press.

———. 1992. "Anthropology, Law, and Transnational Processes." *Annual Review of Anthropology* 21: 357–79.

Milward, Alan S. 1992. *The European Rescue of the Nation-State*. London: Routledge.

Mingay, Gordon E. 1989a. "'Rural War': The Life and Times of Captain Swing." In id., ed., *The Unquiet Countryside*, pp. 36–51. London: Routledge.

———, ed. 1989b. *The Rural Idyll*. London: Routledge.

———. 1990. *A Social History of the English Countryside*. London: Routledge.

Mitchell, W. J. T. 1980. "Foreword." In id., ed., *On Narrative*, pp. vii–x. Chicago: University of Chicago Press.

———. 1986. *Iconology: Image, Text, Ideology*. Chicago: University of Chicago Press.

———. 1994a. "Introduction." In id., ed, *Landscape and Power*, pp. 1–4. Chicago: University of Chicago Press.

———. 1994b. "Imperial Landscape." In id., ed., *Landscape and Power*, pp. 5–34. Chicago: University of Chicago Press.

Moore, C. W., W. J. T. Mitchell, and W. Turnbull Jr. 1989. *The Poetics of Gardens*. Cambridge, Mass.: MIT Press.

Moore, Sally Falk. 1973. "Law and Social Change: The Semi-Autonomous Social Field as an Appropriate Subject of Study." *Law and Society Review* 7: 719–46.

———. 1976. *Law as Process: An Anthropological Approach*. London: Routledge & Kegan Paul.

———. 1986. *Social Facts and Fabrications: "Customary Law" on Kilimanjaro, 1880–1980*. Cambridge: Cambridge University Press.

Mosse, George L. 1985. *Nationalism and Sexuality: Respectability and Abnormal Sexuality in Modern Europe*. Madison: University of Wisconsin Press.

Moxon-Browne, Edward. 1993. "Social Europe." In J. Lodge, ed., *The European Community and the Challenge of the Future*, pp. 152–62. 2d ed. London: Pinter.

Murphy, Alexander. 1991. "Regions as Social Constructs: The Gap between Theory and Practice." *Progress in Human Geography* 15, 1: 22–35.

———. 1993. "Emerging Regional Linkages within the European Community: Challenging the Dominance of the State." *Tijdschrift voor Econ. en Soc. Geografie / Journal of Economic and Social Geography* 84, 2: 103–18.

Nadel-Klein, Jane. 1991. "Reweaving the Fringe: Localism, Tradition, and Representation in British Ethnography." *American Ethnologist* 18: 500–517.

Nairn, Tom. 1977. *The Break-Up of Britain: Crisis and Neo-Nationalism*. London: NLB.

———. 1988. *The Enchanted Glass: Britain and Its Monarchy*. London: Radius.

Nancy, Jean-Luc. 1991. *The Inoperative Community*. Translated by Peter Connor, Lisa Garbus, Michael Holland, and Simona Sawhney. Edited by Peter Connor. Minneapolis: University of Minnesota Press. Originally published as *La Communauté désoeuvrée*.

Napier, A. David. 1992. "Culture as Self: The Stranger Within." In id., *Foreign Bodies: Performance, Art, and Symbolic Anthropology*, pp. 139–75. Berkeley and Los Angeles: University of California Press.

Nelson, Brian, David Roberts, and Walter Viet, eds. 1992. *The Idea of Europe: Problems of National and Transnational Identity*. New York: Berg.

Nichols, John Gough, ed. 1846. *The Chronicle of Calais in the Reigns of Henry VII and Henry VIII to the year 1540.* London: Camden Society.

Nock, O. S. 1947. *The Railways of Britain: Past and Present.* London: B. T. Batsford.

Norton, A. 1992. *The Principle of Subsidiarity and its Implications for Local Government.* Birmingham: Institute of Local Government Studies and the School of Public Policy, University of Birmingham.

Oelschlaeger, Max. 1991. *The Idea of Wilderness.* New Haven, Conn.: Yale University Press.

O'Neil, O. 1994. "Justice and Boundaries." In C. Brown, ed., *Political Restructuring in Europe: Ethical Perspectives*, pp. 69–88. London: Routledge.

Ong, Walter J. 1967. *The Presence of the Word: Some Prolegomena for Cultural and Religious History.* New Haven, Conn.: Yale University Press.

Open Spaces Society. 1993. *Beating the Bounds: List of Events on Sunday 16 May 1993, Rogation Sunday.* Henley-on-Thames, Oxon.: Open Spaces Society.

———. 1994. *Beating the Bounds: List of Events on Sunday 8 May 1994, Rogation Sunday.* Henley-on-Thames, Oxon.: Open Spaces Society.

———. N.d. *. . . And What Will You Be Doing on Rogation Sunday?* Henley-on-Thames, Oxon.: Open Spaces Society.

Ordish, George. 1985. *The Living Garden: The 400-Year History of An English Garden.* Boston: Houghton Mifflin.

Panofsky, Erwin. 1991 [1927]. *Perspective as Symbolic Form.* Translated by Christopher S. Wood. New York: Zone Books.

Parry, C. 1968. "The Function of Law in the International Community." In M. Sorensen, ed., *Manual of Public International Law*, pp. 1–54. London: Macmillan.

Pateman, Carole. 1988. *The Sexual Contract.* Stanford: Stanford University Press.

Pevsner, Sir Nikolaus. 1956. *The Englishness of English Art.* Reprint. London: Penguin Books, 1993.

Pick, D. 1994. "Pro Patria: Blocking the Tunnel." *Ecumene* 1: 77–94.

Pickvance, C. 1991. "The Difficulty of Control and the Ease of Structural Reform: British Local Government in the 1980s." In id. and E. Preteceille, eds., *State Restructuring and Local Power: A Comparative Perspective*, pp. 48–88. London: Pinter.

Pimlott, J. A. R. 1947. *The Englishman's Holiday.* New York: Harvester Press.

Pinder, John. 1991. "Public Opinion and European Union: Thatcher versus the People of Europe." In K. Reif and R. Inglehart, eds., *Eurobarometer: The Dynamics of European Public Opinion*, pp. 101–22. New York: St. Martin's Press.

Pocock, J. G. A. 1987 [1957]. *The Ancient Constitution and Feudal Law: A Study of English Historical Thought in the Seventeenth Century.* Cambridge: Cambridge University Press.

Poignant, Roslyn. 1992. "Surveying the Field of View: The Making of the Royal Anthropological Institute Photographic Collection." In E. Edwards, ed., *Anthropology and Photography, 1860–1920*, pp. 42–73. New Haven, Conn.: Yale University Press in association with the Royal Anthropological Institute, London.

PoliceSpeak. 1993. *Police Communications and Language and the Channel Tunnel, Report.* Cambridge: PoliceSpeak Publications.

Porteous, J. Douglas. 1976. "Home: The Territorial Core." *Geographical Review* 66: 383–90.

———. 1990. *Landscapes of the Mind: Worlds of Sense and Metaphor.* Toronto: University of Toronto Press.

Pred, Allan. 1990. *Making Histories and Constructing Human Geographies: The Local Transformation of Practice, Power Relations, and Consciousness.* Boulder, Colo.: Westview Press.

Prescott, J. R. V. 1987. *Political Frontiers and Boundaries.* London: Unwin Hyman.

Preston, J. 1992. "Local Government." In S. Bulmer, S. George, and A. Scott, eds., *The United Kingdom and EC Membership Evaluated*, pp. 111–23. New York: St. Martin's Press.

Pue, Wesley W. 1990. "Wrestling with Law: (Geographical) Specificity vs. (Legal) Abstraction." *Urban Geography* 11, 6: 566–85.

Pugh, Simon. 1988. *Garden, Nature, Language (Cultural Politics).* Manchester: Manchester University Press.

———, ed. 1990. *Reading Landscape: Country, City, Capital.* Manchester: Manchester University Press.

Purdy, Trudi, ed. 1993. *A Taste of the South: An Anthology of Poems about the South.* Peterborough: Arrival Press.

Rapport, Nigel J. 1993. *Diverse World-Views in an English Village.* Edinburgh: Edinburgh University Press.

Ratcliffe, P. 1992. "British Perceptions of 'Europe.'" *International Journal of Sociology*, special issue, *Europe: Beyond Geography*, 22, 1–2: 110–29.

Rawlings, R. 1994. "Legal Politics: The United Kingdom and Ratification of the Treaty of European Union. Parts I and II." *Public Law* (Summer): 254–78; (Autumn): 367–91.

Read, L. F. 1989. "Private Bill Procedure: Is There a Better Way?" In *New Orders, New Rules, New Assessments—in Practice.* Paper from a conference organized by Bar Council and the Law Society, Oxford, September 1989. London: Sweet & Maxwell.

Reed, Michael. 1984. "Anglo-Saxon Charter Bounders." In id., ed., *Discovering Past Landscapes*, pp. 261–306. London: Croom Helm.

Renan, Ernest. 1990 [1882]. "What Is a Nation?" Reprinted in H. Bhabha, ed., *Nation and Narration*, pp. 8–22. London: Routledge.

Rhodes, Deborah L. 1989. *Justice and Gender: Sex Discrimination and the Law.* Cambridge, Mass.: Harvard University Press.

Rhodes, R. A. W. 1985. "Intergovernmental Relations in the United Kingdom." In Y. Meny and V. Wright, eds., *Centre-Periphery Relations in Western Europe*, pp. 33–78. London: George Allen & Unwin.

———. 1991. "Now Nobody Understands the System: The Changing Face of Local Government." In P. Norton, ed., *New Directions in British Politics?: Essays on the Evolving Constitution*, pp. 83–112. Aldershot, Hants.: Edward Elgar.

Robins, Kevin. 1993. "Prisoners of the City: Whatever Could a Postmodern City Be?" In E. Carter, J. Donald, and J. Squires, eds., *Space and Place: Theories of Identity and Location*, pp. 303–30. London: Lawrence & Wishart.

Robinson, A. H. 1990. "Regional Identity in Tomorrow's EC and the Case of North England." *EIU European Trends* 2: 68–76.

Robinson, Mary. 1992. "A Question of Law: The European Legacy." In R. Kearney, ed., *Visions of Europe*, pp. 133–43. Dublin: Wolfhound Press.

Robinson, R. E. 1991. "Introduction: Railway Imperialism." In C. B. Davis and K. E. Wilburn, eds., *Railway Imperialism*, pp. 1–6. New York: Greenwood Press.

Rokkan, S., and D. W. Urwin. 1982. "Introduction: Centers and Peripheries in Western Europe." In id., eds., *The Politics of Territorial Identity: Studies in European Regionalism*, pp. 1–18. London: Sage.

Rokkan, S., D. Urwin, F. H. Aarebrot, P. Malaba, and T. Sande. 1987. *Center-Periphery Structures in Europe*. Frankfurt: Campus Verlag.

Rootes, Andrew. 1980. *Front Line County: Kent at War, 1939–45*. London: Robert Hale.

Rosas, A. 1993. "The Decline of Sovereignty: Legal Perspectives." In J. Iivonen, ed., *The Future of the Nation-State in Europe*, pp. 130–58. Aldershot, Hants.: Edward Elgar.

Rose, Carol M. 1994. *Property and Persuasion: Essays on the History, Theory, and Rhetoric of Ownership*. Boulder, Colo.: Westview Press.

Rose, Gillian. 1993. *Feminism and Geography: The Limits of Geographical Knowledge*. Minneapolis: University of Minnesota Press.

Rose, N., and P. Miller. 1992. "Political Power beyond the State: Problematics of Government." *British Journal of Sociology* 43: 173–205.

Ross, R. J. S. 1990. "The Relative Decline of Relative Autonomy: Global Capitalism and the Political Economy of the State." In E. S. Greenberg and T. F. Mayer, eds., *Changes in the State: Causes and Consequences*, pp. 206–23. Newbury Park, Calif.: Sage Publications.

Ross, Stephanie. 1998. *What Gardens Mean*. Chicago: University of Chicago Press.

Rotenberg, Robert. 1995. *Landscape and Power in Vienna*. Baltimore: Johns Hopkins University Press.

Rotman, Brian. 1993. *Signifying Nothing: The Semiotics of Zero*. Stanford: Stanford University Press.

Rumley, Denis, and Julian V. Minghi, eds. 1991. *The Geography of Border Landscapes*. London: Routledge.

Rustin, M. 1994. "Unfinished Business: From Thatcherite Modernization to Incomplete Modernity." In M. Perryman, ed., *Altered States: Postmodernism, Politics, Culture*, pp. 73–93. London: Lawrence & Wishart.

Sack, Robert D. 1986. *Human Territoriality: Its Theory and History*. Cambridge: Cambridge University Press.

Sahlins, Peter. 1989. *Boundaries: The Making of France and Spain in the Pyrenees*. Berkeley and Los Angeles: University of California Press.

———. 1990. "Natural Frontiers Revisited: France's Boundaries since the Seventeenth Century." *American Historical Review* 95, 4: 1423–51.

Said, Edward. 1978. *Orientalism*. New York: Pantheon Books. Reprints, Random House, Vintage Books, 1979, 1994.

Salem, T. F. 1991. "Regionalism: The Awakening Paradigm in World Politics." *Journal of History and Politics*, special issue, *Regionalism and Theory*, 9: 143–60.

Sampson, Anthony. 1992. *The Essential Anatomy of Britain: Democracy in Crisis*. London: Hodder & Stoughton. 1st U.S. ed., San Diego: Harcourt Brace, 1993.

Samuel, Raphael, ed. 1989. *Patriotism: The Making and Unmaking of British National Identity*. 2 vols. London: Routledge.

Sandeman, G. A. C. 1908. *Calais Under English Rule*. Oxford: Blackwell.

Sandys, Charles F. S. A. 1851. *A History of Gavelkind and Other Remarkable Customs of Kent*. Reprint. London: John Russel Smith, 1981.

Santos, Boaventura de Sousa. 1985. "On Modes of Production of Law and Social Power." *International Journal of the Sociology of Law* 13: 299–336.

———. 1987. "Law: A Map of Misreading. Toward a Postmodern Conception of Law." *Journal of Law and Society* 14, 3: 279–302.

———. 1992. "State, Law and Community in the World System: An Introduction." *Social and Legal Studies* 1: 131–42.

———. 1995. *Toward a New Common Sense: Law, Science and Politics in the Paradigmatic Transition*. New York: Routledge.

Sassen, Saskia. 1991. *The Global City: New York, London, Tokyo*. Princeton, N.J.: Princeton University Press.

———. 1994a. *Cities in a World Economy*. Thousand Oakes, Calif.: Pine Forge Press.

———. 1994b. "The Global City: A New Frontier?" *Contention* 3, 3: 39–52.

———. 1994c. "Ethnicity and Space in the Global City: A New Frontier." In Seamus Dunn, ed., *Managing Divided Cities*, pp. 13–29. London: Ryburn Publishing / Keele University Press.

Savage, M. 1989. "Spatial Differences in Modern Britain." In C. Hamnett, L. McDowell, and P. Sarre, eds., *Restructuring Britain: The Changing Social Structure*, pp. 244–68. London: Sage.

Schaefer, G. F. 1991. "Institutional Choices: The Rise and Fall of Subsidiarity." *Futures* (September): 681–94.

Schama, Simon. 1995. *Landscape and Memory*. New York: Knopf.

———. 1996. "Mad Cows and Englishmen." *New Yorker*, 8 April, pp. 61–62.

Schivelbusch, Wolfgang. 1986. *The Railway Journey: The Industrialization of Time and Space in the Nineteenth Century*. Berkeley and Los Angeles: University of California Press.

Segrest, Dale. 1994. *Conscience and Command: A Motive Theory of Law*. Atlanta: Scholars Press.

Shapiro, B. 1974. "Codification of the Laws in Seventeenth-Century England." *Wisconsin Law Review*, no. 2 (1974): 428–65.

Shapiro, Michael J. 1992. *Reading the Postmodern Polity: Political Theory as Textual Practice*. Minneapolis: University of Minnesota Press.

Sharpe, L. J. 1987. "The West European State: The Territorial Dimension." In R. A. W. Rhodes and V. Wright, eds., *Tensions in the Territorial Politics of Western Europe*, pp. 148–67. London: Frank Cass.

Sheate, W. R. 1992. "Lobbying for Effective Environmental Assessment." *Long Range Planning* 25, 4: 90–98.

Shepard, Paul. 1967. *Man in the Landscape: A Historic View of the Esthetics of Nature*. New York: Knopf.

Shoard, Marion. 1987. *This Land Is Our Land: The Struggle for Britain's Countryside*. London: Paladin Grafton Books.

Shore, Cris. 1995. "Transcending the Nation-State? The European Commission and the (Re)-Discovery of Europe." Paper presented at Kent University Seminar "Reappraising the Force of Tradition," April 1995.

Shore, Cris, and Annabel Black. 1994a. "The European Communities and the Construction of Europe." *Anthropology Today* 8, 3: 10–15.

———. 1994b. "Citizens: Europe and the Construction of European Identity." In V. A. Goddard, J. R. Llobera, and C. Shore, eds., *The Anthropology of Europe: Identity and Boundaries in Conflict*, pp. 275–98. Providence, R.I.: Berg.

Silbey, Susan S. 1992. "Making a Place for Cultural Analyses of Law." *Law and Social Inquiry* 17, 1: 39–48.

Simmel, Georg. 1950. "Metropolis and Mental Life." Translated by K. Woff in *The Sociology of Georg Simmel*, pp. 409–24. Glencoe, Ill.: Free Press.

———. 1994. "Bridge and Door." *Theory, Culture and Society* 11: 5–10.

Simmons, I. G. 1993. *Interpreting Nature: Cultural Constructions of the Environment*. London: Routledge.

Simo, Melanie L. 1988. *Loudon and the Landscape: From Country Seat to Metropolis, 1783–1843*. New Haven, Conn.: Yale University Press.

Simon, J. 1992. "'In Another Kind of Wood': Michel Foucault and Sociolegal Studies." *Law and Social Inquiry* 17, 1: 49–56.

Sinclair, M. T., and Page, S. J. 1993. "The Euroregion: A New Framework for Tourism and Regional Development." *Regional Studies* 27, 5: 475–83.

Skurski, J., and F. Coronil. 1993. "Country and City in a Postcolonial Landscape: Double Discourse and the Geo-Politics of Truth in Latin America."

In D. L. Dworkin and L. G. Roman, eds., *Views Beyond the Border Country: Raymond Williams and Cultural Politics*, pp. 231–59. London: Routledge.

Slowe, Peter M. 1990. *Geography and Political Power: The Geography of Nations and States*. London: Routledge.

Smart, Carol. 1989. *Feminism and the Power of Law*. New York: Routledge.

Smith, Anthony D. 1997. "National Identity and European Unity." In P. Gowan and P. Anderson, eds., *The Question of Europe*, pp. 318–44. London: Verso.

Smith, M. 1992. "Modernization, Globalization and the Nation-State." In A. G. McGrew, P. G. Lewis et al., eds., *Global Politics: Globalization and the Nation-State*, pp. 253–68. Cambridge: Polity Press.

Smith, Neil. 1984. *Uneven Development: Nature, Capital and the Production of Space*. Oxford: Blackwell.

Sontag, Susan. 1989. *AIDS and Its Metaphors*. New York: Farrar, Straus & Giroux.

Special Report from the Select Committee on the Channel Tunnel Bill (Session 1986–87). 1986. London: HMS Office.

Spengler, Oswald. 1928. *The Decline of the West*. Vol. 2. New York: Knopf.

Stanley, Christopher. 1995. "Law of Space, Space of Law: Part 1: Orientation via Goodrich and contra Harvey." *International Journal of the Sociology of Law* 23: 1–21.

Starr, June, and Jane F. Collier, eds. 1989. *History and Power in the Study of Law: New Directions in Legal Anthropology*. Ithaca, N.Y.: Cornell University Press.

Stephenson, J. 1993. "Britain and Europe in the Later Twentieth Century: Identity, Sovereignty, Peculiarity." In M. Fulbrook, ed., *National Histories and European History*, pp. 231–54. Boulder, Colo.: Westview Press.

Stewart, S. 1966. *The Enclosed Garden: The Tradition and the Image in Seventeenth-Century Poetry*. Madison: University of Wisconsin Press.

Stilgoe, John R. 1983. *Metropolitan Corridor: Railroads and the American Scene*. New Haven, Conn.: Yale University Press.

———. 1994. *Alongshore*. New Haven, Conn.: Yale University Press.

Strathern, Marilyn. 1992. *After Nature: English Kinship in the Late Twentieth Century*. Cambridge: Cambridge University Press.

Summerson, John. 1945. *Georgian England*. Reprint. London: Penguin Books, 1991.

Swift, Graham. 1996. *Last Orders*. A novel. London: Picador.

Taussig, Michael T. 1997. *The Magic of the State*. New York: Routledge.

Taylor, John. 1994. *A Dream of England: Landscape, Photography and the Tourist's Imagination*. Manchester: Manchester University Press.

Theroux, Paul. 1983. *The Kingdom by the Sea: A Journey around Great Britain*. London: Hamish Hamilton; Boston: Houghton Mifflin.

Thomas, Keith. 1983. *Man and the Natural World: Changing Attitudes in England, 1500–1800*. London: Penguin Books.

Thomas, R. H. G. 1972. *London's First Railway—The London & Greenwich.* London: B. T. Batsford.

Thomé de Gamond, Aimé. 1870. *Atlas Containing the Plans and Sections of the Submarine Tunnel between England and France.* . . . London: Savill.

Thompson, E. P. 1993. *Customs in Common.* New York: New Press.

Thrift, Nigel. 1990. "Transport and Communication, 1730–1914." In R. A. Dodgshon and R. A. Butlin, eds., *An Historical Geography of England and Wales*, pp. 453–86. 2d ed. London: Academic Press.

————. 1995. "Taking Aim at the Heart of the Region." In D. Gregory, R. Martin, and G. Smith, eds., *Human Geography: Society, Space, and Social Science*, pp. 200–231. Minneapolis: University of Minnesota Press.

Tilly, Charles. 1994. *Globalization Threatens Labor's Rights.* Center for Studies of Social Change, Working Paper No. 182. New York: New School for Social Research, 1994.

Tocqueville, Alexis de. 1979. *De Tocqueville: Journeys to England and Ireland.* Edited by J. P. Mayer. New York: Arno Press.

Torpey, John. 1995. "The Rise of the Passport System." Paper presented at the annual meeting of the Law and Society Association, Toronto, Canada, 1–4 June.

Tuan, Yi-Fu. 1974. *Topophilia: A Study of Environmental Perception, Attitudes and Values.* Englewood Cliffs, N.J.: Prentice-Hall.

Turner, M. 1984. "The Landscape of Parliamentary Enclosure." In M. Reed, ed., *Discovering Past Landscapes*, pp. 132–66. London: Croom Helm.

Urry, John. 1984. "Englishmen, Celts, and Iberians: The Ethnographic Survey of the United Kingdom, 1892–1899." In G. W. Stocking, ed., *History of Anthropology*, vol. 2: *Functionalism Historicized: Essays on British Anthropology*, pp. 83–105. Madison: University of Wisconsin Press.

————. 1990. *The Tourist Gaze: Leisure and Travel in Contemporary Societies.* London: Sage.

————. 1992. "Tourism, Travel and the Modern Subject." Paper presented at British Sociological Club, Moscow, Colloquium. BSCM Transactions 1.

Urwin, Derek W. 1982. "Territorial Structures and Political Developments in the United Kingdom." In S. Rokkan and D. W. Urwin, eds., *The Politics of Territorial Identity: Studies in European Regionalism*, pp. 19–74. London: Sage.

Vaughan, William. 1993. "The British Landscape Tradition." In N. Alfrey et al., *Towards a New Landscape*, pp. 84–101. London: Bernard Jacobson.

Verdery, Katherine. 1994. "Beyond the Nation in Eastern Europe." *Social Text* 38: 1–20.

Vickerman, Roger W. 1991. "Transport Infrastructure in the European Community: New Developments, Regional Implications and Evaluation." In id., ed., *Infrastructure and Regional Development.* London: Pion.

Viegas, J., and U. Blum. 1993. "High Speed Railways in Europe." In D. Banister and J. Berechman, eds., *Transport in a Unified Europe*, pp. 75–90. Amsterdam: Elsevier.

Vine, P. A. L. 1972. *The Royal Military Canal.* Newton Abbot, Devon: David & Charles.

Viswanathan, G. 1993. "Raymond Williams and British Colonialism: The Limits of Metropolitan Cultural Theory." In D. L. Dworkin and L. G. Roman, eds., *Views beyond the Border Country: Raymond Williams and Cultural Politics,* pp. 217–30. New York: Routledge.

Voltaire [François-Marie Arouet]. 1981 [1759]. *Candide.* New York: Bantam Books.

Wæver, O., B. Buzan, M. Kelstrup, and P. Lemaitre. 1993. *Identity, Migration and the New Security Agenda in Europe.* New York: St. Martin's Press.

Waldron, Jeremy. 1990. *The Law.* London: Routledge.

Wallace, Anne D. 1993. *Walking, Literature and English Culture.* Oxford: Clarendon Press.

Wallace, William. 1997. "The Nation-State—Rescue or Retreat." In P. Gowan and P. Anderson, eds., *The Question of Europe,* pp. 21–50. London: Verso.

Wallerstein, Immanuel. 1983. *Historical Capitalism; with Capitalist Civilization.* London: Verso.

Walsh, Kevin. 1992. *The Representation of the Past: Museums and Heritage in a Post-Modern World.* London: Routledge.

Ward, Ian. 1996. *A Critical Introduction to European Law.* London: Butterworths.

Warner, Marina. 1994. *Six Myths of Our Times: Little Angels, Little Monsters, Beautiful Beasts, and More.* New York: Random House, Vintage Books.

Waters, Michael. 1988. *The Garden in Victorian Literature.* England: Scholar Press.

Webber, F. 1991. "From Ethnocentrism to Euro-racism." *Race and Class* 32, 3: 11–18.

Weber, Eugene. 1979. *Peasants into Frenchmen: The Modernization of Rural France, 1870–1914.* London: Chatto & Windus.

Weber, Max. 1946. "Politics as a Vocation." In H. H. Gerth and C. W. Mills, eds., *From Max Weber: Essays in Sociology.* New York: Oxford University Press.

———. 1954. *Law in Economy and Society.* Translated by E. Shils and M. Rheinstein. New York: Simon & Schuster.

———. 1958. *The City.* New York: Free Press.

Welfare, D. 1992. "An Anachronism with Relevance: The Revival of the House of Lords in the 1980s and Its Defence of Local Government." *Parliamentary Affairs* 45, 2: 205–19.

Wheeler, W. 1994. "Nostalgia Isn't Nasty: The Postmodernising of Parliamentary Democracy." In M. Perryman, ed., *Altered States: Postmodernism, Politics, Culture,* pp. 94–109. London: Lawrence & Wishart.

White, H. P. 1970. *Southern England.* Vol. 2 of *A Regional History of the Railways of Great Britain.* Newton Abbot, Devon: David & Charles.

Whittaker, Nicholas. 1997. *Platform Souls: The Trainspotter as Twentieth-Century Hero*. London: Trafalgar Square.

Wieviorka, M. 1993. "Racism and Modernity in Present-Day Europe." *Thesis Eleven* 35: 51–61.

Williams, Raymond. 1973. *The Country and the City*. New York: Oxford University Press.

———. 1989a. "Decentralism and the Politics of Place." In id., *Resources of Hope: Culture, Democracy, Socialism*, pp. 238–44. London: Verso.

———. 1989b. "Between Country and City." In id., *Resources of Hope: Culture, Democracy, Socialism*, pp. 227–37. London: Verso.

Williams, Richard H. 1993. "Spatial Planning for an Integrated Europe." In J. Lodge, ed., *The European Community and the Challenge of the Future*, pp. 348–59. 2d ed. London: Pinter.

Williamson, Tom. 1995. *Polite Landscapes: Gardens and Society in Eighteenth-Century England*. Baltimore: Johns Hopkins University Press.

Williamson, Tom, and Liz Bellamy. 1987. *Property and Landscape: A Social History of Land Ownership and the English Countryside*. London: George Philip.

Wilson, Keith. 1994. *Channel Tunnel Visions, 1850–1945*. London: Hambledon Press.

Wilson, Thomas M. 1993. "An Anthropology of the European Community." In id. and M. Estellie Smith, eds., *Cultural Change and the New Europe: Perspectives on the European Community*, pp. 1–24. Boulder, Colo.: Westview Press.

Wilson, Thomas M., and M. Estellie Smith, eds. 1993. *Cultural Change and the New Europe: Perspectives on the European Community*. Boulder, Colo.: Westview Press.

Wilson, Thomas M., and Hastings Donnan, eds. 1998. *Border Identities: Nation and State at International Frontiers*. Cambridge: Cambridge University Press.

Winstanley, M. 1981. "Voices from the Past: Rural Kent at the Close of an Era." In G. E. Mingay, ed., *The Victorian Countryside*, 2: 626–38. London: Routledge & Kegan Paul.

Wood, Denis, with J. Fels. 1992. *The Power of Maps*. New York: Guildford Press.

Worcester, R. M. 1990. "European Attitudes to the European Community and to 1992." *International Journal of Public Opinion Research* 2, 3: 227–48.

Worpole, K. 1994. "The New 'City States'"? In M. Perryman, ed., *Altered States: Postmodernism, Politics, Culture*, pp. 157–73. London: Lawrence & Wishart.

Wright, Christopher. 1975. *Kent through the Years*. London: B. T. Batsford.

Wright, Patrick. 1985. *On Living in an Old Country*. London: Verso.

———. 1994. "Harvesting a Future from Rocky Ground." *Guardian*, 14 May 1994, p. 31.

Wright, R. 1938. *The Story of Gardening.* New York: Garden City Publishing Co.

Young, Alison, and Austin Sarat. 1994. "Introduction to 'Beyond Criticism: Law, Power and Ethics.'" *Social and Legal Studies* 3: 323–31.

Zukin, Sharon. 1991. *Landscapes of Power: From Detroit to Disney World.* Berkeley and Los Angeles: University of California Press.

Zulaika, Joseba. 1998. "Tropics of Terror: From Guernica's 'Natives' to 'Global Terrorists.'" *Social Identities: Journal for the Study of Race, Nation and Culture* 4, 1: 93–108.

Index